China, India and Beyond

GLOBAL DEVELOPMENT NETWORK

Series editor: George Mavrotas, *Chief Economist, Global Development Network*

Meeting the challenge of development in the contemporary age of globalization demands greater empirical knowledge. While most research emanates from the developed world, the Global Development Network series is designed to give voice to researchers from the developing and transition world – those experiencing first-hand the promises and pitfalls of development. This series presents the best examples of innovative and policy-relevant research from such diverse countries as Nigeria and China, India and Argentina, Russia and Egypt. It encompasses all major development topics ranging from the details of privatization and social safety nets to broad strategies to realize the Millennium Development Goals and achieve the greatest possible progress in developing countries.

Titles in the series include:

Testing Global Interdependence
Issues on Trade, Aid, Migration and Development
Edited by Ernest Aryeetey and Natalia Dinello

Political Institutions and Development
Failed Expectations and Renewed Hopes
Edited by Natalia Dinello and Vladimir Popov

Economic Reform in Developing Countries
Reach, Range, Reason
Edited by José María Fanelli and Lyn Squire

China, India and Beyond
Development Drivers and Limitations
Edited by Natalia Dinello and Wang Shaoguang

China, India and Beyond

Development Drivers and Limitations

Edited by

Natalia Dinello

Principal Political Scientist,
Global Development Network, New Delhi, India

Wang Shaoguang

Professor,
Chinese University of Hong Kong and Tsinghua University, China

GLOBAL DEVELOPMENT NETWORK

Edward Elgar
Cheltenham, UK • Northampton, MA, USA

Published by
Edward Elgar Publishing Limited
The Lypiatts
15 Lansdown Road
Cheltenham
Glos GL50 2JA
UK

Edward Elgar Publishing, Inc.
William Pratt House
9 Dewey Court
Northampton
Massachusetts 01060
USA

A catalogue record for this book
is available from the British Library

Library of Congress Control Number: 2008937417

ISBN 978 1 84720 695 4

Printed and bound in Great Britain by MPG Books Ltd, Bodmin, Cornwall

Contents

Notes on the Contributors   *vii*

Foreword: The Asian Miracle and its Implications, by Lawrence Summers   *xi*

Introduction by Natalia Dinello and Wang Shaoguang   *xvi*

Acknowledgements   *xxv*

PART ONE – CHINA'S BOOM AND INDIA'S GROWTH   1

1.   Perspectives on China's Economic Growth: Prospects and   3
     Wider Impact
     Linda Y. Yueh

2.   India's Growth: Past and Future   23
     Shankar Acharya

3.   Asian Century or Multipolar Century?   46
     David Dollar

PART TWO – DRIVERS AND LIMITATIONS OF DEVELOPMENT   71

4.   Specialization Patterns under Trade Liberalization: Evidence   73
     from India and China
     Choorikkadan Veeramani

5.   Sources of China's Export Growth   98
     Roberto Álvarez and Sebastián Claro

6.   Trade Liberalization and R&D Investment: 119
     Evidence from Manufacturing Firms in India
     Mavannoor Parameswaran

7.   Public–Private Partnership in the Provision of Health Care   143
     Services to the Poor in India
     A. Venkat Raman and James Warner Björkman

8. Labor Market Informalization and Implications for   173
    Sustainable Growth
    Du Yang, Cai Fang and Wang Meiyan

9. Financing China's Entrepreneurs: The Role of Legislative   199
    Membership
    Wubiao Zhou

10. Grassroots Democracy, Accountability and Income Distribution: 225
    Evidence from Rural China
    Yan Shen and Yang Yao

Index   247

Notes on the Contributors

SHANKAR ACHARYA is a member of the Board of Governors and an honorary professor at the Indian Council for Research on International Economic Relations (ICRIER). He was chief economic adviser to the government of India from 1993 to 2000.

ROBERTO ÁLVAREZ is a senior economist at the research department of the Central Bank of Chile and a researcher at the Centre for Innovation and Entrepreneurship, University of Chile. He received a B.A. in economics from the University of Chile and M.A. and Ph.D. degrees from the University of California – Los Angeles. His research focuses on international trade, evaluation of state-sponsored programs, innovation and productivity.

JAMES WARNER BJÖRKMAN is professor of public policy and Administration at the Institute of Social Studies, The Hague, and professor of public administration and development at Leiden University. He has been a visiting professor at the University of Namibia and the International Centre for the Promotion of Enterprise in Ljubljana, Slovenia. Björkman has also taught at the University of Wisconsin and served as executive director of the International Institute of Comparative Government in Lausanne, Switzerland. He holds a doctorate in political science from Yale University.

CAI FANG holds a Ph.D. in economics from the Graduate School of the Chinese Academy of Social Sciences (CASS). Currently he is director of the Institute of Population and Labor Economics, CASS; dean of the Department of Population Studies, Graduate School of CASS; and director of the Center for Human Resources Research, CASS. His research focuses on development theory and policy, agricultural policy, economic reform in China, labor economics and demographic economics.

SEBASTIÁN CLARO is associate professor of economics at Pontificia Universidad Catolica de Chile, and since December 2007 he has been a board member of the Central Bank of Chile. He received a B.A. degree in economics from the Pontificia Universidad Catolica de Chile and an M.A. and Ph.D. in economics from the University of California – Los Angeles. His research has mainly focused on the economic transition in China, with special emphasis on the implications of trade and capital market integration for domestic firms, as well as the impact of China's growth in other developing economies.

NATALIA DINELLO has earned doctorate degrees from the University of Pittsburgh and the Soviet Academy of Science. In her current position as Political Environment Scanning Adviser at the United Nations Population Fund, she is responsible for monitoring and analyzing the external environment for the purpose of better strategy development and implementation. In her previous position as Principal Political Scientist at the Secretariat of the Global Development Network, she designed and implemented strategies and programs for building research capacity in developing and transition economies. She served as executive editor of the *Global Development Network Series* until August 2007 and co-edited three volumes in the series.

DAVID DOLLAR is the World Bank country director for China and Mongolia and has been based in Beijing since 2004. Prior to that he worked in the research complex of the Bank for nine years. He has published a wide range of research papers on trade and growth, growth and poverty, aid effectiveness and economic reform in China and Vietnam. Dollar was the Bank's country economist for Vietnam from 1989 to 1995. Prior to joining the Bank he taught in the economics department at the University of California – Los Angeles. He has a Ph.D. in economics from New York University and a B.A. in Asian Studies from Dartmouth College.

DU YANG is a professor at the Institute of Population and Labor Economics, Chinese Academy of Social Sciences. He earned a Ph.D. in economics from the University of Zhejiang in 1999. Much of his research uses primary source data collected in the Chinese labor market to understand how China's rapidly changing economic and policy environment affects the behavior of households and individuals. His studies have focused primarily on migrants, urban labor markets, how national policies affect households/individuals and the implications of labor market development on economic growth.

MAVANNOOR PARAMESWARAN is a lecturer at the Centre for Development Studies, Trivandrum, India. He holds a Ph.D. in economics from Jawaharlal Nehru University, New Delhi, India. His areas of research include industrial economics, growth economics and International Trade.

A. VENKAT RAMAN is an associate professor at the Faculty of Management Studies, University of Delhi, and teaches courses in human resource management and health services management. A graduate of the Tata Institute of Social Sciences, Bombay, Raman holds Ph.D. in management from Delhi University. He had been a visiting fellow at the Institute of Social Studies, The Hague, and has been associated with the World Bank Institute, USAID, DFID, GTZ, Population Council, and Population Foundation of India. He is currently working on PPP policy for health sector for the state of Madhya Pradesh and Delhi. His research interests include organizational reforms, human resource management, public-private partnership, and capacity building in the health sector.

YAN SHEN is an associate professor at China Center for Economic Research (CCER), Beijing University. She received her Bachelor in economics from Beijing University in 1997, and her Ph.D. in economics at the University of Southern California in 2003. Her research interests include applied micro-econometrics and economic development in China.

LAWRENCE SUMMERS is President Emeritus of Harvard University and served as secretary of the treasury of the United States from 1999 to 2000. Summers earned a doctorate in economics from Harvard University in 1982 and frequently taught at the university in subsequent years. Summers took leave from Harvard in 1991 to return to Washington, as vice president of development economics and chief economist of the World Bank. Two years later he was named undersecretary of the treasury for international affairs, and on July 2, 1999, the US Senate confirmed Summers as secretary of the treasury.

CHOORIKKADAN VEERAMANI is a visiting fellow at the Indira Gandhi Institute of Development Research Mumbai, India. He was previously a fellow at the Indian Council for Research on International Economic Relations (ICRIER), New Delhi, and an assistant professor at the Indian Institute of Technology, Bombay. Veeramani holds a doctorate in economics from Jawaharlal Nehru University. His areas of research include international trade, industrial development and economic reforms in India.

WANG MEIYAN is an associate professor at the Institute of Population and Labor Economics of the Chinese Academy of Social Sciences, Beijing.

WANG SHAOGUANG is professor of political science at the Chinese University of Hong Kong and the chief editor of the *China Review*, an interdisciplinary journal on greater China. He studied for his LL.B. at Peking University and his Ph.D. at Cornell University. He taught at Tijiao High School in Wuhan from 1972 to 1977 and Yale University from 1990 to 2000.

YANG YAO is a professor and deputy director of the China Center for Economic Research (CCER), Beijing University. He earned a B.S. in geography and an M.S. in economics from Beijing University and a doctorate in agricultural and applied economics from the University of Wisconsin-Madison. He currently serves as the acting director of CCER for academic affairs and editor of *China Economic Quarterly*.

LINDA Y. YUEH is a fellow in economics at St. Edmund Hall, University of Oxford. She is a visiting professor at the Economics Department of the London Business School and previously worked at the Economics Department at the London School of Economics and Political Science. Yueh is an associate of the Centre for Economic Performance at LSE, and Queen Elizabeth House (Department of International Development) at the University of Oxford. She practiced international corporate law while resident in New York, Beijing and Hong Kong prior to entering academia. Her research interests are in macroeconomics, economic growth and development, economic transition, and law and economics. She originated the Economic Development and Growth book series by World Scientific Publishing.

WUBIAO ZHOU is an assistant professor of sociology in the School of Humanities and Social Sciences at Nanyang Technological University, Singapore. He received his Ph.D. in sociology from Cornell University in 2006 and B.A. in sociology and law from Peking University in 1996. His current research areas include entrepreneurship, corporate governance and R&D.

Foreword: The Asian Miracle and its Implications

Lawrence Summers

The topic of this book is well chosen. No other event is as important today as the rise of Asia – centered on China and followed by India. To better understand how miraculous it is, a comparison with other important events of all times is in order.

The eighteenth-century industrialization and modernization era was called the Industrial Revolution because it introduced ground-breaking changes. At the beginning of that revolution, living standards in Europe were less than twice higher than in Athens 2,000 years earlier. Yet, because of the Industrial Revolution, within a single human life span (then only about 40 years), it was possible to imagine that living standards would increase by 50 per cent. As the revolution spread to the United States, it became possible to envision that within a singe human life span, living standards could increase by as much as a factor of four or five. What is happening in Asia today is much more spectacular. At a 6.5 per cent growth rate of per capita living standards (which is less than the average of the last ten years for China), living standards rise 100-fold within a single human life span! They rise more than living standards have increased in the United States since the country gained independence in 1776. And this is not an isolated event affecting a few people in some niche of the world. This is an event affecting a third or more of humanity, if one takes into account the populations of China and India and looks to the remainder of Asia.

An economic event with such a dramatic increase in living standards of a third of humanity is likely to exceed the impact of either the Renaissance or the Industrial Revolution. When historians record the history of our time 300 years from now, current developments in Asia – which change the lives of so many people, so quickly and have numerous ramifications for the global system – will be considered the most important story of the day. Developments in the Middle East – the region's conflicts, troubles and achievements – will probably be considered the second story in its importance. And the end of the Cold War – the 50-year struggle between the two economic and political systems – will be assigned only third place in contemporary history.

The Asian miracle should engage anyone concerned with development. Traditionally, discussions on development refer to the ways affluent societies can assist developing countries in order to achieve better socioeconomic outcomes improving people's lives. Even though such discussions are relevant in respect to Asia, the focus on assistance is not sufficient. The development of Asia is so significant, and the impact of a growing Asia on the global economy is so substantial, that many other questions need to be raised. Let me highlight here three major aspects of what the rise of Asia means for the world – indicating the issues rather than providing answers.

GLOBAL FLOW OF CAPITAL

We live in a world where mature industrialized economies with high standards of living grow much slower than emerging economies with far lower standards of living. If you ask an economist who lived on Mars for the last two decades about the direction of the capital flow under these conditions, he or she would most probably say 'from mature core to the rapidly growing periphery.' Wrong! The present-day net flow of capital is from emerging Asia to the industrialized core. And this trend is likely to continue – on an expanding scale – in the future. The most rapidly growing China is the world's largest lender, while the United States, the world's largest power, is the greatest borrower. This paradox should engage us because it is not clear how sustainable it can be and how desirable it is even if it can be sustained.

The numbers are impressive. China has accumulated a trillion dollars. Developing Asia has accumulated $2 trillion. The vast majority of this capital is held in US treasury bills or similar instruments at a less than 2 per cent yield in real terms or close to zero in local terms, if the growth of those societies and the likely capital appreciation are taken into account. Two trillion dollars which are invested at no return signal lost opportunities for productive investment and for productive consumption – for enabling people to enjoy the present and the fruits of prosperity in the future. To be sure, adequate reserves for insurance are an imperative. As US secretary of the treasury, I advocated the accumulation of reserves to avoid a liquidity crisis similar to the one experienced by Asia a decade ago. But $2 trillion dollars in reserve certainly constitute a paradox.

Contemporary tendencies in the global flow of capital also raise a long-run question about recipients of this capital. How long can the United States run a deficit as large as it is running? Will the confidence to lend still be there as the $2 trillion turn into $4 trillion? Will there be a willingness to accept exports from Asia and imports to the United States which are concomitant to this large capital imbalance? How can this issue be best addressed? This is the first series of questions posed by the rise of Asia.

GLOBAL FLOW OF GOODS AND SERVICES

The second issue is that of profound distributional consequences of the Asian miracle. For the global distribution of income, the rise of China and India is by far the best thing which has ever happened. Globally, the situation of humanity is improving, and the condition of the poorest on the planet is improving most rapidly. So, citizens of China and India and other emerging nations are enormous winners from the latest developments. Moreover, those with the wherewithal to take advantage of new opportunities are also enormous winners: major financial institutions, leaders of large multinational corporations and those with the ability to create ideas or sell sophisticated products in expanded global markets.

However, there exists a vast global middle – workers from Michigan, farmers from Mexico and merchants from Morocco – for whom this phenomenon of globalization may not be favorable. This global middle does not have the capacity to be at the cutting edge of the global economy to benefit from its opportunities and at the same time cannot compete on price with labor from China or India. Of course, protectionism carries many dangers, while there are enormous consumer benefits from the rise of Asia. But the question about the impact of Asia's miraculous emergence on the vast global middle and how it should be cushioned is neither well researched nor resolved. In the meantime, the impatience of the polity in many places is increasing.

GLOBAL FLOW OF INFLUENCE AND POWER

In defining the third question let me start with the historical observation that whenever there is an important change in the distribution of relative economic strength, the geopolitical consequences are profound. *Dangerous Nation* by Robert Kagan (Knopf, 2006) describes how people who lived in Mexico, the Caribbean, the Philippines or west of the Mississippi River between 1607 and 1898 perceived the United States. Kagan's book is quite sobering for an American. History is less benign and more complex than standard US history textbooks may suggest. And it teaches some lessons on how narrow minded responses to rising economic power bred frustration and conflict.

China, India and other developing countries make impressive efforts to understand the US and European perspectives as well as perspectives of international organizations. However, no effort of comparable intensity goes on within the United States, Europe and international organizations to grasp the hopes, fears, aspirations and worries of these societies which are so rapidly transforming. Returning to the previous point, the rate of change in Asia is far greater than anything that ever happened in the United States. And the present-day impact of Asia on the United States and the industrialized world is enormous, involving a particularly dramatic effect on the global middle. That is why this subject is going to dominate the history of our time and why we owe it thoughtful and careful consideration.

IMPORTANCE OF ECONOMIC RESEARCH

This book is a result of economic research conducted by scholars affiliated with the Global Development Network (GDN). I am an ardent believer in research and its capacity to contribute to understanding the present and anticipating the future. A few anecdotes would highlight its importance.

In 1995, soon after President Ernesto Zedillo, the current chair of the GDN Board of Directors, came to power in Mexico, his country faced a very severe financial challenge. To contain the crisis, the United States and the International Monetary Fund were engaged in lending money to Mexico on an extraordinary scale, tens of billions of dollars. When I met with President Zedillo – upon President Bill Clinton's request – to assess the situation and share the perspective of the US administration, our conversation went much beyond the scheduled meeting items. The President of Mexico started discussing a variety of research which had been done on the economics of information, adverse selection, moral hazard and what it meant for credit rationing and the possible impacts on increasing interest rates. So, on a dark day of financial crisis, the president of that nation was profoundly concerned about results of economic research.

Some time later there was another financial crisis in China, and I was sent by President Clinton to meet with the then Chinese Prime Minister Zhu Rongji. At some point in the discussion, Mr. Zhu said: 'Tell me, Professor Summers, who is correct – Stanley Fischer or Joseph Stiglitz – in assessing what should be done with monetary policy in the context of a crisis?' He proceeded to tell all about his previous meeting with [the Nobel Prize Winner in Economics] Merton Miller and Miller's views on issuing put options with respect to the *renminbi* and whether they would diminish effectiveness. More recently, I spoke to a student who traded in environmental permits for carbon on the

European exchange, and he discussed a variety of theories on how the relative prices of carbon permits in Europe would move with carbon permits in China. And again I realized that the world has been changed by the results of economic research.

To give one more example, it is now a commonplace idea that the reason people go hungry is because they lack the wherewithal to *buy* food – not because there is no food. This is now an insight which informs all efforts to respond to famines. When I went to a graduate school 30 years ago, this was not a common belief. At that time, it was thought that the world needs to figure out how to produce more food. And if the world figures out how to produce more food, famines will disappear. This change in the perspective is also a result of economic research. Therefore, we should not underestimate the importance of intellectual debates which identify factors of success or failure: the incentive schemes that determine whether teachers show up for work, the resource allocation schemes that determine whether syringes are available to provide immunization, questions about pricing of water which are literally matters of life and death for hundreds of people around the world.

This book assembles social science research on the most important topic of our time. It is particularly helpful that GDN brings out the voices of scholars from the developing world – those who are underrepresented in contemporary literature and whose views are invaluable for managing the global economy. Every phenomenon has two sides – positive and negative, drivers and limitations. By analyzing the two sides of the rise of China and India, this book should enrich our understanding of the Asian miracle and contribute to its balanced interpretation.

Introduction

China and India: Is the Glass Half-Full or Half-Empty?

Natalia Dinello and Wang Shaoguang

China and India have captured the attention and imagination of economists, business people, political observers and the general public in the early years of the new century. However, the stories about their rise and prospects vary significantly. Three different narratives have acquired prominence in the social science literature.

First, some authors have dubbed the twenty-first century the 'Asian century', with China and India serving as engines of global development. As indicated by David Kelly and Ramkishen Rajan (2006, 1), 'With the exception of the crisis period in 1997–1999, Asia has been the world's fastest growing region for the last three decades'. Hubert Schmitz (2007, 1) claimed, 'The speed of industrialization in China and other Asian countries is breathtaking. They are not just catching up, they have begun to drive the changes in the rest of the world'. In earlier publications, Jim Rohwer (1995) placed Asia's spectacular rise in historical and global perspectives,[1] while Nicholas Kristof and Sheryl WuDunn (2001) showed how Asia managed to recover from the 1997 crisis to become stronger than ever.

The views that single out Asia – and 'Chindia' in particular – have solid foundations. The 'Four Little Dragons' (also known as the 'East Asian Tigers') – Hong Kong, Taiwan, Singapore and South Korea – impressed the world with high growth rates and rapid industrialization from the early 1960s through the 1990s. The Giant Dragons – China and India – have demonstrated unprecedentedly high and continuous growth rates in the last two decades. They have also spurred overwhelming interest because of their large size; together they account for 37.5 per cent of the world's population and 6.4 per cent of world output and income (Winters and Yusuf 2007, 1). Considering China's hardware (a dynamic manufacturing sector) and India's software (an extremely successful IT industry), many observers think that these two countries can overtake the world.

The second school of thought recognizes that China and India are currently at the forefront of world development. However, while applauding their achievements, it denies the existence of the phenomenon of Chindia. Most of the analysts sharing this view believe that China significantly outperforms India, although some claim that it is the other way around. Yasheng Huang and Tarun Khanna in a now-famous article in *Foreign Policy* alleged that India's path is more promising compared with China's due to the extraordinary success of homegrown entrepreneurship (Huang and Khanna 2003).

The third narrative is much more skeptical and pessimistic. It questions not only the phenomenon of Chindia, but also argues that the impact of either of these two countries on the world is limited, and the prospect of continued growth is doubtful in the long run. For example, Pranab Bardhan writes: 'Severe structural and institutional problems will hobble them [China and India] for years to come. At this point, the hype about the Indian economy seems patently premature, and the risks on the horizon for the Chinese polity – and hence for economic stability – highly underestimated' (Bardhan 2005). Indeed, both China and India are still very poor countries, illiteracy in India remains very high and agriculture continues to be a dominant sector.

The authors of this volume do not share the third view. Instead, they are consistent in acknowledging the significance of China and India for the global economy. Nevertheless, there are variations in their perceptions of how much the rise of China and India matters for the world and how sustainable the growth of China and India can be. In his foreword to this book, Lawrence Summers compares the present-day 'Asian miracle' with the eighteenth-century Industrial Revolution and finds Asia much more 'miraculous' – 'the most important story of the day', he contends (xi). Summers' exuberant view is not shared by all contributors. David Dollar, for example, is much more sober. He questions the notion of the Asian miracle and prefers to highlight China's outstanding performance, that leaves India much behind: 'The "rise of Asia" is something of a myth', he writes. 'During 1990–2005 China accounted for 28 per cent of global growth, measured at purchasing power parity (PPP). India accounted for 9 per cent. The rest of developing Asia, with nearly a billion people, accounted for only 7 per cent, the same as Latin America. Hence there is no general success of Asian developing economies'. Furthermore, 'There is too much heterogeneity within Asia to make "Asian Century" a very useful concept' (48). Similarly Linda Yueh underscores the exceptional progress of China: 'When adjusted for PPP, China is currently the world's second-largest economy. It is also the world's largest country in terms of population (and potential market), a leading destination for foreign direct investment and the one of the three largest traders' (3).

The difference in the interpretation of the present and the forecasts of the future boil down to the perception of the balance between drivers and limitations of development. Those who see the glass half-full or sometimes absolutely full emphasize the drivers of China's and India's development, such as strong human capital and technological progress, flexible labor markets, openness to the global economy and institutional environments which enable growth. Those who see the glass half-empty focus their attention on existing limitations of growth such as infrastructure bottlenecks, trade imbalances, resource scarcity, environmental degradation and too cozy relations between state and business.

This book seeks to test models and assertions with evidence from practitioners in these two countries. The book is organized in two parts. The first part provides an overview of economic growth in China and India and compares these countries' recent progress with that of the rest of Asia. The second part empirically analyzes the drivers and limitations of their growth, primarily based on micro-level data and covering a broad set of topics ranging from international trade and investment to health care and grassroots democracy.

The book is comprised of papers presented at the Eighth Annual Global Development Conference, held in Beijing, China, in January 2007. The conference was organized by the Global Development Network (GDN), an organization with the dual mission of building research capacity in social science and bridging research and policy. Similar to previous publications in the Global Development Network Series, that are designed to give voice to researchers from the developing and transition world (Aryeetey and Dinello 2007; Dinello and Popov 2007; Squire and Fanelli 2008), this book brings together recognized scholars from both developing and developed countries as well as lesser known researchers from developing countries, whose contribution to international social science literature should be noticed and regarded on its merits. Consistent with GDN's mission of promoting high-quality research in all disciplines of social science, the book assembles articles by authors representing economics, political science and sociology.

DRIVERS OF DEVELOPMENT

Asia-watchers have suggested a variety of factors driving China's development. Dollar, for example, contends that China has grown better than its developing neighbors because it started its reform with a better base of human capital, has been more open to foreign trade and investment, and created good investment climates in coastal cities. To further analyze factors stimulating China's growth, the following sections highlight drivers identified by Dollar – human capital, trade liberalization and a favorable investment climate – as well as other causes of accelerated development – technological progress, flexible labor markets, and the institutional environment – which are far from perfect but, nevertheless, enable growth.

Human Capital and Technological Progress

Many students of human capital are quick to refer to China's superior literacy rate. However, the higher literacy rate in China, including female literacy (87 per cent, compared with 45 per cent in India) is considered to be a legacy of the past. Despite the disruption caused by the Chinese social and economic experiments of the 1950s, 1960s and 1970s, the revolution did produce a literate population. At the same time, India boasts an advanced research community and highly sophisticated professionals, particularly in information technology (IT) and pharmaceuticals. While China's growth was driven by manufactured exports which exploited its skillful yet cheap labor, India is now relying on the human capital of its professional elite to move forward. According to Kripalani and Engardio, 'If India can turn into a fast-growth economy, it will be the first developing country that used its brainpower, not natural resources or the raw muscle of factory labor, as the catalyst' (2003, 70). Confirming the importance of human capital, the four case studies presented at GDN's 2006 conference – two from India (the software and space industries) and two from China (the automotive and personal computer industries) – have shown that it is possible for developing countries to catch up technologically with developed countries. Furthermore, both countries put great emphasis on skills development, not only as government policy, but also as a cultural practice deeply rooted in Chinese values as well as among India's upper castes (Altenburg, Schmitz and Stamm 2006, 30).

Dollar acknowledges China's historical advantage in terms of literacy, citing extensive data and studies by Christian Morrisson and Fabrice Murtin (2005) as well as by Robert Barro and Jong-Wha Lee (2000): 'Already in 1870, 21 per cent of adults in China were literate – since nearly all of these would have been males, this means that about 40 per cent of adult males were literate. … In 1990, even though China was poorer than India or RODA [the rest of developing Asia], it had a more educated population' (89). Dollar also points to another aspect of China's superiority in human capital – infant mortality data, that are a good summary indicator of health status: 'In 1990 China's infant mortality rate was 38 per 1,000, far below India's 80 or RODA's 69' (50).

Contemplating the relative terms of human capital development in the near and medium future, some scholars draw attention to India's 'demographic dividend'. China faces the non-enviable position of having become old (due to the aging population) before becoming rich. But India stands to benefit from the growth dividend of its young population (Kelly and Rajan 2006, 11). However, as Acharya notes, India's prospective advantage depends on the country's ability to educate the next generation (38).

Leaving the future aside, it is nevertheless China which today is successfully building on its human capital 'must transform from a growth model based on productivity advances from factor reallocation to one which is fuelled by technological advancement and innovation' (19). As indicated by Yueh in Chapter 1, 'The need to improve domestic productivity has led China to become one of the largest investors in research and development in the 2000s' (17). Human capital and technological progress, as signaled by the R&D expenditure, are thus widely used in China to stimulate the intensive growth which has become the country's trademark.

Labor Market Flexibility

Radical reforms are usually painful. But they often produce unexpected means to adapt to change which, although not perfect, can partially relieve the pains and further drive development. Chapter 8 by Yang Du, Fang Cai and Meiyan Wang, in the second part of the book, discusses labor market informalization in China as a way to adjust to the process of dismantling of the communist-era employment system, known as 'breaking the iron rice bowl'. Informal employment has many disadvantages compared with formal employment, such as lower earnings, longer working hours, inadequate work conditions and the lack of social protection. But it is still better than unemployment and – due to its low costs, market dependency and flexibility in hiring and firing – it can increase labor mobility, create additional opportunities for investment and contribute to sustainable development.

Relying on China's Comprehensive Labor Statistics Reporting System and a household survey, Du, Cai and Wang show that informal employment has been growing in post-reform China. They provide evidence that the flexibility offered by informal employment has promoted a form of work which offers greater security than the existing social security system, even though this is not an excuse for neglecting state-sponsored social security. Informal employment has been the main path for developing a labor market in China, and allowing wage rates to be determined by the market is a key source of growth in this labor-abundant country. Equipped with their findings, these researchers caution the Chinese government that its zeal to further regulate the labor market could destroy the informal sector's positive effects on job creation and poverty reduction. They also advocate enhancing education and providing training in order to gradually formalize employment, while preserving labor market flexibility.

Openness

As noted by Dollar, the Chinese refer to their reform program as *Gai ge kai fang* which translates as 'change the system, open the door', while the whole reform program is often called the 'open door' policy. Having first welcomed foreign direct investment (FDI) into 'special economic zones', China has become the world's largest recipient of investment flows. Trade liberalization was another key component of Chinese reform: ... after joining the World Trade Organization China's average tariffs have dropped below 10 per cent, and to around 5 per cent for manufactured imports (52). Yueh also emphasizes the importance of China's outward-looking development model. 'For an economy of its size, China has a high degree of openness (70 per cent when measured as exports plus imports as a proportion of GDP), as compared with 37 per cent for the comparatively open United Kingdom and 20 per cent for the more closed United States' (3).

Writing about India, Acharya finds the same trend. The country's 'economy in 2006 is far more open to external trade, investment and technology than it was 15 years ago' (28). In Chapter 6 Mavannor Parameswaran similarly contends, 'India is moving from an import substituting and inward-oriented trade policy regime toward a more open and liberal trade policy regime' (120). These views are consistent with that of L. Alan Winters and Shahid Yusuf (2007, 9): 'China's trade expansion since 1978 has been legendary, and, since the early 1990s, India also has taken off.' Moreover, both countries have been the most attractive FDI destinations in the world – ahead of the United States (Kelly and Rajan 2006, 9).

But although China and India are similar in their drive toward openness, China is much ahead of India. 'China has done more to open its economy to the global market', Dollar notes, 'while significant numbers of its coastal cities have created sound investment climates for private investment. The result has been a remarkable growth dynamic. India has followed a similar path, but more slowly in terms of opening up the economy and with less success in creating good investment climates' (54). Acharya expresses this difference between the two countries even more emphatically, protesting, 'The prevailing fashion of bracketing India's rise with China's exceptionally dynamic development under rubrics like "China and India Rising" may mask more than it reveals' (41). Acharya's comparison of India's 'good' versus China's 'extraordinary' development in the last 25 years largely hinges on his evaluation of the degree and pace of opening up their economies: 'While India has been a gradual "globalizer", China's surging development has been far more intensively based on global trade and capital flows' (41).

Trade Liberalization and its Impact

Part 2 of the volume continues the focus on development, concentrating specifically on drivers of and barriers to development. Echoing Acharya, in Chapter 4 Choorikkadan Veeramani contrasts China's dramatic opening up since 1978 with India's 'cautious liberalization' launched in the 1980s and highlights such consequences of trade liberalization as the expansion of intra-industry trade[2] versus inter-industry trade.[3] This distinction is crucial, because if the intensity of intra-industry trade increases with the reduction of trade barriers, this would undermine a common argument that import liberalization leads to the demise of domestic industries in the developing countries. Also, intra-industry adjustment is associated with relatively low costs because it entails workers' movement within industries rather than between them. Based on his research, Veeramani comes to the conclusion that by 2005 the manufacturing industries of China and India show roughly similar intensity of intra-industry trade. Growth of intra-industry trade reflects greater specialization in unique varieties and product lines by the individual plants in China and India, demonstrating that the large majority of domestic industries and firms in both China and India can successfully compete and survive under liberal trade regimes via specialization in narrow product lines. This finding gives ammunition to supporters of globalization, by providing empirical evidence that the elimination of trade barriers is consistent with developing countries' interests.

While Veeramani discusses the impact of trade liberalization on China and India, Chapter 5 examines the sources of China's export growth and analyzes how trade liberalization in China affects the rest of the world. Based on the detailed data on Chilean imports between 1990 and 2005, Roberto Álvarez and Sebastián Claro first show that China's strong export penetration relative to other countries is mainly explained by an increase in the intensive margin; that is, an increase in the volume of exports in product categories which are also exported by other countries. Surprisingly, the main source of growth in the intensive margin is explained by an increase in exported quantities, without a significant fall in the relative price of Chinese products. One explanation for this apparent paradox is an increase in the willingness to pay for quality Chinese products relative to the rest of the world. Their study provides direct and indirect evidence of the growing sophistication of China's export mix.

In particular, it demonstrates that exports from China have increased their similarity with exports from rich countries, and that the quality of Chinese exports has improved over time. The research findings confirm that product quality does indeed matter, and that it is an important dimension of Chinese export growth. They also corroborate Dani Rodrik's (2006) evidence that, given China's level of income per capita, the country has a sophisticated export mix because a high share of its exports corresponds to products mainly exported by high-income countries.

Parameswaran analyzes a very different type of trade liberalization impact – the effect on firms' R&D investment. This analysis adds to the debate on whether a more open trade policy regime accelerates the technological prowess and growth of an economy. Parameswaran shows that exporting firms have greater incentive to invest in R&D, suggesting that trade liberalization and the subsequent removal of the anti-export bias of the system can encourage innovation and technological progress. Moreover, he finds that the impact of import competition depends on the domestic market structure. Specifically, import competition promotes investment in R&D only in those industries where the market structure is highly concentrated; otherwise, it has a negative impact.

Thus, the study reveals the conditional nature of the impact of trade liberalization and thereby highlights the need for complementary policies to make domestic conditions favorable. To improve innovation and technological progress of the domestic industry, trade policy should be aligned with suitable industrial policy. In particular, industrial policy should help firms achieve a scale of operation viable for undertaking various productivity-enhancing investments. An example would be a removal of legal barriers on entry and exit and removing restrictions on the scale of operations, mergers and amalgamation, which would allow an industry to adjust to the liberal trade policy regime by increasing its technological standards.

The three empirical studies of the impacts of trade liberalization send the same message: liberal trade regimes can be beneficial to both developed and developing countries and to both exporters and importers. Moreover, countries' accomplishments – whether an improvement in product quality or meeting challenges of import competition – are generally well rewarded. However, taking advantage of trade under conditions of economic openness requires mastering the art of adjustment. Specialization in unique varieties and product lines may be an effective response to import liberalization. An improvement in product quality can go together with price reduction as a result of surging productivity. Finally, trade policy should be complemented with effective industrial policy to achieve innovation and greater productivity.

FDI and Investment Climate

This book also discusses the factors responsible for the inflow of FDI into China and India, building on previous studies. China's foreign-investment boom is largely attributed to the power of the Chinese diaspora worldwide. Most investment comes to China from Hong Kong, Macau and Taiwan. This phenomenon is sometimes called 'China plus': China plus key neighbors and China plus multinational companies which have established their factories in the country (Schmitz 2007, 2). Compared with the Chinese, the Indian diaspora is much less connected to the homeland.

In Chapter 3 Dollar emphasizes that the 'opening up' measures had such substantial impact because they were accompanied by improvements in investment climate. Claiming that this is probably one of the least understood features of China's recent development, he refers to Chinese coastal cities which developed good investment climates which, in turn, catapulted the private sector into the leading sector of the economy and made it highly profitable. For example, while Indian firms lose 7.9 per cent of their output due to unreliable power supplies, the comparable figure for firms located in coastal Chinese cities is 1.0 per cent; while it takes an average of 6.6 days for imports to clear customs in India, it is only 3.2 days in Chinese cities (54). In general, there are fewer constraints on the private sector in China. For example, it takes 90 days to start a business in India, but only 30 days in China (Dollar, Hallward-Driemeier, Shi, Wallsten, Wang and Xu 2003, 3).

However, even though FDI is widely recognized as a driver of economic development, not all observers are euphoric about China's over-reliance on this channel. In his provocatively titled book, *Selling China*, Yasheng Huang (2003) argues that China's reliance on FDI reflects the huge deficiencies and lower competitiveness of its corporate sector. While India receives little FDI, it has cultivated impressive entrepreneurship within leading global companies such as Infosys, Wipro and Tata Consultancy Services.

Another paradox is that China's incredible economic openness is not supported by political openness. This mismatch, due to the country's authoritarian (closed and strongly regulated) political system, may jeopardize the sustainability of China's development in the long run. Conversely, India is an open society in the political sense, but it displays limited economic openness. The question about the relative importance of economic (FDI and trade) versus political openness (democracy and freedoms) as drivers of development naturally raises the issue of institutions.

Institutions

Thanks to reforms the general institutional environment in both countries is improving, although they still leave much to be desired. The courts are slow and corruption is rampant in China as well as India. Both China and India ranked 70th on the 2006 Transparency International Corruption Perceptions Index, while the 'cleanest' nations included Finland, Iceland and New Zealand. Private property rights are not sufficiently protected in China, and in India, contracts are not always enforced, ownership of land is often unclear and the bureaucracy is slow.

Some observers, nonetheless, claim that the 'soft' infrastructure of institutions, including legal institutions, is better in India. Questioning the image of India lagging behind China, Huang and Khanna (2003, 78) write: 'Although India's courts are notoriously inefficient, they at least comprise a functioning independent judiciary. Property rights are not fully secure, but the protection of private ownership is certainly far stronger than in China. The rule of law, a legacy of the British rule, generally prevails'. Furthermore, while China has no institutional framework for managing dissent, India is considered to be a 'messy democracy', and its government does not interfere much in private sector activities apart from providing a regulatory framework. As a result, home-grown entrepreneurship flourishes in India, while China 'has imposed substantial legal and regulatory constraints on indigenous, private firms' (Huang and Khanna 2003, 76).

Chapter 10 by Yan Shen and Yang Yao challenges the near consensus that China lacks democratic institutions. The authors focus on the country's grassroots democracy, that they interpret as 'a significant milestone in China's progression toward a full democracy' (243). In 1987, the National People's Congress (NPC) passed a tentative version of the Organic Law on the Village Committee, that started a ten-year-long experiment with village elections. In 1998, the NPC formally passed the law and elections quickly spread throughout the whole country. Yan and Yao admit, 'The elections hardly take place in a friendly institutional environment' (225). Within the village, the authority of the elected village committee is seriously constrained, if not superseded, by the Communist Party committee. Outside a village, the township and county governments still maintain a heavy hand in village affairs. Also, the decentralized nature of the election may make it easier for local elites to capture local politics. Nevertheless, based on survey data, the researchers come to the striking conclusion that despite all constraints on village democracy, such interference actually improves accountability and income distribution in the community. This finding has significant policy implications for the current debate on China. First, it shows that grassroots democracy can work even in a distorted institutional environment. Second, villagers can quickly learn how to run a functioning democracy and steer it toward serving their interests. Third, the reduction in income inequality can be achieved through the villages' pro-poor actions, such as increasing productive investments. The Chinese experience thus defies the conventional wisdom that democracy necessarily leads to policies focused on redistribution.

Yan and Yao's conclusions challenge Acharya's contention that democratic populism is a significant source of fiscal stress. Referring to the advent of India's United Progressive Alliance government in 2004 and its populist expenditure programs, such as the National Rural Employment Guarantee scheme, Acharya asserts that 'the possibility of significant public pay increases [and, as a result, fiscal pressure] is obviously high' (35). The difference in the perceptions between Yan and Yao, on one hand, and Acharya, on the other, may be due to the difference in the focus of their analysis – the small-scale village elections versus national democracy. Yan and Yao maintain, 'Within the village context of lineage and other intimate ties, it may be easier for the villagers to reach more productive decisions than to fight for more short-term redistribution' (244). In contrast, large-scale democracies are inevitably less flexible and less mobile and, as a result, have to resort to manageable 'short cuts', such as arbitrary pay raises and income redistribution schemes to satisfy their constituencies.

Similar to the lack of agreement on the fiscal implications of democracy, the impact of democracy on development also remains a contentious issue. Theoretically, democracy is beneficial for development (see, for example, Sen 1999). But the empirical evidence to support this assertion is scarce, leading Dollar to conclude: 'In developing Asia there is no clear relationship between political systems and good economic governance' (57–58). Dollar goes on to elaborate his point:

> Leaving developed countries out of the analysis, there is no correlation between democracy as measured by Freedom House and ICRG's [International Country Risk Guide] property rights/rule of law index ... In the very long run there is likely to be a relationship – all the fully industrialized countries have both good economic governance and liberal democracy. But the lack of correlation between democracy and economic governance among developing countries suggests that the relationship is a long-run one, and probably a complex one with causality running both ways (58).

This mixed evidence about institutions confirms the major finding of the previous book in the Global Development Network Series, *Political Institutions and Development* (Dinello and Popov 2007), that highlighted the failed expectation that there is one optimal institutional design which can be successfully applied to any country. Based on macro- and micro-level studies, *Political Institutions and Development* showed that institutions are highly context-dependent and time-sensitive and must be tailored to local conditions. Consistent with this understanding, China and India may require quite different institutional designs to resolve similar problems, such as corruption, insufficient protection of property rights and slow bureaucracy. Both Indian-style 'messy democracy' or Chinese-style gradual democratization, starting with village elections, should build on local advantages and be effectively customized to meet the existing challenges and further promote development.

BARRIERS TO DEVELOPMENT AND CHALLENGES AHEAD

When assessing China's and India's recent development and its sustainability, skeptics tend to focus on existing limitations on growth. Some of these challenges are short-term (for example, infrastructure bottlenecks for India, trade imbalances for China, the international economic environment for both); some medium-term (resource scarcity, environmental degradation and growing inequality); and others are structural (i.e., cozy relations between state and business). The analysis of limitations included in this book does not necessarily apply to both countries. But the collection of studies gives an overall sense of the factors which weaken these countries' economic growth and endanger their social development.

Short-Term Limitations

In Chapter 2 Acharya writes extensively about the 'legendary problems' of India's infrastructure; issues which reflect failures in public sector performance and governance. Referring to World Bank data, he indicates that over 60 per cent of Indian manufacturing firms own generator sets (only 27 per cent in China), and India's combined real cost of power is almost 40 per cent higher than China's. The quantity and quality of roads is also a serious choke point. While there has been some progress in recent years with national highway development, state and rural road networks are woefully inadequate, especially in poorer regions. Urban infrastructure, especially water and sewerage, is another major constraint for rapid industrial development and urbanization (35).

Compared with India's creaking seaports, airports, roads and power supplies (Kelly and Rajan 2006, 9–10) China has considerable physical infrastructure (in particular highways, telephone service and energy supply). At the same time, China's 'institutional infrastructure' – such as the banking, legal and judicial systems – is frail. Yueh maintains that China has 'weak formal institutions, particularly those required to support contracting and to reduce the risk of appropriation' (11). Nevertheless, China, with its exceptional economic growth, has relatively more resources to address this weakness. As noted by T.N. Srinivasan (2004, 7), 'The potential budgetary impact of addressing the non-performing loans of state-owned banks in India is more serious than in the case of China because of the better fiscal health of China'.

In the immediate future, the trade imbalance between China and the United States is a real worry. The current situation is not sustainable, and China needs to shift its production away from exports and toward internal needs such as better social services and higher household consumption. Dollar is quite categorical in outlining possible consequences of the trade imbalance: 'If the two countries do not cooperate on resolving the trade imbalance through higher savings in the United States and greater consumption in China (including public spending on health and education), there could be a nasty global recession with high US dollar interest rates and sharply falling commodity prices, that would create a very poor environment for the rest of the developing world' (48–49).

Moreover, although the international economic environment has been so far favorable to the development of China and India, its preservation is not guaranteed, and there can be negative consequences for both China and India if this environment deteriorates. Focusing on consequences for India, Acharya writes: 'The chances of some slackening in the growth of world output and trade are clearly rising. Just as the Indian economy has benefited from strong global expansion in the last four years, so it may expect to bear some downside risks from slower world growth in the years ahead' (39).

Medium-Term Limitations

Many observers believe that strong economic growth in China and India puts heavy pressure on global natural resources and significantly increases environmental pollution (Winters and Yusuf 2007, 16; OECD 2005). Dollar describes the related concerns about impending resource scarcity and deterioration of the environment in relation to China. He points to the very high rates of resource consumption by the Chinese economy: 'Over the past 15 years China's oil imports have been growing rapidly … and [the country] has emerged as the second-largest importer behind the United States. Before long it will emerge as the largest importer' (61). He also highlights the country's incredible inefficiency in the use of resources, particularly energy. High resource consumption, compounded by their inefficient use has resulted in high levels of pollution, especially air pollution. Considering these unfortunate circumstances, Dollar predicts, 'In the medium term, the resource-intensity of China's growth is not sustainable' (47).

Growing inequality is another medium-term challenge facing China. Although China has achieved the most rapid poverty reduction in human history over the last 30 years, that trend has begun to reverse in recent years, raising concerns about whether the country's future transformation would be balanced. The rural–urban differences are the most obvious dimension of inequality in China, in fact ranking as one of the worst in the world for this indicator. Another important dimension is the large gap between coastal and interior provinces. While the rural–urban differences fuel massive migration from the countryside to cities, the regional disparities boost migration across the country. Already about 200 million people have relocated. In the next 10–15 years, another 200 million will likely follow suit. Such migration may be a source of growth as people move from lower- to higher-productivity employment, but it is an enormous challenge to ensure that migration on such a gigantic scale proceeds smoothly.

On top of rural–urban and regional disparities, there are also growing inequities within the countryside and among urban residents. As Dollar admits, China's Gini coefficient (0.41) is not high compared with larger Latin American countries (Brazil's Gini coefficient is 0.58 and Mexico's is 0.50). But still the rapid recent increase in inequality is a real concern. Due to inadequate public expenditure, 'China, ironically, has one of the most privatized health care and education systems in the world in which the majority of expenditure is paid for privately, out of peoples' pockets' (63). This, in turn, results in slower social improvements (for example, a slower decline in infant mortality) than expected. The top political leadership in China has recognized this problem, that is reflected in Beijing's current focus on developing a more 'harmonious society'.

Compared with China, social development in India is even more difficult, as there are fewer resources to invest due to lower rates of economic growth. Consequently, many social services have crumbled. Approximately 29 per cent of India's population (almost 300 million people) live below the poverty line and depend on free health services from the public sector. But as shown by Raman and Björkman in Chapter 7, deficiencies in India's public health system force the poor to seek services from the private sector, that has grown remarkably. Based on 16 case studies of public–private partnerships in nine states of India, Raman and Björkman find that if well designed and implemented in stages, public–private partnerships have proven to be an innovative mechanism to deliver health services to the poor. However, given current limitations, the public sector must build capacity within its own institutions in order to optimize the benefits of partnerships. They also contend that while it is unfair to describe such partnerships as 'privatization', they are no substitute for more efficient governance of the public sector health system.

The overall quality of health services in India leaves much to be desired. Acharya notes that the staff in primary health clinics in many Indian states are not as competent as their counterparts in other developing countries, such as Tanzania and Indonesia (39). Policies and programs for education and skills development are yet one more weak spot for India. Even though school enrolment rates have climbed over time, the actual cognitive skills acquired in schools (even simple reading and arithmetic) are still very low (Pratham 2006). Government-led programs in critical social sectors suffer from the lack of reform impetus. Unless health care and education are significantly improved, India will not be able to retain its competitive edge in an increasingly globalized, knowledge-based world economy.

India's feeble agriculture sector constitutes another serious drag on the economy. As Acharya points out, 'The share of agriculture in GDP has declined to hardly 20 per cent. But agriculture is still the principal occupation of nearly 60 per cent of the labor force. Thus improving the performance of this sector is essential to alleviate poverty and contain rising regional and income inequalities' (38). However, since the mid-1990s, the growth of agriculture has dropped to barely 2 per cent, compared with earlier trend rates ranging between 2.5 and 3.0 per cent. There are many reasons behind this frailty, including 'declining public investment by cash-strapped states, grossly inadequate maintenance of irrigation assets, falling water tables, inadequate rural road networks, unresponsive research and extension services, soil damage from excessive area use (encouraged by high subsidies), weak credit delivery and a distorted incentive structure which impedes diversification away from food grains' (37). To revitalize agriculture, India needs greater investments in (and maintenance of) rural infrastructure such as irrigation, roads and soil conservation, and it must reinvigorate the present systems of agricultural research and application. These are difficult tasks for India's state governments, given their weak financial and administrative capabilities.

Structural Challenges

Yueh regards the 'close relationship among the state, state-owned enterprises and state-owned banks' as 'the core of the structural problems in China's transition path' (3). This coziness manifests itself at the national as well as the provincial level. The state's deep involvement in the economy – i.e., soft budget constraints due to refinancing of loss-making enterprises – undermines firm discipline and contributes to their inefficiency.

Continuing the theme of improper relationships between state and business, in Chapter 9 Wubiao Zhou confirms that many Chinese entrepreneurs are eager to obtain a political position in order to promote their enterprises. Membership in China's People's Congress (PC) and People's Political Consultative Conference (PPCC) are among the most attractive positions for private entrepreneurs, because they carry with them substantial legitimacy and social capital benefits. Based on the 2000 National Survey of Chinese Private Enterprises, that includes data on more than 3,000 private firms from all 31 Chinese provinces, Zhou's study suggests that even though the PC and PPCC have little real political power and simply endorse Communist Party decisions, memberships in these bodies can facilitate access to bank loans for private entrepreneurs. This is very important because the private sector, especially small- or medium-sized private firms, have great difficulties securing loans from China's state-owned or state-regulated banks.

The research on financing China's entrepreneurs is part of a broader debate on how state–business coziness affects economic development. Zhou demonstrates that because of the unfriendly regulatory environment, Chinese entrepreneurs have resorted to political strategies and networks to resolve their financing problem. Such entrepreneurial political behavior may involve rent seeking and corruption. The competition among entrepreneurs for legislative posts creates opportunities for local party officials to extract bribes from competitors. Corruption may also emerge when an entrepreneur uses high-status contacts to establish relationship lending or to intervene in bank credit decisions. Nevertheless, Zhou is less straightforward than Yueh in characterizing this phenomenon as purely negative. He makes a distinction between the consequences of state–business coziness in the short and long run and argues that his findings provide some support to the view that corruption may serve as temporary grease for the wheels of commerce. However, in the long run state favoritism discourages many other private entrepreneurs and will inevitably constrain economic development.

Finally, the book focuses on India's labor market rigidities as enormous structural obstacles. In the last 20 years the country's labor force has grown to more than 400 million people. Yet India's non-agricultural employment in the private organized sector (units employing more than 10 workers) has stagnated below 9 million people. Acharya faults India's complex and rigid labor laws, perhaps the most restrictive labor laws in the world, which impede 'firing and hiring' (35–36). These laws, while protecting those with organized sector jobs, strongly discourage new employment in the formal sector. 'Without significant reform of existing labor laws', he writes, 'India's cheap labor advantages remain hugely underutilized' (36). This also poses a political challenge because the bulk of the country's forthcoming 'demographic dividend' will occur in the poor, slow-growing and populous states of central and eastern India.

*   *   *

This volume's cross-country comparison of drivers of and barriers to growth reveals similarities as well as differences between China and India. In terms of drivers, both states rely on research as an important factor of development, have considerably opened their economies to international trade and foreign investment, and have made efforts to improve their institutional environments. China, however, is much ahead of India in terms of literacy and other indicators of human development and has achieved record exports and attracted record FDI. On the other hand, India enjoys a 'demographic dividend' and the exceptional brainpower of its research community. It also has a better 'soft' institutional infrastructure, due to the country's long legacy of democracy and respect for the rule of law.

At the same time, both countries face serious limitations in their development. Regarding India, this book highlights the 'legendary' bottlenecks in its 'hard' infrastructure and low quality, high-cost health services. China's development is troubled by an enormous trade imbalance with the United States and grave concerns about the inefficient use of resources and environmental degradation. Both China and India are plagued by inefficient social sectors and high, increasing social inequality. The only limitation on India which is not characteristic of China is its labor market rigidity. Instead, China benefits from labor market flexibility, that promotes employment and fuels growth.

Depending on the combination of stimuli and constraints on development as well as their relative intensity, evaluations of these countries' progress range from euphoric to disparaging. An impression of the 'glass half-full' more often refers to China than India. Although there are common weaknesses, China is usually viewed as a greater achiever, that also boasts vaster resources to resolve existing bottlenecks. The final judgment has, however, many sources and many facets. And it is these numerous ingredients of success versus failure – and their delicate balance – that will interest readers of this book.

NOTES

1. As evidence of this extraordinary growth, for example, China's per capita income doubled in only 10 years following 1978, while the United States' per capita income doubled in 50 years following 1840.
2. Refers to the simultaneous presence of imports and exports of the products of a given industry.
3. Refers to export increase from one set of industries and import increase in another.

BIBLIOGRAPHY

Altenburg, Tilman, Hubert Schmitz and Andreas Stamm (2006), 'Building Knowledge-Based Competitive Advantages in China and India: Lessons and Consequences for Other Developing Countries', paper presented at the workshop 'Asian and Other Drivers of Global Change', Seventh Annual Global Development Conference, St. Petersburg, 18–19 January 2006.

Aryeetey, Ernest and Natalia Dinello (2007), *Testing Global Interdependence: Issues on Trade, Aid, Migration and Development*, Cheltenham, UK – Northampton, MA: Edward Elgar.

Bardhan, Pranab (2005), 'China, India Superpower? Not So Fast!', *YaleGlobal*, (25 October), available at: http://yaleglobal.yale.edu/display.article?id=6407.

Barro, Robert and Jong-Wha Lee (2000), 'International Data on Educational Attainment: Updates and Implications', Cambridge, MA, National Bureau of Economic Research (NBER) Working Paper No. 7911.

Bezlova, Antoaneta (2007), 'China Still Beating the African Drum', *Asia Times Online*, (18 May).

Bhalla, Surjit (2007), *Second among Equals: The Middle Class Kingdoms of India and China*, Washington DC: Institute of International Economics.

Chaudhuri, Shubham and Martin Ravallion (2007), 'Partially Awakened Giants: Uneven Growth in China and India', in L. Alan Winters and Shahid Yusuf (eds), *Dancing with Giants: China, India and the Global Economy*, Washington: World Bank, pp. 175–210.

Cui, Li and Murtaza Syed (2007), 'The Shifting Structure of China's Trade and Production,' Washington, DC, IMF Working Paper No. WP/07/214.

Dinello, Natalia and Vladimir Popov (eds), (2007), *Political Institutions and Development: Failed Expectations and Renewed Hopes*, Cheltenham, UK – Northampton, MA: Edward Elgar.

Dollar, David et al. (2003), *Investment Climate Assessment: Improving the Investment Climate in China*, Washington: World Bank and International Finance Corporation.

Dumbaugh, Kerry and Mark P. Sullivan (2005), 'China's Growing Interest in Latin America', Congressional Research Service Report for Congress, No. RS22119.

Geda, Alemayehu (2006), 'Asian Drivers (China and India) and African Manufacturing: Issues and Challenges', paper presented at the AERC-AFDB International Conference on Accelerating Africa's Development Five Years into the Twenty-First Century, 22–24 November, Tunis, Tunisia.

Huang, Yasheng (2003), *Selling China: Foreign Direct Investment During the Reform Era*, New York: Cambridge University Press.

Huang, Yasheng and Tarun Khanna (2003), 'Can India Overtake China', *Foreign Policy* (July/August): 74–81.

International Monetary Fund (2007), *Global Finance Stability Report: Market Developments and Issues*, Washington, DC: IMF.

'It's the People, Stupid' (2005), *Economist*, (5 March): 3.

Kaplinsky, Raphael, Dorothy McCormick and Mike Morris (2006), 'The Impact of China on Sub-Saharan Africa', unpublished paper, available at: http://www.uk.cn/uploadfiles/2006428172021581.doc.

Kelly, David and Ramkishen Rajan (2006), 'Introduction to Managing Globalization: Lessons from China and India', in David Kelly, Ramkishen Rajan and Gillian Goh (eds), *Managing Globalization: Lessons from China and India*, Singapore: World Scientific Press.

Kripalani, Manjeet and Pete Engardio (2003), 'The Rise of India', *Business Week*, (8 December): 70.

Kristof, Nicholas and Sheryl WuDunn (2001), *Thunder from the East: Portrait of a Rising Asia*, New York: Alfred A. Knopf.

Morrisson, Christian and Fabrice Murtin (2005), 'The World Distribution of Human Capital, Life Expectancy and Income: A Multi-Dimensional Approach', unpublished paper available at: http://www.paris-jourdan.ens.fr/ydepot/semin/texte0506/MUR2005WOR.pdf.

Mwega, Francis (2007), 'China, India and Africa: Prospects and Challenges', revised version of a paper presented at the AERC-AFDB International Conference on Accelerating Africa's Development Five Years into the Twenty-First Century, 22–24 November, Tunis, Tunisia.

National Bureau of Statistics of China (2007), *Annual Statistical Bulletin on the 2006 National Economic and Social Development of the People's Republic of China*, (23 May), available at: http://www.fdi.gov.cn.

Organization for Economic Cooperation and Development (2005), *Governance in China*, Paris: OECD.

Pamlin, Dennis and Long Baijin (2007), 'China's Outward Investment Flows', WWF report available at: http://assets.panda.org/downloads/wwf_re_think_chinese_outward_investment.pdf.

Pratham (2006), 'Annual Status of Education Report', Mumbai: Pratham Resource Centre.

Rodrik, Dani (2006), 'What's So Special about China's Exports?', Cambridge, MA, Harvard University, John F. Kennedy School of Government, Working Paper No. 06-001.

Rohwer, Jim (1995), *Asia Rising*, New York: Simon and Schuster.

Sachs, Jeffrey (2007), 'China's Lessons for the World Bank', *Guardian*, (24 May).

Schmitz, Hubert (2007), 'The Rise of the East: What Does It Mean for Development Studies?', *IDS Bulletin*, **38** (2).

Sen, Amartya (1999), *Development as Freedom*, New York: Alfred A. Knopf.

Squire, Lyn and José Fanelli (eds), (2008), *Economic Reform in Developing Countries: Reach, Range, Reason*, Cheltenham, UK – Northampton, MA: Edward Elgar.

Srinivasan, T.N. (2004), 'China and India: Economic Performance, Competition and Cooperation: An Update', p. 7, unpublished paper available at: www/econ.yale/edu/~srinivas.

Transparency International (annual), *Corruption Perceptions Index*, Berlin, Transparency International.

United Nations Development Programme (2006), *Human Development Report 2006: Beyond Scarcity: Power, Poverty and the Global Water Crisis*, New York: Palgrave Macmillan.

Wallis, William (2007), 'China Pledges $20 bn for Africa', *Financial Times*, (18 May).

Winters L. Alan and Shahid Yusuf (2007), 'Introduction: Dancing with Giants', in L. Alan Wintersand Shahid Yusuf (eds), *Dancing with Giants: China, India and the Global Economy*, Washington: World Bank, pp. 1–25.

World Trade Organization (2006), *International Trade Statistics 2006*, Geneva: WTO.

'L[atin]. America Sees China as Large Investor', (2006), Xinhua (14 April).

Zafar, Ali (2007), 'The Growing Relationship Between China and Sub-Saharan Africa: Macroeconomic, Trade, Investment, and Aid Links', *World Bank Research Observer*, **22** (1), 103–30.

Acknowledgements

This book is the result of the Global Development Network's efforts to promote policy-relevant social science research on development. Published as part of the GDN Series, it assembles papers from the 2007 Global Development Research Medals competition and the Eighth Annual Global Development Conference held under the theme 'Shaping a New Global Reality: The Rise of Asia and Its Implications' (Beijing, China, January 2007). The editors and contributors would like to thank the GDN Secretariat staff, technical editor Ann Robertson, and the staff of Edward Elgar Publishing, Ltd. Without their help and support this book would not be possible.

PART ONE

China's Boom and India's Growth

1. Perspectives on China's Economic Growth: Prospects and Wider Impact

Linda Y. Yueh

China has been a remarkably successful economy since its adoption of market-oriented reforms in 1978. As Figure 1.1 shows, China's real GDP growth has averaged over 9 per cent per year from 1979 to 2005.

China rapidly propelled itself to become the world's fourth-largest economy (see Figure 1.2). When adjusted for purchasing power parity (PPP), China is currently the world's second-largest economy. It is also the world's largest country in terms of population (and potential market), a leading destination for foreign direct investment (FDI), and one of the three largest traders. At the same time, China is a developing country with a per capita GDP which only recently exceeded $1,000 and still has a substantial amount of poverty. Despite its aggregate size, China's per capita GDP suggests that it has sizable growth potential, as China's average income is substantially below that of Organization for Economic Cooperation and Development (OECD) countries of comparable size.

China's record, however, masks structural problems in its economy. The progress and nature of market-oriented reforms will in large part determine its growth prospects. Specifically, China will need to address the large portfolios of non-performing loans held by state-owned banks (SOBs), rising unemployment in various forms, and institutional frailties. These challenges are a consequence of the 'gradualist' reform path undertaken by China as it transitions from a centrally planned to a more market-oriented economy. They are also a result of China's status as a developing country, needing to confront the challenges of economic development, as well as an underdeveloped set of institutional structures in the economy, namely, the rule of law and mechanisms to ensure contractual security. However, China's prospects will also depend on its integration with the global economy. For an economy of its size, China has a high degree of openness (70 per cent when measured as exports plus imports as a proportion of GDP), as compared with 37 per cent for the comparatively open United Kingdom and 20 per cent for the more closed United States. Thus,

Figure 1.1   Real GDP Growth in China, 1979–2005

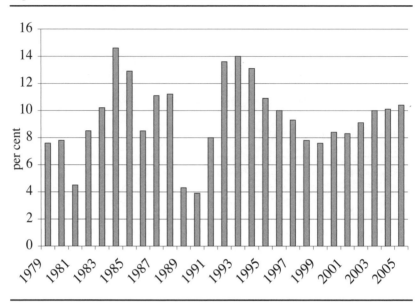

Source: *China Statistical Yearbook* (various years).

China's global integration will also inform its prospects. But, China's size further means that its growth will also affect the global economy.

This chapter has four parts. The first is a review of China's economic reform strategy and why the 'easy-to-hard' sequence makes China face certain challenges today. This is followed by an evaluation of China's development prospects and then the determinants of growth in the context of China's relationship with the global economy. Finally, the chapter assesses the structural problems inherent in the Chinese economy which may thwart its growth prospects.

CHINA'S PATH TO ECONOMIC REFORM

China's approach to economic growth must be viewed within the context of its status as a transition economy which is also a developing country. China has been in transition for nearly 30 years from a centrally planned economy which had followed Soviet-style heavy industrialization. China adopted its pro-market reforms gradually or incrementally, slowly introducing market forces into an administered economy.

Figure 1.2   China Compared with OECD Countries, 1980–2004

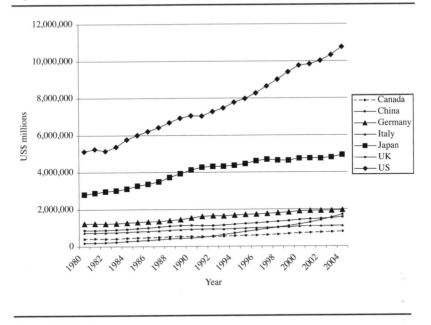

Source: World Bank.

China's Reform Path

Economic reform in China is a partial reform strategy characterized by institutional innovations and regional experimentation (e.g., Qian and Xu 1993; Fan 1994). Reform began in the countryside and the early successes were seen in the township and village enterprises (TVEs) in rural areas. The creation of TVEs in 1979 injected industry and market-orientated mindsets into the rural economy, that was characterized by abundant and surplus labor. Further, the Household Responsibility System gave residual ownership to farmers so that they could retain some return on their effort within a framework of communal ownership of land. These reforms re-oriented national saving to households, injected incentives into an economy which did not recognize private property and re-allocated the essential factor of labor from agriculture to more productive enterprises. Output grew rapidly in the early 1980s, as seen in Figure 1.1, leading to the observation that China's growth began in the countryside (Riskin 1987).

Buoyed by the successful experiments in the countryside, the authorities introduced further reform into urban areas in 1984. Managers in state-owned enterprises (SOEs) were granted more autonomy and allowed to retain a portion of profits through the new Contract Responsibility System. Wage reform introduced a performance element into pay scales (Yueh 2004). Urban reforms further bolstered the status and income of urban residents, who had been favored in the administered economy (Knight and Song 1999). Urban residents enjoyed the 'iron rice bowl' (guaranteed lifetime employment) and social security provisions provided by the *danwei* (work unit) which were not available to rural residents. This 'urban bias' enabled China to undergo industrialization, and the favorable treatment of urban residents maintained stability – a critical element of a gradualist transition path.

Indeed, stability is essential to maintaining a 'dual-track' transition. When allowing enterprises to sell part of their output at market prices, the authorities must be able to control the sale of goods to the administered part of the market in order to implement a partial-liberalization strategy (Murphy, Schleifer and Vishny 1992). However, at the same time, China sustained a degree of decentralization that permitted experiments to take place so that market-oriented reform could be introduced without affecting the economy as a whole. This approach further allowed the authorities the flexibility to adapt to changing circumstances rather than follow a prescribed plan of reform.

The final prong of China's reform approach is the 'open-door' policy. China created special economic zones (SEZs), initially in southern provinces, which were essentially export-processing zones open to international trade and foreign investment (Lardy 1998). The introduction of market forces into SEZs allowed the government to experiment with a limited degree of opening. These measures began in 1979, but did not take off until 1992 when Deng Xiaoping famously toured the earliest SEZs in Fujian and Guangdong. Since then, China has created further forms of SEZs, such as Free-Trade Zones and High-Technology Development Zones (HTDZs), which are geared at attracting foreign investment in technology sectors and promoting research and development (R&D). The resulting growth of high- and medium-technology goods represents the impressive upgrading of Chinese exports (Lall and Albaladejo 2004). Moreover, China has been transformed from an economy with an export-to-GDP ratio of 15 per cent in 1990 to 30 per cent in 2000. In the span of a decade, China reached the market share which the East Asian 'tiger' economies achieved at the peak of their export-led growth (Yueh 2006).

Finally, the transition strategy undertaken by China during the reform period is considered a 'dual track' reform path because there are both planned and market components. Understanding the evolution of this 'incrementalist' or 'gradualist' strategy sheds light on why the structural problems underpinning China's economy are predictable.

'Gradualism' versus 'Shock Therapy'

China appeared to reject a 'shock therapy' approach to transition because reasonable economic conditions existed when the first reforms were adopted (Riskin 1987). 'Gradualism' was preferred to the more radical reform programs, that were similar to the rapid introduction of market forces adopted later in much of Eastern Europe and the former Soviet Union (EE/FSU). For China in 1978, the rate of economic growth was an impressive 12.3 per cent,[1] a rate which reflected well on the socialist economic system. In contrast, the EE/FSU societies in the late 1980s and early 1990s accepted a shock-therapy package, but under different circumstances, such as weak central governments. Gradualism had been tried before the 1989 revolutions without great success. The ability to adopt gradualism or radical change seems dependent on how much the economy had stagnated and declined at the time of reform. The lower the growth potential of the old system, the stronger the incentives and political will to pursue radical reform.

Gradualism is related to initial conditions and economic structure in other ways as well. This approach is more likely to be successful in an underdeveloped and underindustrialized economy with a large, rural, surplus labor force. Rural incomes had been falling compared with the urban population in China. The pre-existence of a declining sector, such as agriculture, results in a population of people who possess a strong demand for opportunities and who will also constitute a new labor force.

Thus, there are two main conditions which facilitate successful incrementalist reform. First, China started its reforms before the state sector was in drastic decline, so that heavy subsidies were not needed, unlike the situation of Soviet firms in the late 1980s. Second, the start of rural reform and the accompanying liberalization of private economic activities in the presence of a large rural labor surplus generated growth rapid enough to outpace the speed of increasing SOE subsidies.

Further, stability is required to provide enough control over the economy to maintain quantity ceilings and to ensure that goods are sold at both administered and market prices (Murphy, Schleifer and Vishny 1992).[2] And, on the eve of reform, the state sector must be sufficiently viable so that the levels of continuing transfers to the state sector do not surpass the growth in the non-state sector.

Lack of an Objective Model

China also did not have the focus that the EE/FSU economies had, namely, to adopt a largely privately owned economy and rejoin Europe. For China, the motivation was the recognition that a centrally planned economy was no longer viable and changes were required to promote economic growth. Consequently, without a definite model in mind, China underwent a lengthy path of adjusting reform objectives: from 'a planned economy with some market adjustment', to 'a combination of plan and market' to 'a socialist market economy'. This path was adaptive rather than deliberate. With the rise and success of the non-state sector and the decline of the state sector, popular sentiment started to shift toward the market system and the government's objective shifted and adapted accordingly.

Regional Experimentation

Much of the innovation and many of the advances which occurred in the process of reform were less by design and more a result of the Chinese government's pragmatic flexibility. Some of the gradual changes are more accurately characterized as adjustments to practical circumstances. For example, one of the key steps in starting the reform process was the advent of the Household Responsibility System. Banned in 1979, it was accepted when it became widely practiced by rural residents anyway. This adaptation occurred again when the rural economy was liberalized, when TVEs emerged as the dynamic engine of growth in the 1980s.

Generally, the Chinese government approach can be described as 'no encouragement, no ban' (Naughton 1995). Experiments encompassing different reform programs at various governmental levels were encouraged, including the creation of special economic zones. SEZs were specially designated areas in which export-oriented companies were permitted to flourish and become foreign-invested, such as Shenzhen. Special treatment was subsequently given to different regions and local initiatives were respected.

One reason for this success may be the type of coordination found in China (see Qian and Xu 1993 for a formal exposition). M-form structures of coordination are based on minimal interdependence among regions or industries, so that experimentation in one area of industry can be completed without its success or failure causing disruptions across the economy. A U-form organization is characterized as 'top-down' because of more interdependence; thus, experimentation could affect the whole system. M-form is more conducive to experimentation than U-form hierarchies. China perhaps resembled the M-form as a result of the decentralization which preceded the reform period, that accounts for the success of experiments in heralding further reforms.

The Theory of 'Partial Reform'

Beijing adopted a partial-reform process in which some markets were liberalized and permitted to sell output at market prices, but they were also required to sell to state firms at administered prices. This 'dual-track' system has been extended to cover almost all economic transactions in China. Although the reforms were not accompanied by immediate privatization, the resulting arrangements generated new forms of economic organizations. The most important is the creation of a non-state sector parallel to the state one. Much of China's dynamic growth can be attributed to the non-state sector, consisting of private and semi-private enterprises, including community-owned industrial enterprises, foreign joint ventures and individually owned businesses.

The appeal of this approach is in part to honor 'implicit contracts' built on expectations under a socialist system. This reduces market efficiency and instead reflects vested interests, but maintaining such distorted incentives lessens resistance to reform.

The success of this approach depends mainly on the success of the new track (Fan 1994). If the growth rate of the new sector is higher than that of the old sector, then the old state-run system will eventually shrink as a proportion of the economy. Similarly, if the old administered track stops expanding and the new market-oriented track grows, the transition will eventually consist of the new market economy (Fan 1994). For example, price reform on food items began in 1982; by 1992 market prices were nearly twice that of official prices. When governmental controls were removed after a decade, convergence occurred, and food sold at officially set prices accounted for less than 15 per cent of total consumption. Under these conditions, convergence did not cause a 'shock'. In the foreign exchange market, unification of the official exchange rate and the 'swap market exchange rate' occurred at the end of 1993, when the differential between the two rates was about 50 per cent. At that time, only 20 per cent of such transactions were still subject to the official exchange rate. The 'rationed' component did not shrink in absolute size but relatively with respect to the 'new track'.

Despite the reforms, the old track has expanded in absolute size during the reform period. This is because the government has frequently taken from the more productive sectors to compensate those who suffer losses due to transformation and to expand the older sectors. The old track does not shrink as expected (Fan 1994).

'Easy-to-Hard' Reform Sequence

There were a number of problems generated by the devolution of decision-making powers to local governments and increased autonomy for enterprises. The gradualist approach is in actuality an 'easy-to-hard' reform sequence. It addresses the easy problems first and leaves the hard ones until later. A radical approach would do the opposite: maximize efficiency gains rather than minimize implementation costs. However, restructuring may be easier with the gradualist approach.

When a transition strategy is more concerned with implementing reform and overcoming opposition than introducing rapid and complete marketization, it often leaves the difficult issues unresolved. However, restructuring may be easier with the gradualist approach, as it minimizes the political opposition to, and the costs of, reform. As the following look at China shows, different conditions can produce a different optimum sequence.

DEVELOPMENT PROSPECTS

There are a number of structural issues in the Chinese economy which are a consequence of the gradualist approach to market-oriented reforms.

Soft-Budget Constraints

The primary structural problem is the close relationship among the state, state-owned enterprises and state-owned banks at both the national and provincial levels. The presence of soft budget constraints means firms lack discipline and will be inclined to be inefficient. The state, as it owns both the SOEs and the SOBs, can finance SOEs through direct transfers or indirectly through policy loans from state-owned banks. The non-performing loans problem in China can be traced to the use of bank financing and money creation to fuel transfers to SOEs (Brandt and Zhu 2000). The SOEs, however, are not just enterprises, they also provide social security benefits and allow the government to maintain full employment. Despite the lack of efficiency of SOEs, they did not shed labor until the large-scale layoffs of the mid-1990s, when China's official urban unemployment rate first exceeded 3.5 per cent. Unemployment, more broadly defined to include laid-off workers and other forms of non-employment, is much higher than the official estimates (Knight and Xue 2006). The lack of a social safety net, combined with concerns about instability and restructuring the state-owned enterprises and banks, adds up to a difficult challenge for China (Bai et al. 2000).

The urban reforms have produced a decentralized state sector where fairly autonomous local governments, local SOEs and local SOBs have become increasingly important in determining resource allocation, while the central government's influence has waned. The decentralization reforms may have indeed improved the technical efficiency of the state sector, but by the standards of allocative efficiency and intertemporal stability the decentralized state sector is a major institutional cause of macroeconomic instability and the divergent development of regional economies. Thus, soft budget constraints remain a difficult issue for SOE reform in China. The debate over corporatization of SOEs versus full privatization will affect not only the viability of the enterprises, but also the provision of social security benefits for the populace and have an impact on the stability of the banking sector.

Urban Bias

The second set of issues centers on the 'urban bias' which fuelled industrialization but has resulted in a significant urban–rural income gap. Rural incomes are less than one-third of urban incomes and grow at a much slower pace. Recent initiatives such as eliminating grain taxes and investing in interior regions have attempted to stimulate the rural economy. However, the estimated 70–200 million rural migrants who have moved to urban areas are symptomatic of this divide.

Moreover, the agricultural sector is declining as a proportion of GDP (see Figure 1.3), although this sector still employs just under half of China's workers and nearly 60 per cent of China's population remains rural. As comparative advantage shifts against agriculture in China, its limited arable land becomes more evident. In addition, the slowing contributions from the TVEs, that were early engines of growth, contribute to the relatively slower improvement in the livelihoods of the rural population.

Weak Formal Institutions

The final set of structural issues centers on weak formal institutions, particularly those required to support contracting and to reduce the risk of appropriation, typical measures of institutional soundness in the growth literature (Acemoglu, Johnson and Robinson 2005). China has not had formal property rights conventionally defined, and Beijing only granted protection equal to public property to private property in March 2004, when the provision was included in the constitution. Yet China's phenomenal growth has taken place with residual claimant rights in its partially marketized economy, the so-called institutional innovations. Specifically, the Household Responsibility System

Figure 1.3   Sectoral Composition of GDP

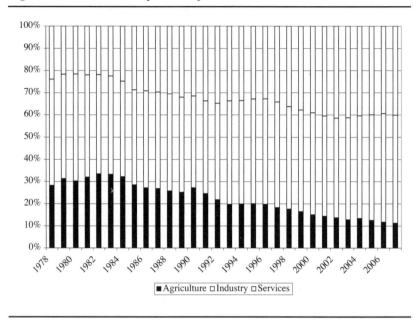

Legend: ■ Agriculture □ Industry □ Services

Source: *China Statistical Yearbook* (various years).

was implemented to great success in the rural economy in the late 1970s, while the Contract Responsibility System was instigated in urban areas in the 1980s so that farmers and enterprises could retain some portion of profits above the amount contracted to the state without an outright change to private ownership. This system of informal property rights extended to China's treatment of multinational corporations investing in China.

Since the open-door policy of the mid-1980s and its take-off in the early 1990s, China has rapidly become one of the world's top destinations for foreign direct investment, trailing only the United States and United Kingdom in terms of stock of investment. Unlike most developing countries, China has exercised strict controls over the nature of inward investment. Until recently, the predominant form of FDI was joint ventures, where Chinese and foreign partners set up either equity or cooperative joint ventures. Equity joint ventures partition returns on the basis of the invested capital, while returns are contractually defined in cooperative joint ventures. Both forms, however, were vested in essentially contractually determined rights. The uncertainty which might have been generated by China's particular system of property rights, however, did not seem to deter potential foreign investors. Because of the lack of private property rights in the rest of the Chinese economy, in some ways the joint venture laws provided more protection to foreign-invested enterprises (FIEs) than accorded to Chinese non-state firms, such as *getihu* (sole proprietorships) and small- and medium-sized enterprises.

China thus successfully established a system of contract-based rights spanning its institutional innovations, such as those governing households, firms and even local governments, as well as with regard to FIEs. This system of legally defined – but arguably informal – property rights also seemed to stimulate China's impressive economic growth during the reform period despite its incomplete legal system. In a framework of informal property rights, enforcement would seemingly be of considerable significance; yet, China's legal and regulatory systems lag behind its contractually defined obligations and growing body of laws. These approximate market structures will come under increasing scrutiny with the advent of international economic law.

For economic development to continue in China, these structural issues linked to its gradualist transition will need to be addressed.

ECONOMIC GROWTH AND GLOBAL INTEGRATION

China's gradualist path has resulted in largely extensive growth which is premised on increasing factors of production as compared with intensive growth, that refers to growth in technologically driven productivity improvements. The country's large, surplus, rural labor force has already been mentioned. Studies show that China's growth is less associated with gains in real productivity over the reform period and more with increases in factor accumulation (e.g., the evidence cited in Wang and Yao 2001). As an example, surplus labor in the agricultural sector was efficiently re-allocated with the creation of TVEs to absorb rural employment. This is not to discount the improvements gained from introducing market-oriented incentives (Groves et al. 1995). However, the bulk of the empirical evidence indicates that China's growth is more similar to the East Asian tigers' factor accumulation process, that is only associated with small increases in real productivity (Chow 1994). A growth spurt is unlikely as extensive growth reaches its limits due to diminishing returns, limits of capacity, slower population growth, etc. Early growth based on extensive growth should lead to a dramatic slowdown, as seen in other socialist economies, such as the Soviet Union between 1950 and the 1970s.

Sustaining economic growth through factor accumulation is a limited strategy due to China's aging population and its already high rates of labor force participation. Therefore, one of the main challenges is to sustain growth via productivity advances. This can be achieved through factor reallocation, such

China, India and Beyond

Figure 1.4   Composition of GDP in China

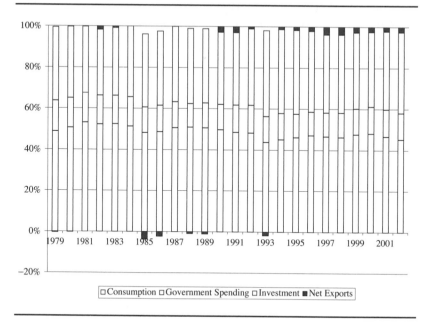

Source: *China Statistical Yearbook* (various years).

as more efficiently utilizing China's abundant labor force. However, although there is still much surplus labor in China's SOEs and SOBs, the restrictions on mobility between rural and urban *hukou* holders (the household registration system which controls residency) has resulted in areas such as Guangdong reporting a shortage of millions of workers. Knight and Yueh (2004) offer one measure of the low degree of mobility in Chinese labor markets, finding that, in 1999, 78 per cent of urban residents had only held one job in their lifetime.

Growth can also come about through the re-orientation of capital stock. However, as China is already industrialized, seen in Figure 1.3, the creation of new capital stock is a challenge, particularly given its underdeveloped capital markets and lack of market instruments to channel investment into more productive assets. Interest rates, for example, were only liberalized in October 2004. Figure 1.4 shows the fairly constant level of investment in China and the large role which it plays in generating national income.

Although fixed asset investment continues to grow quickly, the challenge will be to generate investment in R&D and technological advancements rather than increasing real estate construction. As with many developing countries, China has had low levels of investment in R&D, instead adopting or imitating

Figure 1.5   China's Total Exports to the Rest of the World, 1985–2005

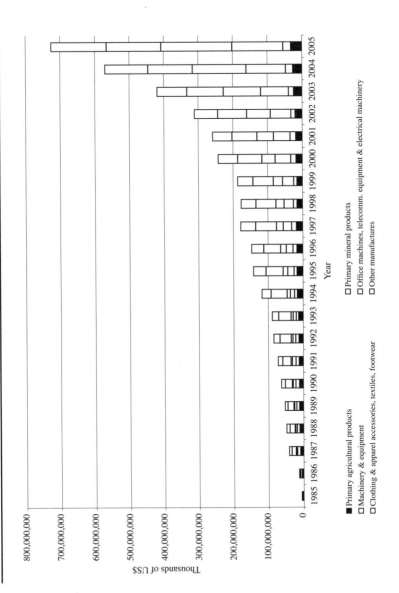

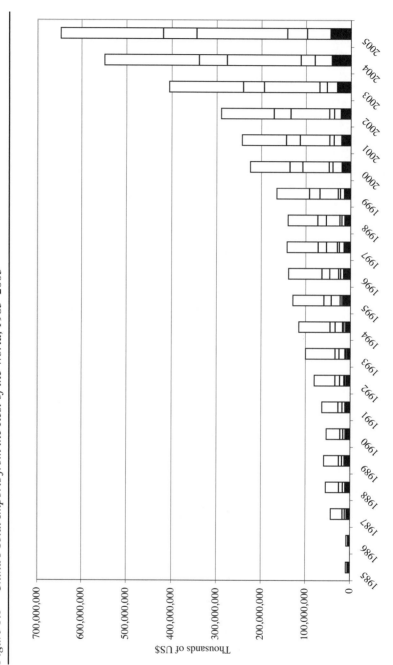

Figure 1.6   China's Total Imports from the Rest of the World, 1985–2005

the technology of advanced economies through foreign investment and capital inflows. This process is well known in development and is termed 'catching up'. At low levels of growth, the resulting rate of growth can thus be substantial.

China appears to be targeting its strategy toward promoting investment in technology sectors, such as the Shanghai–Pudong science park. China's creation of HTDZs and its early focus on joint ventures – frequently accompanied by technology transfer agreements – were intended to serve this purpose. However, although FDI has been impressive in China, it comprises about 10 per cent of total annual investment and some of it likely comes from 'round-tripping', whereby Chinese capital leaves the country and returns to gain benefits as 'foreign' investment. Indeed, the need to improve productivity has led China to become one of the largest investors in research and development in the 2000s. Beijing has begun to better educate scientific personnel and improve infrastructure. Coupled with access to foreign capital and global markets, China is attempting to increase the technological component of its growth model to sustain a rate of growth which would otherwise begin to slow due to limits on factor accumulation.

China's forays into the global economy, however, are not limited to improving the skill intensity of its manufactured goods. Figures 1.5 and 1.6 show the composition of China's exports and imports, divided into several commodity groupings.

The figures reveal the dominance of manufactures and telecommunications equipment, reflecting China's place in global supply chains. The existence of intra-industry trade, particularly vertical trade, suggests a degree of global integration which is consistent with the high degree of foreign-invested enterprises, that have accounted for more than half of all exports since the mid-1990s (Yueh 2006). On the import side, a further notable feature is the rapid growth of energy and raw materials imports.

These trade patterns can provide a source of growth while China reforms its domestic economy. Its integration into global supply chains, including in the high-technology sector, will enable China to imitate the technology of developed countries and potentially allow it to catch up. Second, global markets provide another avenue of growth which can help the non-state sector expand while China undertakes difficult reforms in the state sector. Moreover, since joining the World Trade Organization (WTO) in 2001, China has also become part of a rules-based trading system which exposes it to the best-practice standards of international economic law which can aid the development of its market-supporting institutions.

The downside of globalization, however, is three-fold. First, it puts increasing pressure on the agriculture sector and rural economy. Second, China's increasingly liberalized trade and financial sector generates pressures on its banking system and exchange rate, revealing the fragility of its transition economy and susceptibility to macroeconomic crises. Finally, China's terms-of-trade have deteriorated by an estimated 17 per cent since 1980 (UNCTAD 2004). The fall in export prices relative to import prices, coupled with an exchange rate which has appreciated little relative to its recent trade surpluses, indicate a lower standard of living for the Chinese populace than its growth would otherwise suggest. Overall, however, globalization holds the potential for stimulating economic growth along with improving China's much needed institutional foundation, while the downsides can be considered short-term structural issues. China's size, however, further means that its relationship with the rest of the world will be influenced by its larger footprint.

China's trade patterns affect the rest of the world in several areas. There will be winners and losers at the national and sub-national levels. In terms of primary products including energy, countries which sell to China (e.g., African states) may well experience an improvement in their terms of trade. However, countries which buy the same items as China (e.g., OECD countries) will lose. The picture for manufactured goods is more complex. Countries which sell to China, particularly those which are part of the vertical supply chains located in China (e.g., Asian firms), will do well (Yueh 2006). Multinational corporations, as sources of the global supply chains, will also gain. These countries and companies will further benefit from China's rise, as Beijing fulfills more of its World Trade Organization obligations and opens its sizable domestic market, increasing the prospect for horizontal FDI whereby China becomes a notable market. But countries which sell similar goods (e.g., Chile) will lose (Lall and Weiss 2005). Those countries which buy from China (e.g., European Union members and the United States) will experience a terms-of-trade improvement and benefit (Kaplinsky 2006). Generally, up to this time, China has lowered the price of manufactured goods worldwide, contributing to low interest rates, low inflation and a strong growth environment (Rogoff 2006).

At the sub-national level, the picture is yet more complex, and it is determined by wages, cost and comparative advantage. China is characterized by tremendous wage differences, with wages on the coast now twice as high on average as those in the interior, although they were the same just a decade or so ago. There is evidence that China's exports embody a substantial amount of skills upgrading (Rodrik 2006), but foreign-invested enterprises have produced more than half of all exports since the mid-1990s. Given this mixed picture of wages and costs, it is not straightforward to characterize China's comparative advantage and therefore its wider implications. The expectation is that there will be sectoral shrinkages affecting unskilled workers in other countries and downward pressure on wages. Moreover, for developed countries in particular, it is difficult to disentangle the effects of skill-biased technical change from the effects of globalization (Machin and Van Reenen 1998). The impact on wages is further affected by the estimated increased profitability of multinational corporations, that has somewhat mitigated the impact on labor and wages in developed countries (Grossman and Rossi-Hansberg 2006).

The impact of China on other countries will depend on their trade patterns, terms-of-trade, exchange rates and domestic productivity, and not every sector will become uncompetitive as a result. However, the global integration of an economy the size of China will entail structural adjustments in other countries, and the process can be challenging. So far, the net China effect has been to contribute to a lower-than-expected global inflationary environment (Rogoff 2006). Nevertheless, the reaction of the rest of the world to China's rise has been cautious, and protectionist sentiments are growing louder.

China's wider economic impact has been varied, but it has contributed significantly to the growth of the global economy as a result of its rapid growth rate (Dollar 2008). Its global integration further suggests that a slowdown in China will affect global trade and consumption. Taken together, China's fate is increasingly tied to the global economy, and its prospects will therefore affect the rest of the world.

CONCLUSION

China has performed admirably well since market-oriented reforms were introduced in 1978. This chapter has analyzed the nature of its development path and growth model, that have resulted in a set of unresolved structural issues in the Chinese economy. These issues are exacerbated by China's accession to the WTO in December 2001 and the challenges associated with opening to the global economy, although global integration itself offers numerous benefits for China.

Given the easy-to-hard sequence which characterizes China's reform strategy, there are many challenges that lie ahead. The coincidence of the 'hard' issues with opening the economy to global trade provides possible ways to grow within the constraints of a partial reform strategy. In particular, China must transform from a growth model based on productivity advances from factor reallocation to one which is fuelled by technological advancement and innovation. The challenges of China's continued development will test the ultimate success of a 'gradualist' reform strategy in an economy increasingly open to global factors, including international economic law.

Unsurprisingly, given its size, the effects of China's rise have been felt in the global economy. Countries which have experienced an improvement in their terms-of-trade have benefited from China's rise, while others have had to contend with declining sectors and increased competition as a result of China's growth. China's rise has seemingly benefited the global economy, but it has also increased the need to be productive and generated structural change in other countries. Given the openness of the Chinese economy, its own fate is increasingly tied to the health of the global economy, while, at the same time, it is affecting the very growth of the rest of the world. In this respect China befits its status as one of the largest economies in world and one that is more open than others of comparable size.

This chapter has outlined China's reform approach and focused on the elements of China's transition from a centrally planned to a more market-oriented economy. Structural problems which continue to plague its development prospects were viewed in the context of China as a transition economy also contending with the issues of a developing country. Next, economic growth and global integration were discussed as a way of further analyzing the prospects of sustained growth. China's continuing development, therefore, is possible if it can address the hard issues and structural problems facing its transition and development. It will need to focus on redressing the downsides of globalization and become more conscious of its impact on the global economy due to growing protectionist sentiments. Global integration is important for China, but its significant degree of openness also means that it will be susceptible to downturns in the global economy. Moreover, the wide impact of China's global integration raises further challenges for other countries to assess and manage the effects on their economy. Therefore, China's economic growth prospects remain positive, but challenges do remain. China's wider impact has been felt, but these effects are only beginning to be understood.

NOTES

1. There are always concerns over the measurement of growth and other statistics in both the pre-reform and reform periods. Suffice it to say that the economic situation in 1978 was not dire; thus, the impetus for a more radical type of reform was not present.
2. Murphy, Schleifer and Vishny (1992) show that the government's ability to impose and maintain quantity ceilings for goods and services sold at 'market prices' explains the success of China and the lack of success of the former Soviet Union in undertaking a gradual transition from central planning.

BIBLIOGRAPHY

Acemoglu, Daron, Simon Johnson and James A. Robinson (2005), 'Institutions as the Fundamental Cause of Long-Run Growth', in Philippe Aghion and Steven Durlauf (eds), *Handbook of Economic Growth*, Amsterdam: Elsevier, pp. 386–472.
Bai, Chong-En, David D. Li, Zhigang Tao and Yijiang Wang (2000), 'A Multitask

Theory of Enterprise Reform', *Journal of Comparative Economics*, **28** (4), 716–38.

Brandt, Loren and Xiaodong Zhu (2000), 'Redistribution in a Decentralizing Economy: Growth and Inflation in Reform China', *Journal of Political Economy*, **108** (2), 422–51.

Chow, Gregory C. (1994), *Understanding China's Economy*, Singapore: World Scientific.

Dollar, David (2008), 'Asian Century or Multipolar Century?', in Natalia Dinello and Wang Shaoguang (eds), *China, India and Beyond: Development Drivers and Limitations*, Cheltenham, UK; and Northampton, MA, US: Edward Elgar, pp. 46–69.

Fan, Gang (1994), 'Incremental Change and Dual-Track Transition: Understanding the Case of China', *Economic Policy*, **19** (Supp.), 99–122.

Grossman, Gene and Esteban Rossi-Hansberg (2006), 'The Rise of Offshoring: It's Not Wine for Cloth Anymore', paper presented at the Federal Reserve Bank of Kansas City conference 'The New Economic Geography: Effects and Policy Implications', Jackson Hole, WY, 24–26 August 2006.

Groves, Theodore, Yongmiao Hong, John McMillan and Barry Naughton (1995), 'China's Evolving Managerial Market', *Journal of Political Economy*, **103** (4), 873–92.

Kaplinsky, Raphael (2006), 'Revisiting the Revisited Terms of Trade: Will China make a Difference?', *World Development*, **34** (6), 981–95.

Knight, John and Lina Song (1999), *The Rural-Urban Divide: Economic Disparities and Interactions in China*, New York: Oxford University Press.

Knight, John and Jinjun Xue (2006), 'How High is Urban Unemployment in China?', *Journal of Chinese Economic and Business Studies*, **4** (2), 91–107.

Knight, John and Linda Yueh (2004), 'Job Mobility of Residents and Migrants in Urban China', *Journal of Comparative Economics*, **32** (4), pp. 637–60.

Lall, Sanjaya and Manuel Albaladejo (2004), 'The Competitive Impact of China on Manufactured Exports by Emerging Economies in Asia', *World Development*, **32** (9), pp. 1441–66.

Lall, Sanjaya and John Weiss (2005), 'China's Competitive Threat to Latin America: An Analysis for 1990–2002', Oxford, UK, University of Oxford, Queen Elizabeth House Working Paper No. 120.

Lardy, Nicholas R. (1998), *China's Unfinished Economic Revolution*, Washington, DC: Brookings Institution.

Machin, Stephen and John Van Reenen (1998), 'Technology and Changes in the Skill Structure: Evidence from Seven OECD Countries', *Quarterly Journal of Economics*, **113** (4), 1215–44.

Murphy, Kevin M., Andrei Schleifer and Robert W. Vishny (1992), 'The Transition to a Market Economy: Pitfalls of Partial Reform', *Quarterly Journal of Economics,* **107** (3), 889–906.

National Bureau of Statistics (multiple years), *China Statistical Yearbook,* Beijing: China Statistics Press.

Naughton, Barry (1995), *Growing out of the Plan*, New York: Cambridge University Press.

Qian, Yingyi and Chenggang Xu (1993), 'The M-form Hierarchy and China's Economic Reform', *European Economic Review*, **37** (2/3), 541–8.

Riskin, Carl (1987), *China's Political Economy*, New York: Oxford University Press.

Rodrik, Dani (2006), 'What's So Special About China's Exports?', Cambridge, MA,

National Bureau of Economic Research (NBER) Working Paper No. 11947.

Rogoff, Kenneth (2006), 'Impact of Globalization on Monetary Policy', paper presented at the Federal Reserve Bank of Kansas City conference 'The New Economic Geography: Effects and Policy Implications', Jackson Hole, WY, 24–26 August 2006.

UNCTAD (2004), *UNCTAD Handbook of Statistics*, Geneva: United Nations Conference on Trade and Development.

Wang, Yan and Yudong Yao (2003), 'Sources of China's Economic Growth: 1952–99: Incorporating Human Capital Accumulation', *China Economic Review*, **14** (1), 32–52.

Yueh, Linda (2004), 'Wage Reforms in China During the 1990s', *Asian Economic Journal*, **18** (2), 149–64.

——(2006), 'China's Competitiveness, Intra-Industry and Intra-Regional Trade in Asia', in Yang Yao and Linda Yueh (eds), *Globalisation and Economic Growth in China*, Singapore: World Scientific, pp. 139–58.

2. India's Growth: Past and Future

Shankar Acharya

India and China are often bracketed together as Asia's 'Giant Dragons', set to dominate the global economy in the twenty-first century. However, as this chapter shows, India's economic rise in global commerce, capital and energy has been much more gradual than China's and is likely to remain so, thus posing few adjustment problems for the rest of the world.

This chapter is divided into five sections. First, it briefly reviews India's growth performance since 1950 and indicates a few salient features and turning points. Second, it discusses some of the major drivers of India's current growth momentum (which has averaged more than 8 per cent since 2003) and raised widespread expectations (at least, in India) that growth of more than 8 per cent has become the new norm for the Indian economy. Third, it points to some of the risks and vulnerabilities which could stall the current dynamism if corrective action is not taken. Fourth, it appraises the country's medium-term growth prospects. Finally, it assesses some implications of India's rise for the world economy.

INDIA'S GROWTH PERFORMANCE, 1950–2006

Table 2.1 summarizes India's growth experience since the middle of the twentieth century. For the first 30 years, economic growth averaged a modest 3.6 per cent, with per capita growth of a meager 1.4 per cent per year.[1] Those were the heydays of state-led, import-substituting industrialization, especially after the 1957 foreign exchange crisis and the heavy industrialization bias of the Second Five Year Plan (1956–61). While this strategy registered some success in raising the level of resource mobilization and investment in the economy, it turned out to be hugely costly in terms of economic efficiency. The inefficiencies stemmed not just from the adoption of a statist, inward-looking policy stance at a time of rapidly expanding world trade, but also from the extremely detailed, dysfunctional and corruption-breeding controls which were imposed on industry and trade (Bhagwati and Desai 1970).

23

Table 2.1   *Growth of GDP and Major Sectors (percentage per year[a])*

Year	1951–52 to 1980–81 (1)	1981–82 to 1990–91 (2)	1992–93 to 1996–97 (3)	1997–98 to 2001–02 (4)	2002–03 to 2005–06 (5)	1992–93 to 2005–06 (6)	1981–82 to 2005–06 (7)
Agriculture and allied	2.5	3.5	4.7	2.0	1.9	3.0	3.0
Industry[b]	5.3	7.1	7.6	4.4	8.0	6.6	6.5
Services	4.5	6.7	7.6	8.2	8.9	8.2	7.4
GDP	3.6	5.6	6.7	5.5	7.0	6.4	5.9
GDP per capita	1.4	3.4	4.6	3.6	5.3	4.4	3.8

Notes:
a. India's economic and financial data are organized according to fiscal years running form April to March. Thus in this and subsequent tables, '1950–51' refers to the year running from 1 April 1950 to 31 March 1951.
b. Industry includes construction.
Source: Central Statistical Office.

Still, India's 3.6 per cent GDP growth rate was four times greater than the 0.9 per cent growth estimated for the previous half century of British colonial rule (Table 2.2). Moreover the growth was reasonably sustained, with no extended periods of decline. Nor were there inflationary bouts of the kind which plagued many countries in Latin America. However, growth was far below potential and much less than the 7–8 per cent rates being achieved in some countries of East Asia and Latin America. Worst of all, the proportion of the Indian population living below even a minimalist poverty line actually increased from 45 per cent to 51 per cent (Table 2.3).

Growth accelerated significantly in the 1980s to 5.6 per cent and per capita growth more than doubled, to 3.4 per cent a year. This acceleration was due to a number of factors, including the early efforts at industrial and trade liberalization and tax reform during the 1980s, a step-up in public investment, better agricultural performance and an increasingly expansionist – almost profligate – fiscal policy. Fiscal controls weakened, while deficits mounted and spilled over to the external sector, requiring growing recourse to external borrowing on commercial terms. Against a background of a low export–GDP

Table 2. 2　Economic Growth: Pre-independence (percentage per year)

Year	1900–46	1900–29	1930–46
GDP	0.9	0.9	0.8
Population	0.8	0.5	1.3
Per capita GDP	0.1	0.4	–0.5

Source: Sivasubramonian (2000).

Table 2.3　Percentage of People Below Poverty Line, 1951–52 to 1999–2000: Official Estimates

Year	Rural	Urban	All India
1951–52	47.4	35.5	45.3
1977–78	53.1	45.2	51.3
1983	45.7	40.8	44.5
1993–94	37.3	32.4	36.0
1999–2000	26.8	24.1	26.1

Source: Planning Commission, Government of India.

ratio, rising trade and current account deficits, and a deteriorating external debt profile, the 1990 Gulf War and consequent oil price spike tipped India's balance of payments into crisis in 1991.

Although the policy reforms of the 1980s were modest in comparison with those undertaken in the 1990s, their productivity 'bang for the buck' seems to have been high (see Table 2.4).[2] Perhaps this was a case whereby modest improvements in a highly distorted policy environment yielded significant gains.

The new Congress government of June 1991, with future prime minister Manmohan Singh as minister of finance, took emergency measures to restore external and domestic confidence in the economy and its management.[3] It devalued the rupee, cut the fiscal deficit and mobilized special balance-of-payments financing from the International Monetary Fund (IMF) and the World Bank. Even more important, the government seized the opportunity offered by the crisis to launch an array of long overdue and wide-ranging economic reforms, including external sector liberalization, industry deregulation, tax and finance reforms and a more commercial approach to the public sector (see Table 2.5).[4]

The economy responded swiftly and positively to these reforms. After virtual stagnation in 1991–92, GDP growth surged over the next five years to clock a record five-year average of 6.7 per cent. In this high-growth Eighth-Plan

Table 2.4   *Growth of GDP, Total Factor Input and Total Factor Productivity (percentage per year)*

	1950–51 to 1966–67	1967–68 to 1980–81	1981–82 to 1990–91	1991–92 to 1999–2000
GDP	3.8	3.4	5.3	6.5
Total Factor Input (TFI)	2.4	2.7	3.3	3.9
Total Factor Productivity (TFP)	1.4	0.7	2.0	2.6
Proportion of Growth Explained by TFP (%)	37.6	20.8	37.7	39.7

Note: For each sub-period, GDP, TFI and TFP are trend growth rates.
Source: Acharya, Ahluwalia, Krishna and Patnaik (2003).

period, all major sectors (agriculture, industry, services) grew noticeably faster than in the pre-crisis decade. The acceleration in the growth of agricultural value added is particularly interesting, given the often repeated criticism that the economic reforms of the early 1990s neglected the agricultural sector.

The factors which explain this remarkable and broad-based growth surge in the period 1992–97 appear to include:

- Productivity gains from the deregulation of trade, industry and finance, especially in industrial and service sectors;
- The surge in export growth at about 20 per cent per year (in dollar terms) for three successive years beginning 1993–94, thanks to the substantial devaluation in real effective terms in the early 1990s and a freer policy regime for industry, foreign trade and payments;
- The investment boom of 1993–96, that exerted expansionary effects on both supply and demand, especially in industry. The investment boom itself was probably driven by a combination of factors including the unleashing of entrepreneurial energies by economic reforms, the swift loosening of the foreign exchange bottleneck, confidence in broadly consistent governmental policy signals and the easier availability of funds for investment (both through borrowing and new equity issues);
- The partial success in fiscal consolidation, that kept a check on government borrowings and facilitated expansion of aggregate savings and investments;
- Improvement in the terms of trade for agriculture resulting from a combination of higher procurement prices for important crops and lower trade protection for manufactures;

- Available capacity in key infrastructure sectors, notably power; and
- A buoyant world economy which supported expansion of foreign trade and private capital inflows.

The growth momentum slowed to an average of 5.5 per cent in the Ninth Plan period (1997–2002), after averaging 6.7 per cent in the previous five years. Several factors contributed to this deceleration, including the significant increase in fiscal deficits (mainly due to large public pay increases following the Fifth Pay Commission) and the associated decline in public savings. Economic reforms slackened after 1995 as coalition governance became the norm, while agricultural growth significantly slowed for a variety of reasons. Finally, India felt the repercussions of a marked downswing in the industrial cycle and an increasingly unsupportive international economic environment, including the Asian financial crisis of 1997–98, rising energy prices and the global recession of 2001. Indeed, India's economic growth in 1997–2002 might have been even weaker without the unexpected and somewhat inexplicable strong growth in the services sector, that clocked an average of 8.2 per cent, despite industrial growth of only 4.4 per cent.[5] The services sector accounted for almost 70 per cent of all growth in this period.

Economic reforms picked up pace in 2000–2004, fiscal deficits trended down after 2002 and the world economy rebounded strongly in 2002–2006. These factors supported a broad-based upswing in Indian industrial output and investment from the second half of 2002. Growth of industrial valued added surged to 8 per cent in 2002–2006. With the continued strong growth of services (at nearly 9 per cent), GDP growth climbed to an average of 7 per cent, despite the continued sluggishness of agriculture. Between 2003 and 2006 overall economic growth averaged over 8 per cent. This latest economic surge raises the interesting issue of whether India's trend growth rate has accelerated to 8 per cent (or higher) from its previous level of around 6 per cent. This question is explored below.

MAIN DRIVERS OF RECENT ECONOMIC GROWTH

There are least seven major elements driving India's surge in economic growth in the 1990s, starting with the momentum built from 25 years of strong economic growth.

Momentum

Over the past 30 years, very few developing countries have sustained decent per capita growth for two decades or more (Acharya 2006b). Specifically, out

*Table 2.5	Main Economic Reforms of 1991–93*

Fiscal
- Reduction of the fiscal deficit.
- Launching of reform of major tax reforms.

External Sector
- Devaluation and transition to a market-determined exchange rate.
- Phased reduction of import licensing (quantitative restrictions).
- Phased reduction of peak custom duties.
- Policies to encourage direct and portfolio foreign investment.
- Monitoring and controls over external borrowing, especially short term.
- Build-up of foreign exchange reserves.
- Amendment of FERA to reduce restrictions on firms.

Industry
- Virtual abolition of industrial licensing.
- Abolition of separate permission needed by 'MRTP houses'.
- Sharp reduction of industries 'reserved' for the public sector.
- Freer access to foreign technology.

Agriculture
- More remunerative procurement prices for cereals.
- Reduction in protection to the manufacturing sector.

Financial Sector
- Phasing in of Basle prudential norms.
- Reduction of reserve requirements for banks (CRR and SLR).
- Gradual freeing up of interest rates.
- Legislative empowerment of SEBI.
- Establishment of the National Stock Exchange.
- Abolition of government control over capital issues.

Public Sector
- Disinvestment program begun.
- Greater autonomy/accountability for public enterprises.

of 117 developing countries with a population of over half a million, only 12 countries achieved per capita growth of more than 3 per cent per year in 1980–2002, with at least 2 per cent growth in the 1980s and 1990s. As shown in Table 2.6, these 12 countries are: China, Vietnam, South Korea, Chile, Mauritius, Malaysia, India, Thailand, Bhutan, Sri Lanka, Botswana and Indonesia. The number falls to nine if restricted to populations of at least 3 million. Nine of these 12 countries are in Asia and, fortunately, they include the three most populous: China, India and Indonesia. Over the full 25 years (1981–2006), India's per capita growth has averaged almost 4 per cent per year.

Sustained improvements in standards of living of this magnitude bring their own growth-reinforcing elements. People come to think more positively about the future and base their savings, investment and production decisions on an expectation of continued growth. Electorates in India's democracy come to expect development and hold government performance to higher standards, despite disappointments. Companies think big when they invest.

Openness

The Indian economy in 2006 is far more open to external trade, investment and technology than it was 15 years ago.[6] Table 2.7 presents some key comparative indicators. For example, peak import duties on manufactures have come down from over 200 per cent to 12.5 per cent, a remarkable reduction by any standard. The regime of tight, detailed and discretionary import controls has been almost completely dismantled. The exchange rate was devalued and made market-responsive (1991–93). The policies toward foreign portfolio and direct investment have been greatly liberalized. As a result, the ratio of traded goods to GDP has more than doubled from less than 15 per cent to nearly 33 per cent. Because of the sustained boom in software exports and worker remittances, the ratio of current receipts (goods exports + gross invisibles) has more than tripled from 8 per cent to over 24 per cent of GDP. Foreign investment has risen from negligible levels to $20 billion in 2005–2006.

After initial periods of sometimes painful adjustment in the 1990s, Indian industry has thrived in the more open and competitive environment. The explosion in software and information technology (IT) enabled service exports, that rose from zero in 1991 to $24 billion in 2005–2006. Anecdotal evidence suggests that small-scale units have benefited greatly from the much freer access to traded raw materials, components and designs. Perhaps most importantly, the old mindset of 'foreign exchange scarcity' – and the welter of bad economic policies it spawned – has been effectively banished. Interestingly, the 'opening up' has also strengthened foreign exchange reserves and debt service ratios.

*Table 2.6   Good Growth Performers of Recent Decades: Average Annual
             Per Capita Growth (%)*

Country	1980–2002	1990s	1980s	Population in 2000 (Millions)
China	8.2	8.6	7.7	1262
Vietnam	4.6	5.7	1.9	78
South Korea	6.1	5.0	7.4	47
Chile	3.3	4.3	2.1	15
Mauritius	4.4	4.1	4.9	1
Malaysia	3.4	3.7	3.1	23
India	3.6	3.6	3.6	1016
Thailand	4.6	3.4	6.0	61
Bhutan	4.3	3.4	5.4	1
Sri Lanka	3.1	3.1	3.1	18
Botswana	4.7	2.7	7.2	2
Indonesia	3.5	2.6	4.4	206

Source: World Bank (2005).

Table 2.7   Toward a More Open Economy

	1990–91	2005–2006
Peak import duties (manufacturers)	200% plus	12.5%
Import controls	Tight, detailed	Almost gone
Trade (goods) / GDP ratio (%)	14.6	32.7
Current Receipts / GDP (%)	8.0	24.5
Software exports ($ billion)	Nil	23.6
Worker remittances ($ billion)	2.1	24.6
Foreign investment ($ billion)	Negligible	20.2
Foreign currency reserves ($ billion, 31 March)	2.2	145.1
Debt service ratio (%)	35.3	10.2

Source: Reserve Bank of India, Annual Report, 2005–2006, except for first two rows.

Strong Companies, Modern Capital Markets

The 1990s brought far-reaching reforms in India's capital markets. The
Securities and Exchange Board of India was statutorily empowered in 1992

and quickly moved to improve standards of disclosure and transparency. The new electronic-trade-based National Stock Exchange was established in 1993 and set high technical and governance standards, that soon had to be emulated by the much older (and sometimes scam-plagued) Bombay Stock Exchange. Depositories legislation was enacted and soon paperless trading became the norm. Brokers were encouraged to incorporate, and futures markets were nurtured. These and other reforms transformed Indian capital markets into one of the best in the developing world.

The combination of a modernizing capital market, an increasingly liberal and competitive environment for investment, trade and production, a wealth of entrepreneurial talent and sustained economic growth has facilitated the rise of strong new companies and supported the expansion of the more agile and aggressive among the established firms. For example, Airtel, the leading private telecommunications firm, went from nothing to a multi-billion dollar company in a decade. The same was true for the leading domestic airline, Jet, and IT icons like Infosys, Wipro, TCS and HCL. Old pharmaceutical companies, like Ranbaxy, transformed themselves. New media companies like Zee and NDTV bloomed. Established corporations restructured and flourished (e.g., some Tata companies, Reliance, Bajaj, Mahindra and Hero Honda) or saw their market shares decline. In recent years quite a few Indian companies have expanded through overseas investments and acquisitions, facilitated by direct investments abroad averaging over $2 billion annually since 2003. Tata Steel's successful $7.6 billion bid for Corus in 2006 is a well-publicized example.

Aggregate financial data also point to the strength and expansion of India's corporate sector in recent years. The market capitalization of companies listed on the Bombay Stock Exchange rose nearly 14-fold from $50 billion in 1990–91 to $680 billion in 2005–2006 (Table 2.8). Since 2002 the growth of profits has outpaced the growth of sales of private corporations, indicating rising profit margins. With falling interest rates and growing recourse to internal funding, the share of interest outgo in gross profits dropped sharply from above 50 per cent in the late 1990s to 15 per cent in 2005–2006 (Reserve Bank 2006, Box 1.7). Unsurprisingly, data for the top 1,000 listed companies showed net profits as a percentage of net sales rising from 4.5 per cent in 2001–2002 to 8.9 per cent in 2004–2005 (Business Standard 2006).

Growing Middle Class

In the mid-1990s, shortly after the major economic reforms of 1991–94, there was premature exuberance about India's rising middle class and their acquisitive aspirations. Today there is a much firmer basis for emphasizing the importance of the growing middle class in transforming consumption,

Table 2.8   Rising Middle Class

	1990–91	2005–06
People in households with income (INR 2 million–10 million OR PPP \$20,000–\$1,00,000 approximately)[a]	15 million	100 million
Bombay Stock Exchange market capitalization[b]	\$50 billion	\$680 billion
Cars + UVs sold[c]	205,000	1.319 million
Two-wheelers sold[c]	1.8 million	7.57 million
Telephone connections[d] (million)	5	125[e]

Source:
a. Based on data from NCAER (2005).
b. RBI, Handbook of Statistics on the Indian Economy, 2005–2006.
c. Business Beacon, CMIE and Monthly Review of the Indian Economy, CMIE, October 2006.
d. Business Beacon CMIE and Economic Survey, 2005–2006.
e. December 2005.

production and investment in the Indian economy. Table 2.8 provides a few indicators. Based on surveys by India's National Council of Applied Economic Research (NCAER), about 100 million people now live in households with annual incomes between INR 200,000 and INR 1 million (approximately PPP\$20,000 to 100,000), compared with about 15 million in 1990–1991. With a lower defining threshold, the size of the middle class would be greater. For example, if the middle class cutoff is defined as the 'non-poor' by standards of developed economies, then Bhalla (2007) estimates that 34 per cent of India's population was 'middle class' in 2005 compared with about 10 per cent in 1990.

Purchases of iconic middle class consumption items have certainly soared in the last 15 years (see Table 2.8). Annual sales of cars (including multi-utility vehicles) have risen more than six times to 1.3 million in 2005–2006. Two-wheeler sales have increased more than four times to 7.6 million in 2005–2006. In 1990–91 India had just 5 million fixed telephone connections. By the end of 2005 the number was 125 million, and about two-thirds were mobile connections. Indeed, in October 2006 the new mobile connections were close to 7 million, more than the total of phone connections 15 years ago.

Table 2.9   Share of Working Population (15–59 yrs)

Country	1950	1975	2000	2025	2050
India	55.5	54.0	58.9	64.3	59.7
China	59.0	53.6	65.0	62.1	53.8
Japan	56.9	64.0	62.1	52.8	45.2
United States	60.5	60.0	62.1	56.6	54.6
Western Europe	61.7	58.1	61.3	54.8	50.4

Source: United Nations, World Population Ageing, 1950–2050, at http://www.un.org/esa/population/publications/worldageing19502050/countriesorareas.htm.

Demographic Dividend

The growth potential of India's young population and declining dependency ratio is well known. According to most population projections, the share of the working-age population in total population will continue to rise for the next 30 years or so, long after the decline has set in other major polities like China, the United States, Western Europe and Japan (Table 2.9). These demographics point to a large potential for higher growth through augmented supply of labor and savings. Indeed, these trends have already been at work for over 15 years, helping to raise India's household savings from around 15–16 per cent of GDP in the late 1980s to 22–24 per cent after 2002.[7]

Recent Policies

As noted above, economic reforms slowed after 1995 and then revived somewhat from 2000 to 2004. At the same time, real interest rates declined worldwide, including for India. In India this may have been helped by renewed efforts to reduce burgeoning fiscal deficits at the central level, such as the Fiscal Responsibility and Budget Management Act (2003). The fiscal position of the states (India's regions) also improved from the dire straits which followed the Fifth Pay Commission. The states also adopted fiscal responsibility laws following the recommendations (and conditional debt write-offs) of the Twelfth Finance Commission (India, Government of 2006). Furthermore, tax revenues at both levels of government were buoyed by resurgent economic – especially industrial – growth after 2002–2003.

The net result was a decline in the gross fiscal deficit from almost 10 per cent of GDP in 2001–2002 to 7.5 per cent in 2004–2005 and an even larger decline in the revenue deficit from 7 per cent to 3.7 per cent of GDP (Table 2.10). This was the single most important factor explaining the increase in

Table 2.10   Deficits, Savings and Investment (as percentage of GDP)

Year	1995–96	2001–2002	2004–2005
Gross fiscal deficit (Center and States)	6.5	9.9	7.5
Revenue deficit (Center and states)	3.2	7.0	3.7
Gross domestic savings	25.1	23.6	29.1
(of which government)	(−2.0)	(−6.0)	(−2.7)
Gross domestic investment	26.9	23.0	30.1

Source: Reserve Bank of India, *Handbook of Statistics on the Indian Economy, 2005–2006*; Central Statistical Office data.

aggregate savings from around 24 per cent of GDP in 2001–2002 to 29 per cent in 2004–2005 which, in turn, helped finance the current investment boom.

International Economic Environment

Despite the war in Iraq (2003–) and the high oil prices after 2003, the world economy has grown at almost 5 per cent over the period 2003-2006, propelled by strong growth in the United States and China and some recovery in Japan and Europe. World trade in goods and services has expanded rapidly. This favorable environment has fuelled the rapid growth in exports of goods and services from India, that, in turn, has been a significant driver of economic growth.[8]

RISKS TO FUTURE STRONG GROWTH

However, there are at least seven risks or constraints which could adversely affect the annual 8 per cent growth rate enjoyed by India since 2003. Each of these merits brief elaboration.

Populist Demands for Government Spending

The recent progress in fiscal consolidation, noted above, is real but modest. The overall fiscal deficit remains high at 7.5 per cent of GDP in 2005–2006, while the government debt-to-GDP ratio stays at 80 per cent (compared with about 60 per cent in 1995–2006). While the fiscal responsibility laws enacted by central and state governments (22 out of 28 states have passed such laws so far) are promising, they are not immune to populist pressures. Especially since the advent of the United Progressive Alliance (UPA) government in 2004, populist expenditure programs, such as the National Rural Employment Guarantee scheme – which guarantees at least 100 days of minimum wage pay each year – have gained fresh momentum. The Sixth Pay Commission convened in 2006 and is expected to submit its report by mid-2008, with governmental action likely before the next general election. The possibility of significant public pay increases is obviously high. On the revenue side, the state-level VATs have contributed to revenue buoyancy. But the recent scheme for special economic zones is fraught with unduly generous tax concessions, making the prospects for fiscal consolidation mixed, at best.

Infrastructure Bottlenecks

India's infrastructure problems are legendary and reflect failures in public sector performance and governance. As the World Bank's 2006 study, *Inclusive Growth and Service Delivery: Building on India's Success*, points out, 'The average manufacturer loses 8.4 per cent in sales annually on account of power outages', over 60 per cent of Indian manufacturing firms own generator sets (compared to 27 per cent in China and 17 per cent in Brazil) and India's combined real cost of power is almost 40 per cent higher than China's. The quantity and quality of roads is also a serious bottleneck. While there has been some progress in recent years with national highway development, the state and rural road networks are woefully inadequate, especially in poorer states (Figure 2.1). Urban infrastructure, especially water and sewerage, is another major constraint for rapid industrial development and urbanization (Figure 2.2). The successful example of rapid telecom development is very promising. But unlike telecom, the energy, roads and urban infrastructure sectors are burdened by long histories of a subsidy culture and dual (center and state) constitutional responsibilities. Unless the various infrastructure constraints are addressed swiftly and effectively, it is difficult to see how 8 per cent (or higher) economic growth can be sustained.

Labor Market Rigidities

According to official data, India's non-agricultural employment in the private, organized sector (units employing more than ten workers) has stagnated below 9 million for over 20 years, although the labor force has grown to exceed 400 million. A major cause has been India's complex and rigid labor laws, that

Figure 2.1 Percentage of Habitations Not Connected by Roads, by Indian State

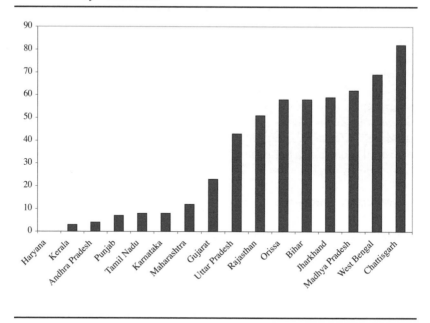

Source: Indian Ministry of Rural Development, as cited in World Bank (2006).

hugely discourage new employment while protecting those with organized-sector jobs.[9] Investment climate surveys by the World Bank indicate that India has some of the most restrictive labor laws in the world, that essentially convert labor (in organized units) into a fixed factor of production (layoffs are extremely difficult) and thereby discourage fresh employment in the organized sector while promoting more 'casualization' and insecurity among the 93 per cent of workers relegated to the unorganized sector. The laws are not just rigid, but also numerous; according to the World Bank, 'A typical firm in Maharashtra thus has to deal with 28 different acts pertaining to labor' (World Bank 2006, 120).

Without significant reform of existing labor laws, India's cheap labor advantages will remain hugely underutilized. Looking to the future, the challenge will increase as the 'demographic dividend' brings further large increases in the labor force. In fact, as I have pointed out elsewhere (Acharya 2004), the economic and political challenge is far greater than normally appreciated, because the bulk of the coming demographic bulge will occur in the poor,

Figure 2.2   Percentage of Population with Access to Sewage Facilities,
by Indian State

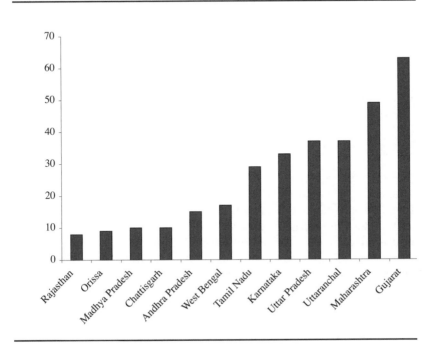

Source: Central Public Health and Environmental Engineering Organization (2000), as cited in World Bank (2006).

slow-growing and populous states of central and eastern India – notably, Uttar Pradesh, Bihar, Orissa and Madhya Pradesh.

Weak Agricultural Performance

Since 1996–97 the growth of agriculture has dropped to barely 2 per cent, compared with earlier rates ranging between 2.5 and 3.0 per cent. The reasons are many and include declining public investment by cash-strapped states, grossly inadequate maintenance of irrigation assets, falling water tables, inadequate rural road networks, unresponsive research and extension services, soil damage from excessive urea use (encouraged by high subsidies), weak credit delivery and a distorted incentive structure which impedes diversification away from food grains. Tackling these problems and revitalizing agriculture will take time, money, understanding and political will. It will also require much greater investments in – and maintenance of – rural infrastructure of irrigation, roads, soil conservation, etc. and reinvigoration of the present systems of agricultural research and outreach. While the central government can play a significant role in revamping systems, the main responsibility for strengthening rural infrastructure lies with the states. However, their financial and administrative capabilities have weakened over time.

The share of agriculture in GDP has declined to hardly 20 per cent. But agriculture is still the principal occupation of nearly 60 per cent of the labor force. Thus improving the performance of this sector is essential to alleviate poverty and contain rising regional and income inequalities.

Pace of Economic Reforms

There is little doubt that economic reforms have slowed since the UPA government assumed office in May 2004.[10] The privatization program has been halted, although the government remains the dominant owner in banking, energy and transport, and the usual ills of public ownership afflict the performance of many enterprises in these key sectors. The legislative proposals of the National Democratic Alliance (NDA) government (1998–2004) to reduce government ownership in public-sector banks to 33 per cent have lapsed and not been renewed. There has been some revival of interest-rate controls and directed credit. Follow-up action on the reformist new Electricity Act (2003) passed by the NDA government has been slow. The pricing of petroleum products has become more politically administered than before. Education policy has focused on introducing caste-based reservations in institutions of higher education, a provision also being considered for private-sector employment. However, efforts to reform labor laws remain stalled, while there has been little progress in agricultural reform.

Indeed, it is surprising that the economy's growth momentum has remained so strong despite the stalling of economic reforms. If the growth dividends of economic reforms occur with a lag, then the paucity of reforms from 2004 to 2007 may take their toll in the years ahead.

Weak Human Resource Policies

The long-run performance of the Indian economy depends on successful policies and programs for education, skill development and health service provision. Yet the government-led programs in these sectors suffer from very serious weaknesses and a lack of reform impetus. For example, the World Bank (2006) cites a number of surveys which show that less than half of government teachers and health workers actually show up at the schools and clinics they supposed to serve serving (the situation is typically worse in poorer states). Even though school enrolment rates have climbed over time, the actual cognitive skill acquired in schools – even simple reading and arithmetic – is still very low (Pratham 2006). In health, at least one survey shows that staff in primary health clinics in Delhi had a greater than 50 per cent chance of prescribing a *harmful* therapy for specified, common ailments (Das and Hammer 2004a, 2004b). The competence of these medical personnel was found to be lower than their peers in Tanzania and substantially worse than their peers in Indonesia. Even in higher education, an area of supposed competence, studies point to enormous problems of quality, quantity and relevance (Aggarwal 2006).

Quite clearly, the current portfolio of policies and programs in these critical sectors need urgent improvement if India is to retain a competitive edge in an increasingly globalized, knowledge-based, world economy.

International Economic Environment

There are indicators suggesting that the international economic environment is deteriorating. The latter half of 2006 witnessed a distinct slowing in the growth of the US economy, still the single most potent locomotive of global growth. The Doha Round of multilateral trade liberalization remains in limbo. Oil prices have been high and rising to new peaks, with little prospect of falling below $70 a barrel. The chances of some slackening in the growth of world output and trade are clearly rising. Just as the Indian economy has benefited from strong global expansion in 2003–2006, so it may also expect to bear some downside risks from slower world growth in the years ahead.

MEDIUM-TERM GROWTH PROSPECTS

Since 2003–2004 there have been quite a few studies projecting sustained, high growth for the Indian economy in the long run, including the Goldman Sachs 'BRICs' report (Wilson and Purushothaman 2003; Rodrik and Subramanian 2004; Kelkar 2004). Their specific projections and time-periods differ: Goldman Sachs foresaw near 6 per cent growth for 50 years; Rodrik and Subramanian projected a minimum of 7 per cent for the next 20 years and Kelkar was even more optimistic at 10 per cent.[11] More recently, with a three-year 8 per cent average already achieved and the current year (2006–2007) likely to register a similar rate, the government's Planning Commission (2006) has outlined GDP growth projections for the fiscal years 2007–2008 through 2011–2012 at 8 to 9 per cent. Bhalla (2007) goes further and foresees 10 per cent growth as almost

Figure 2.3   India's GDP Growth, 1955–2007 (rolling five-year average)

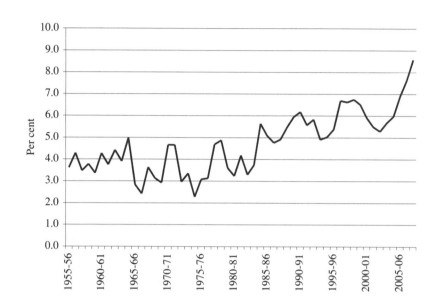

inevitable. Most serious economists in India expect economic growth in the next five years to average at least 8 per cent.

Such optimism is not wholly misplaced. It is based on the continuing strength of the positive factors outlined above, especially continued globalization and 'catch-up', the demographic dividends, the rising middle class, a vibrant entrepreneurial culture, positive expectations of future economic reforms and a generally benign international economic environment. The optimists are not blind to the risks and threats. They simply expect the growth-enhancing tendencies to prevail or, more subtly, for the dynamics of growth to generate solutions to constraints such as infrastructure and education. Figure 2.3 provides encouragement for the bullish outlook.

In my view, the downside factors outlined above should carry more weight in assessing India's medium-term growth prospects. There is a good chance that the currently bullish view of growth expectations is overly influenced by the recent past (2003 onward), a period of strong cyclical upswing in both the global economy and Indian industry. The strength of the cycle could abate in the next few years, and India's growth could revert to a trend rate in the range of 6–7 per cent, perhaps closer to the higher figure. However, even under this

Table 2.11   Medium-Term Growth Expectations

	1992–1993 to 2005–2006	2002–2003 to 2006–2007	2007–2008 to 2011–2012 'Optimist'	'Pessimist'
GDP %	6.4	7.2 *	8–10	6.5–7.0
GDP per capita (%)	4.4	5.5	6.5–8.5	5–5.5

Note: Assuming Reserve Bank projection of 8.0 per cent GDP growth for 2006–2007.

'pessimistic' scenario, annual per capita growth would still be at a historical peak for India (Table 2.11).

Perhaps the most noteworthy point is that medium-term growth expectations for India are so buoyant that the range between optimists and pessimists is placed so high, within a fairly narrow band of about 7–9 per cent. Only time will tell which prediction is closer to reality.

IMPLICATIONS OF INDIA'S RISE

India's growth at an average rate of almost 6 per cent a year over the past quarter century (with per capita growth of nearly 4 per cent annually) is both remarkable and commendable. Certainly, back in 1980, there was almost no respectable scholar or institution predicting such sustained development of this poverty-ridden, populous country. At the same time, the prevailing fashion of bracketing India's rise with China's exceptionally dynamic development under rubrics like 'China and India Rising' may mask more than it reveals. If India's development in the last 25 years has been good, China's has been extraordinary. Furthermore, while India has been a gradual 'globalizer', China's surging development has been far more intensively based on global trade and capital flows.

As a consequence, the global economic impact of China's rise has been much more dramatic in terms of the usual metrics of international economic relations: trade, capital flows and energy. A glance at Table 2.12 confirms this obvious point. The comparison of columns 5 and 6 of the table is especially instructive. It highlights both the dramatic increase in China's engagement with the world economy between 2000 and 2005, as well as the much milder rise in India's international economic integration. For example, China's goods

Table 2.12   China and India: Global Impact

	China		India		Increment (2000–2005)	
	2000 (1)	2005 (2)	2000 (3)	2005 (4)	China (5)	India (6)
Merchandise exports ($billion)[a,b]	249.1	762.4	45.5*	104.7*	513.3	59.2
Share of world exports (%)[e]	3.9	7.3	0.7	0.9	3.4	0.2
Service exports ($ billion) [a,b]	30.4	74.4	16.2*	60.6*	44	44.4
Current account balance ($ billion)[a,b]	20.5	160.8	−2.7*	−10.6*	140.3	−7.6
Foreign exchange reserves ($ billion)[a]	165.6	818.9	37.2	131.0	653.3	93.8
FDI inflow ($ billion)[c]	30.1[#]	72.4	1.7[#]	6.6	42.3	4.9
FDI stock (inward, $ billion)[c]	193.3	317.9	17.5	45.3	124.6	27.8
Oil consumption (million tons)[d]	223.6	327.3	106.1	115.7	103.7	9.6
Primary energy consumption (million tons oil equivalent)[d]	966.7	1554.0	320.4	387.3	587.3	66.9

Notes:
*Data for India refer to fiscal year 2000–2001 and 2005–2006
1990–2000 (annual average)
Sources:
a. International Financial Statistics (December 2006) at http://www.imfstatistics.org/inf.
b. Reserve Bank of India, Handbook of Statistics on the Indian Economy (2005–2006) at www.rbi.org.in.
c. UNCTAD, World Investment Report (2006) at http://www.unctad.org.
d. Statistical Review of World Energy (2006).
e. International Trade Statistics, (2001, 2005) at
   http://www.wto.org/english/res_e/statis_e/statis_e.htm.

exports increased by an amount which was five times the level of India's *total* goods exports in 2005. Similarly, the increase in oil consumption in China was almost equal to India's total oil consumption in 2005.

Aside from the dominant factor of China's full-blooded embrace of global opportunities (compared with the much more hesitant approach adopted by India) there are several other reasons which explain these strikingly different outcomes. First, over the last 25 years, China's per capita growth rate has been about double India's, around 8 per cent as compared with 4 per cent. Second, India's growth has been propelled more by domestic consumption than external demand, as compared with China. Third, China's growth has been powered much more by the rapid growth of industry, especially labor-intensive manufactured exports, while in India the growth of services (mostly non-tradable) has been more dominant. In fact, the share of manufacturing in GDP in 2004 was only 16 per cent in India, but nearly 40 per cent in China.

Even in services, China's total services exports exceeded India's in 2005 and the increment over 2000 was comparable in absolute terms, although much lower in relative ones. The one area where India has displayed China-type growth rates is in regard to software exports, that quadrupled from about $6 billion in 2000–2001 to $24 billion in 2005–2006. But even in 2005–2006 (and despite all the media coverage and hype) the IT (and IT-enabled) services accounted for less than 3 per cent of India's GDP and employed only about 1.3 million workers directly (and perhaps double that number indirectly). By itself this sector cannot be expected to transform India's economy. Although the potential for software export growth remains high, the pace of expansion has moderated as skill shortages have increased, competitors have risen and anti-'outsourcing' sentiments have hardened in importing nations.

In sum, India's economic rise poses few adjustment problems for the rest of the world. That conclusion has certainly been the experience so far, with the limited exception of software exports. It is only fair to acknowledge an alternative view which perceives India's development as simply lagging China's by 10 to 15 years, suggesting that by then India's economic engagement with the global economy will rival China's today (e.g., Bhalla 2007). I don't agree. Instead, the medium-term future is more likely to resemble the past decade's experience. In the coming decade the global economy will have to contend with only one new burgeoning 'giant', as it already has in the past decade. India's economic rise in global commerce, capital and energy transactions is likely to remain gradual and – hopefully – sustained.

NOTES

This study draws liberally on the author's paper, 'India's Growth: Past Performance and Future Prospects', presented at the Tokyo Club Macro Economy conference on 'India and China Rising', Tokyo, 6–7 December 2006.

1. India's economic and financial data are organized according to fiscal years running form April to March. Thus '1950–51' refers to the year running from 1 April 1950 to 31 March 1951.
2. Several different factor productivity studies support this conclusion, including: Acharya et al. (2006); Bosworth and Collins (2003); and Virmani (2004).
3. There has been a great deal written on India's economic reforms and the consequent

performance of the economy, including Acharya (2002a, 2004), Ahluwalia (2002), Kelkar (2004), Kochhar et al. (2006); Panagariya (2004a and 2006) and Virmani (2004). There is a tendency to view the post-1991 economic performance as a single unified experience. I prefer the more nuanced and disaggregated view outlined here.

4. As I have pointed out elsewhere (Acharya 2006a), these reforms are better characterized as 'medium bang' than 'gradualist' (see Ahluwalia 2002).

5. Acharya (2002a, 2003) noted this unusual phenomenon and raised questions about both the quality of the data and the durability of such sharply divergent growth rates of industry and services. More recently, similar doubts have been expressed by Bosworth, Collins and Virmani (2006).

6. The story of India's external liberalization may be found in several places, including Acharya (2002b) and Panagariya (2004b).

7. This could be an important part of the explanation to the puzzle: How does India sustain high growth despite aggregate fiscal deficits above 7 per cent of GDP over the last 20 years?

8. Panagariya (2006) emphasizes this point.

9. The skill and capital-intensive pattern of development of India's modern industrial and services sectors (despite the endowment of abundant unskilled labor) has been noted by many analysts, including Kochhar et al. (2006), Panagariya (2006) and World Bank (2006). All of them point to restrictive labor laws as a major culprit.

10. For a recent review see Acharya (2006c).

11. See Acharya (2004) for a critical assessment of these bullish growth expectations.

BIBLIOGRAPHY

Acharya, Shankar (2002a), 'Macroeconomic Management in the Nineties', *Economic and Political Weekly*, **37** (16), 20 April.

—— (2002b), 'Managing India's External Economic Challenges in the 1990s', in Montek Singh Ahluwalia, Y.V. Reddy and S.S. Tarapore (eds), *Macroeconomics and Monetary Policy*, New York: Oxford University Press, pp. 215–46.

—— (2003), *India's Economy: Some Issues and Answers*, New Delhi: Academic Foundation.

—— (2004), 'India's Growth Prospects, Revisited', *Economic and Political Weekly*, **39** (41), 9 October.

—— (2006a), *Essays on Macro Economic Policy and Growth in India*, New York: Oxford University Press.

—— (2006b), 'Economic Growth: Some Reflections', *Economic and Political Weekly*, **41** (43), 4 November.

—— (2006c): 'Economic Policy: Mid-Term Report', *Business Standard*, [New Delhi] 22 August.

Acharya, Shankar, Isher Ahluwalia, K.L. Krishna and Ila Patnaik (2006), 'India: Economic Growth, 1950–2000', Global Development Network project, 'Explaining Growth', in Kirit Parikh (ed.) *Explaining Growth in South Asia*, New York: Oxford University Press, chapter 3.

Aggarwal, Pawan (2006), 'Higher Education in India: The Need for Change', New Delhi, Indian Council for Research on International Economic Relations (ICRIER) Working Paper No. 180.

Ahluwalia, Montek S. (2002), 'Economic Reforms in India since 1991: Has Gradualism Worked?', *Journal of Economic Perspectives*, **16** (3), 67–88.

Bhagwati, Jagdish and Padma Desai (1970), *India: Planning for Industrialization*, New York: Oxford University Press.

Bhalla, Surjit (2007), *Second Among Equals: The Middle Class Kingdoms of India and China*, Washington, DC: Institute of International Economics.

Bosworth, Barry and Susan Collins (2003), 'The Empirics of Growth: An Update', *Brookings Papers on Economic Activity 2:2003*, Washington, DC: Brookings Institution Press.

Bosworth, Barry, Susan Collins and Arvind Virmani (2006), 'Sources of Growth in the Indian Economy', *India Policy Forum 2006–2007*.

Business Standard (2006), *BS 1000*, January, New Delhi.

Das, Jishnu and Jeffrey Hammer (2004a), 'Strained Mercy: Quality of Medical Care in Delhi', *Economic and Political Weekly*, **39** (9), 28 February.

—— (2004b), 'Money for Nothing; The Dire Straits of Medical Practice in India', Washington DC, World Bank Policy Research Working Paper No. 3269.

India, Government of (2006), Towards Faster and More Inclusive Growth: An Approach to the 11th Five-Year Plan, New Delhi: Planning Commission.

Kelkar, Vijay (2004), 'India: On the Growth Turnpike', *The First Ten K R Narayanan Orations: Essays by Eminent Persons on the Rapidly Transforming Indian Economy*, Canberra: Australian National University, Australia South Asia Research Centre, at http://rspas.anu.edu.au/papers/narayanan/2004oration.pdf.

Kochhar, Kalpana, Raghuram Rajan, Arvind Subramanian and Ioannis Tokatlidis (2006), 'India's Pattern of Development: What happened, What Follows', Cambridge, MA, National Bureau of Economic Research (NBER) Working Paper No. 12023.

NCAER (2005), The Great Indian Middle Class, New Delhi: National Council of Applied Economic Research.

Panagariya, Arvind (2004a), 'India in the 1980s and 1990s: A Triumph of Reforms', *Economic and Political Weekly*, **39** (25), 19 June.

—— (2004b), 'India's Trade Reform', in Arvind Panagariya, Suman Bery and Barry Bosworth (eds), *Indian Policy Forum 2004*, Washington, DC: Brookings Institution.

—— (2006) 'Transforming India', paper presented at Columbia University conference 'India: An Emerging Giant', New York, October.

Parikh, Kirit (ed.) (2006), *Explaining Growth in South Asia*, New York: Oxford University Press.

Pratham (2006), 'Annual Status of Education Report', Mumbai: Pratham Resource Centre.

Reserve Bank of India (2006), *Annual Report, 2005–06*, Mumbai.

Rodrik, Dani and Arvind Subramanian (2004), 'Why India Can Grow at 7 per cent a Year or More', *Economic and Political Weekly*, **39** (16) 17 April.

Sivasubramonian, S. (2000), *The National Income of India in the Twentieth Century*, New York: Oxford University Press.

Virmani, Arvind (2004), 'Sources of India's Economic Growth: Trends in Total Factor Productivity', New Delhi, Indian Council for Research on International Economic Relations (ICRIER) Working Paper No. 131.

Wilson, Dominic and Roopa Purushothaman (2003), 'Dreaming with BRICs: The Path to 2050', New York, Goldman Sachs Global Economic Paper No. 99 at http://www2.goldmansachs.com–insight–research–reports–99.pdf.

World Bank (2005), *Economic Growth in the 1990s: Learning from a Decade of Reform*, Washington DC: World Bank.

—— (2006), *Inclusive Growth and Service Delivery: Building on India's Success*, New Delhi: Macmillan.

3. Asian Century or Multipolar Century?

David Dollar

The most distinctive feature of the modern era of globalization is the emergence of large developing countries, notably China and India, from a long period of self-imposed isolation. In the 15 years between 1990 and 2005, the developing economies of Asia accounted for 44 per cent of global economic growth, measured at purchasing power parity (PPP). The established industrial powers of the Organization for Economic Cooperation and Development (OECD) accounted for 41 per cent. Many observers believe that these trends will continue and that we are on the verge of an 'Asian Century' which will be dominated by Asian economics, politics and culture.

To analyze this topic, I divide Asia into three roughly equal parts – China, India and the rest of developing Asia (RODA) – and compare their economic performances and future prospects. This categorization quickly reveals that the notion of the rise of Asia is something of a myth. In the next section I look at the recent economic performance of China, India and RODA (each of which has, roughly speaking, about a billion people). China's economic performance has been spectacular, and the 'rise of China' is a real phenomenon. India has done well, but over a 15-year period its per capita GDP growth averaged 4 per cent, far behind China's performance. That growth rate has accelerated in recent years, and a key issue for India is whether it can sustain this higher growth. The rest of developing Asia has grown at 2.7 per cent, just slightly better than the world average. Within RODA, there is large heterogeneity, with Thailand and Vietnam growing quite well, while other large economies such as Bangladesh, Indonesia, Myanmar, Pakistan and the Philippines have performed from poor to average. The weaker performances of India and of RODA, compared with China, can be traced to a weaker human capital base, less openness to foreign trade and investment, and a relatively poor investment climate, compared with Chinese coastal locations.

As a result of its rapid growth, China has emerged with significantly higher per capita income than either India or RODA and with higher wages – wages have been rising rapidly in Chinese coastal cities, in real terms. Exchange rate appreciation will strengthen this tendency for China to be the high-wage producer in developing Asia. China has also become a major importer of various natural resources, including oil, natural gas, copper and timber. Looking forward, there are good opportunities for other developing countries to expand trade with China based on greater resource and labor abundance. There is already some shift of labor-intensive manufacturing out of China to other Asian developing countries. But to really reap the potential benefits, Asian developing countries need to continue to open up to foreign trade and investment and to strengthen investment climates. Much of what is important in the investment climate is determined at the local level, so the next period will see intense competition among cities to create good environments and to attract both firms and talent. It is very likely that within Asia some cities will do much better than others in this competition.

As noted, the rise of China is a real phenomenon, and China's continued growth will be increasingly important for the global economy and for developing economies. Below I examine some of the key issues which China faces. The fact that China has grown well for 25 years does not guarantee continued growth. Its demographics, openness and investment climate lay a foundation for further rapid growth for 15 years or so, but the country also faces some new challenges in the short and medium term. In the immediate future, the trade imbalance between China and the rest of the world is a real worry; the current situation is not sustainable and China needs to shift its production away from exports toward internal needs, such as better social services and higher household consumption.

In the medium term, the resource-intensity of China's growth is not sustainable. Energy efficiency has actually declined over the past five years. Inefficient use of energy is contributing to serious pollution problems with very high human costs, and it is also making China increasingly dependent on an imported commodity which is in ever-scarcer supply. The third big issue which China faces is that recent growth has been accompanied by a sharp rise in inequality and by surprisingly little social improvement – so that there is growing popular demand for more public support for education and health and for better designed safety nets.

China's continued success will pose challenges to the rest of the developing world, but also large opportunities. However, if China does not do a good job of addressing these issues, the consequences for the rest of the developing world will be mostly negative. When Beijing does begin to address its key challenges, cooperation between China and the United States will be crucial. If the two countries do not cooperate on resolving the trade imbalance through higher savings in the United States and greater consumption in China (including public spending on health and education), there could be a nasty global recession with high US dollar interest rates and sharply falling commodity prices, that would create a very poor environment for the rest of the developing world.

Looking to the longer term, China and the United States are the two biggest consumers of energy and the two biggest emitters of greenhouse gases. They could cooperate on developing new energy-efficient technologies and capping greenhouse gas emissions. Alternatively, they could compete to try to lock up the declining supply of oil and gas, with negative consequences for global stability and for the global climate. The United Kingdom's 'Stern Review on the Economics of Climate Change' suggests that the economic impact of climate change will be quite devastating for many poor countries, therefore how China and the United States deal with their energy needs will have major ramifications for the developing world.

Given these difficulties, the next century is more likely to be a 'Multipolar Century' than an 'Asian Century'. There is too much heterogeneity within Asia to make 'Asian Century' a very useful concept. If current trends continue, the United States and China will be the main sources of global growth. Good cooperation between Beijing and Washington on important global issues such as maintaining an open trading system, resolving global imbalances, and managing energy scarcity and global climate change could usher in an era of harmony and successful development throughout much of the world. On the other hand, if there is poor cooperation and a lack of progress on these issues, much of the cost will be borne by people in the developing world. If India continues its recent strong growth performance, it will become a third significant force in the global economy, and there are potential scenarios in which China stumbles while India surges. So 'multipolar' seems a good adjective to describe this moment in global economic history.

THE RISE OF ASIA?

The period since 1990 marks an important change in world economic history. For 200 years, the countries of Western Europe and their offshoots (United States, Canada, Australia and New Zealand) grew faster than economies in the rest of the world, dividing the world between 'developed' and 'developing' countries. During this time Japan was the only major country outside of the European sphere which managed to join the club of developed nations. This pattern of the already rich growing faster came to an end during the 1980s. In the 1990s developing countries as a whole grew twice as fast (3.5 per cent per capita) as the developed countries (1.7 per cent per capita). The world has reached an important milestone, whereby about one-half of global GDP, measured at PPP, comes from developing countries. Most of this rapid,

Table 3.1   Global Growth Rates, 1990–2005

	Number of Countries	Pop. (million)	PPP GDP	GDP per capita	Exports
United States	1	296	3.0	1.9	4.7
Japan	1	128	1.3	1.0	3.8
Rest of high income	22	496	2.3	1.8	5.4
China	1	1304	9.6	8.7	15.0
India	1	1095	5.7	4.0	8.9
Rest of developing Asia	17	843	4.5	2.7	8.5
Latin America	29	539	3.0	1.4	7.9
Sub-Saharan Africa	41	711	2.7	0.2	3.9
Eastern Europe/ Central Asia	14	324	0.2	0.1	8.6
Middle East/N Africa	11	275	3.9	2.0	5.9
World	138	6012	3.4	2.0	6.1

Sources: World Development Indicators; World Bank WITS database.

emerging market growth has occurred in Asia, leading to talk of 'the rise of Asia', the theme of this volume.

One immediate problem with the concept of 'the rise of Asia' is that the continent is a large and heterogeneous one. It has about half of the world's population, divided roughly in thirds among China, India and the Rest of Developing Asia (RODA). This last group is quite heterogeneous. The main population centers are Indonesia, Pakistan, Bangladesh, Myanmar, Thailand, Vietnam and the Philippines. Those seven countries have a combined population of 800 million people. Thailand is relatively wealthy and developed, while Myanmar next door is extremely poor and backward.

In 1990 RODA in the aggregate had per capita GDP of $2,421 (measured at PPP), about 50 per cent richer than India ($1,701) or China ($1,597). What has happened since? For the world as a whole, per capita GDP growth was 2 per cent in the 1990–2005 period. Over this period China had spectacular growth of 8.7 per cent per annum. India grew at 4 per cent, while RODA grew at 2.7 per cent (Table 3.1). If I were grading growth performances over the past 15 years, I would give China an A, India B+, and RODA C+. Without China and India, the rest of developing Asia has grown only slightly faster than the world economy as a whole.

While it is useful to talk about growth rates, they also mask important trends in global production. The United States has been growing at a fairly steady rate, around 2 per cent per capita. That sounds very modest. But with a level of

Figure 3.1   Distribution of Increase in Global GDP, 1990–2005 by Region/Country

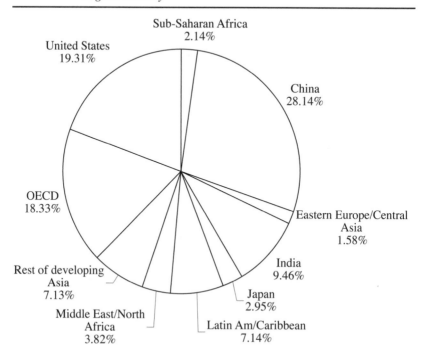

per capita GDP that averaged $33,000 over the 1990–2005 period, that 2 per cent per capita growth generates about $660 in additional goods and services per person per year. China's spectacular growth of 8.7 per cent generated an average increase in goods and services per person of $320 per year during the period.

Based on increased GDP, China and the United States seem to be the two big winners in this era of globalization. China accounted for 28 per cent of the global increase in GDP since 1990, while the United States accounted for 19 per cent (Figure 3.1). Hence China and the United States combined generated nearly half of all global GDP growth in the recent period. India, with 16 per cent of the global population, generated 9 per cent of GDP growth. RODA, with 14 per cent of world population, only generated 7 per cent of growth. The figure is almost identical for Latin America. These numbers suggest that the rise of China is a real phenomenon and the rise of India has good potential, but talk of 'Asia rising' may be misleading. For Asia, outside of China and India, economic performance has been only slightly better than the world average.

There is a similar pattern for trade. One of the features of this modern era of globalization is that trade is growing much faster than GDP, meaning trade integration is deepening, especially for developing countries, many of which had followed inward-oriented strategies up to the 1980s. Global per capita GDP growth has averaged 2 per cent since 1990, aggregate GDP growth 3.4 per cent (adding in population growth), while merchandise export growth has been 6 per cent. For China, export growth has been a spectacular 15.0 per cent per year; for India, 8.9 per cent; for RODA, 8.5 per cent (see Table 3.1).

Since China, India and RODA all had similar per capita GDP in 1990, it is natural to inquire why their growth performances have been so different. This is obviously a complex question involving many factors, but three factors help to explain the divergent growth performances. First, China had a better base of human capital in 1990 compared with India or RODA. Second, over this period China has been more open to foreign trade and investment than India or RODA. Third, China has created a better private sector investment climate than India which, in turn, had a better climate than RODA on average. The qualifier 'on average' is important because Thailand, for example, had quite a good investment climate and grew well, but it is a relatively small part of RODA, dwarfed in size by Indonesia, Bangladesh and Pakistan.

Human Capital

China's human capital advantage has historical roots. Already in 1870, 21 per cent of adults in China were literate. Since nearly all of these would have been males, this means that about 40 per cent of adult males were literate. In South Asia the literacy rate in 1870 was 3 per cent of the adult population, about the same as in Africa. Latin America had a literacy rate of 15 per cent in 1870 (Morrisson and Murtin 2005). In 1990, even though China was poorer than India or RODA, it had a more educated population. Average years of schooling of the adult population in China was 5.2 years in 1990, compared with 3.7 in India or 3.5 for the rest of developing Asia (Barro and Lee 2000). China's superior human capital can be seen as well in infant mortality data, which are a good summary indicator of health status. In 1990 China's infant mortality rate was 38 per 1,000, far below India's 80 or RODA's 69 (Table 3.2). Despite its good human capital, in 1990 China had about the same per capita income as Bangladesh, India, Pakistan and Vietnam and was substantially poorer than Indonesia, Philippines and Thailand. It is hard to get reliable data on wages, but the available data suggest that China had wages somewhat lower than those in Bangladesh, India and Pakistan, and far behind those in the more advanced Asian developing countries (Table 3.3).

Table 3.2   Human Capital Indicators

	Population (millions)	GDP p.c. (2000 US$)	Infant mortality (per 1000)	Years of schooling (adults above 25)
China				
1990	1135	1597	38	5.2
2005	1304	5879	26	5.7
India				
1990	850	1701	80	3.7
2005	1096	3118	61.6	4.8
Bangladesh				
1990	104	1208	100	2.2
2005	142	1786	56.4	2.5
Indonesia				
1990	178	2267	60	3.3
2005	221	3437	29.6	4.7
Myanmar				
1990	41	n.a.	91	2.1
2005	51	n.a.	75.6	2.4
Pakistan				
1990	108	1561	100	2.3
2005	156	2149	80.2	2.5
Philippines				
1990	61	3877	41	7.1
2005	83	4401	26	7.6
Thailand				
1990	55	4552	31	5.4
2005	64	7649	18.2	6.1
Vietnam				
1990	66	1212	38	3.8
2005	83	2739	17.4	n.a.
RODA7				
1990	613	2209	69	3.5
2005	799	3247	45	4.1

Source: World Development Indicators; Barro and Lee (2000).

Table 3.3   *Average Tariffs and Wages in Asia*

	Average import tariff (percent)		Annual manufacturing wages (US$)	
	1990	2004	1980s	2000
Bangladesh	94	18	556	671
India	82	28	1035	1192
Pakistan	65	16	664	844
Vietnam	n.a.	14	n.a.	711
China	40	10	472	1766
Thailand	40	14	2305	2851
Philippines	28	6	1240	2376
Indonesia	21	7	898	3054

Source: UNCTAD TRAINS database; World Development Indicators.

Openness

The Chinese refer to their reform program as *Gai ge kai fang*, that translates as 'change the system, open the door'.[1] The whole reform program is often referred to as the 'open door policy'. Trade liberalization and opening up to direct foreign investment have been key components of Chinese reform. Beijing has not opened the capital account more generally to portfolio flows. By 1990 China's economy was far more open than those of the other low-wage countries in Asia: China's average import tariff was 40 per cent, well below those of Bangladesh (94 per cent), India (82 per cent) or Pakistan (65 per cent). Thailand (40 per cent) had the same average tariff rate in 1990; the Philippines (28 per cent) and Indonesia (21 per cent) were more open still, but with significantly higher wages they were not competing directly with China (Table 3.3). Since joining the World Trade Organization (WTO), China's average tariffs have dropped below 10 per cent, and to around 5 per cent for manufactured imports.[2] Beijing initially welcomed foreign investment into 'special economic zones', but it is important to note that some of these were very large, amounting to urban areas of 20 million people or more. The positive impact of foreign investment in these locations led to a more general opening up of the economy to foreign investment, with the result that China has become the largest recipient of direct investment flows in recent years. Thus, compared to other labor-abundant countries in Asia, China has been more open to foreign trade and investment.

Investment Climate

The opening up measures would not have had such substantial impact if they
had not been accompanied by improvements in investment climate. This is
probably one of the least understood features of China's recent development.
There are literally dozens of Chinese coastal cities which have developed quite
good investment climates. In these cities the private sector accounts for 90
per cent or more of manufacturing assets and production. A genuine Chinese
private sector has emerged, and it is highly profitable – in 2005 the average pre-
tax rate of return for domestic private firms was around 20 per cent, similar to
that for foreign-invested firms (Dollar and Wei 2007). World Bank investment
climate surveys have documented the differences in the objective conditions of
production in Chinese cities, compared with conditions elsewhere in developing
Asia. For example, firms lose considerable output as a result of unreliable
power supply: 3.3 per cent of output in Indonesia, 4.9 per cent in Pakistan,
5.9 per cent in Philippines and 7.9 per cent in India. The figure for coastal
Chinese cities was 1.0 per cent (Table 3.4). Similarly, most manufacturing
firms are importing some parts and materials: customs clearance time for
imports is low in Chinese cities (3.2 days) compared to those in Indonesia (4.8
days), India (6.6), Philippines (7.2), Bangladesh (10.6) or Pakistan (17.1).[3] On
a whole range of practical matters which affect production, Chinese coastal
cities outperform the best locations in Bangladesh, India, Indonesia, Pakistan
and the Philippines. The only large Asian countries which have similarly good
investment climate indicators are Thailand and Vietnam, both of which have
grown quite well – but not as fast as China – in the recent period.

In summary, China, India and RODA entered this recent era of globalization
with similar per capita GDP and wage levels. But China has done more to open
its economy to the global market, while significant numbers of its coastal cities
have created sound investment climates for private investment. The result
has been a remarkable growth dynamic. India has followed a similar path,
but more slowly in terms of opening up the economy and with less success
in creating good investment climates.[4] The rest of developing Asia has some
pockets of notable success such as Malaysia, Thailand and Vietnam, but other
large population centers such as Indonesia, Bangladesh, Pakistan and the
Philippines have been held back, primarily by poor investment climates and
weaker connections to the global market.

Prospects for the Rest of Developing Asia

The world economy and global trade grew well between 1990 and 2005, and
the countries of developing Asia, outside of China, did not take full advantage

Table 3.4   *Production Conditions in Asian Countries*

	Average days to claim imports from customs	Output lost to power outages (percent of sales)
Bangladesh (2002)	10.6	2.8
India (2002)	6.6	7.9
Indonesia (2003)	4.8	3.3
Pakistan (2002)	17.1	4.9
Philippines (2003)	7.2	5.9
Thailand (2004)	3.7	1.4
Vietnam (2005)	3.7	1.3
Coastal China (2005)		
Hangzhou	3.5	0.0
Jiangmen	1.7	2.2
Qingdao	2.0	1.1
Shantou	1.8	0.0
Suzhou	2.6	2.2
Weihai	3.6	0.5
Average of six Chinese cities	3.2	1.0

Sources: www.enterprisesurveys.org; World Bank (2006).

of the opportunities offered by this growth. There is reason to be cautiously optimistic that in the next period India and the economies of RODA will perform better. In the 1990s many of the countries of Asia were competing directly with China, which was a labor-abundant economy which was largely self-sufficient in natural resources. China's success, however, has changed the equation going forward. Wages have risen rapidly in China's coastal cities. Population growth, 1990–2005, was much slower in China (0.9 per cent per year) than in India (1.7 per cent) or RODA (1.8 per cent). So, China will have an increasingly tight labor market, combined with a likely exchange-rate appreciation. Manufacturing wages in China are now two to three times as high as wages in Bangladesh, India, Pakistan or Vietnam (Table 3.3). In China's good coastal locations manufacturing wages now reach $2,400 per year. Compared in a common currency, the wage gap between China and the rest of developing Asia is likely to widen rapidly. Thus, comparative advantage in the more labor-intensive production processes will shift away from China. Indeed, this is already happening.

At the same time, China has emerged as a large net importer of natural resources such as oil, gas, timber, copper and other minerals. Looking ahead, the rest of developing Asia will thus be significantly more labor abundant and more resource abundant than China. Rather than competing with China, as in the recent period, the rest of developing Asia is looking toward an era in which its economies are more complementary to an increasingly developed China – providing good opportunities for mutually beneficial trade. Since China joined the WTO at the end of 2001, its imports from the rest of Asia have been rising at more than 20 per cent per year.

Already there is some evidence of improved economic performance in the rest of developing Asia. For India, per capita growth accelerated from 3.5 per cent in the 1990–2000 period to 5.1 per cent in the subsequent five years. For RODA there was some growth acceleration as well, although less dramatic: from 2.6 per cent per annum (1990–2000) to 2.8 per cent (2000–2005). This acceleration can be seen in some of the major countries of RODA: growth accelerated from 2.0 per cent to 3.8 per cent in Bangladesh; from 5.1 per cent to 6.2 per cent in Vietnam; from 3.2 per cent to 4.0 per cent in Thailand; and from 2.1 per cent to 2.2 per cent in Pakistan.

To fully take advantage of the opportunities arising from growth in China and the global economy, the economies of India and RODA must rectify the main deficiencies which held them back in the recent period: being more closed to global trade and direct investment than China, and having too many severe bottlenecks in the investment climate. Progress on the trade side is easier. Vietnam recently joined the WTO and in the process significantly liberalized its import regime, to an average tariff rate of 14 per cent. Bangladesh (average 2004 tariff of 18 per cent), India (28 per cent) and Pakistan (16 per cent) have lowered their trade barriers, although all are still less open than China (see Table 3.3).

Progress on the investment climate front is more difficult, because typically there are important special interests which benefit from cumbersome customs procedures or complicated regimes of regulations and permits which make it difficult to start and operate firms. Many of the important aspects of the investment climate are actually determined by local government, because local regulations and zoning (over land for example) are critical, and because local governments often have discretion in the implementation of matters which in theory are set at the national level.

Cities are increasingly competing to create better investment climates and attract both firms as well as talented workers. This competition among cities will be one of the hallmarks of the next 15 years. Most of the countries of developing Asia have achieved macroeconomic stability and a trade and investment regime which is open on paper. Competition then moves to the more micro level: which locations can create good environments for firms to start up, access finance, find skilled labor and connect to the global market? The cities which succeed will be the epicenters of growth in the coming period.

Figure 3.2   FH Index vs. ICRG Index: All Countries Except OECD

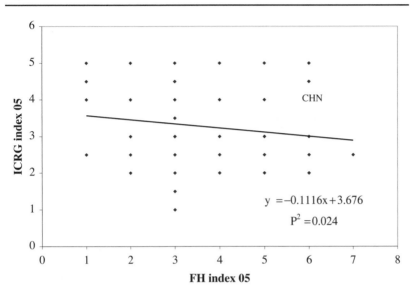

Some critics of globalization have feared that competition would lead to a 'race to the bottom', but in fact the opposite seems to be happening: a 'race to the top'. A 2006 World Bank study of the investment climates in 120 Chinese cities found that the ones which had created a good climate for private investment had also done the best job in terms of meeting social and environmental objectives (World Bank 2006). Wages have risen rapidly in the cities with good investment climates, ushering in other social advances such as low unemployment, low infant mortality and high levels of investment in education. Somewhat surprisingly, the best investment climate cities also had better environmental indicators, such as more clean-air days per year, more green space per capita and more properly treated industrial waste. This correlation likely arises from a number of different sources. The same effective governments which create non-bureaucratic and efficient production environments for private firms seem to be better at meeting human needs as well. Also, as cities prosper and move up the value chain to more sophisticated products, it becomes increasingly important that they have good living environments in order to attract and retrain the best talent. At the high end of the value chain, a good living environment is a crucial part of a good investment climate.

The political side of development is much harder to predict than economic outcomes. Complicating the analysis, there is no clear relationship between political systems and good economic governance in developing Asia. Good economic governance provides wide economic opportunities to the populace through measures such as broad-based public education, a sound investment climate to start firms and openness to the global market to permit division of labor and specialization. While governance is hard to measure, researchers have often used the International Country Risk Guide's Property Rights/Rule of Law index as a summary measure of economic governance and Freedom House's political index as a measure of democracy. Those indicators suggest that, among Asian developing countries, there are democracies with good economic governance (Malaysia, Thailand and India) and democracies where economic governance is poor (Bangladesh, Indonesia, Philippines). Similarly, there are less politically open countries with good economic governance (China, Vietnam) and those where economic governance is poor (Myanmar, Pakistan).

This pattern is similar throughout the developing world. Leaving developed countries out of the analysis, there is no correlation between democracy as measured by Freedom House and ICRG's Property Rights/Rule of Law index (Figure 3.2).[5] In the very long run there is likely to be a relationship – all the fully industrialized countries have both good economic governance and liberal democracy. But the lack of correlation between democracy and economic governance among developing countries suggests that the relationship is a long-run one, and probably a complex one with causality running both ways. Good economic governance leads to sustained growth, higher incomes and a broader civil society, that are promising foundations for political reform. Well-functioning democracy, in turn, provides a mechanism of accountability and checks and balances on decision making which tends to prevent the worst economic mistakes. (While democracies and authoritarian states tend to grow at about the same average rate, the growth rates of authoritarian countries have greater dispersion, suggesting that authoritarian states tend to really get it right or really get it wrong, without much corrective mechanism.)

CHINA'S CHALLENGES

China accounted for 28 per cent of global growth between 1990 and 2005. Going forward, China is likely to account for an even larger share of global growth in the next 15 years. If the growth rate of each region remains the same as in the past 15 years, then China would account for half of all the growth in the world over the next 15. The reason that the same growth rates produce a larger share for China is that its weight in the global economy is increasing rapidly. Now, it is unlikely that China can maintain a spectacular growth rate of around 9 per cent, but it certainly has the potential to continue to grow in the 7 per cent range. Its demographics, good investment climate and growing integration with the global economy mean that the basic foundations of rapid growth remain in place. If China's growth rate averages 7 per cent, while the rest of the world performs as it did in the 1990–2015 period, then China would account for 37 per cent of all global growth in the next period. In that scenario the United States would account for 16 per cent of global growth and India 12 per cent, so that these three large economies would account for about two-thirds of all the growth in the world.

How well the world economy performs will depend a lot on China, and the external environment for other developing countries will depend a lot on China's performance. Because China has had impressive economic success in the past two decades, many outside observers (and investors) naively assume that success will continue. But the past is no guarantee of success; in the immediate future China faces challenges of macroeconomic management which it has not faced before. It also faces medium-term challenges of resource scarcity and growing inequality and social tension. How well China manages these problems will have a large effect on the rest of the world.

Macroeconomic Adjustment

While China has grown well since 1990, it is remarkable the extent of savings and investment this has required. Since 1990 China's investment has been growing more rapidly than consumption – either household or government consumption. Much of this capital formation has been aimed at external markets, and China's export volume has grown much faster than its GDP (so that trade-to-GDP keeps rising). Export orientation has been a good development strategy for China. And in recent years its tendency in that direction has been exacerbated by US policy. The US fiscal stimulus after the 9/11 terrorist attacks was a positive factor in the world, and 2004 was the best year of growth for the world economy in 30 years. But with the US and world economies growing well, there is no longer a macroeconomic justification for such large stimulus. Yet the shift in the US fiscal position – from surplus to deficit – has been on the order of 6–7 percent of GDP. The United States is now set to run large fiscal deficits into the foreseeable future. The deficit, combined with low private savings in the United States, then drives a large external imbalance. The United States is borrowing $800 billion per year from abroad to finance its shortfall of savings. The large US trade deficit is necessary as long as the United States needs this level of external finance.

Thus US policy has acted as a giant vacuum cleaner aimed at a Chinese production machine which was already oriented toward exports. In some sense the US stimulus accelerated development which was likely to take place in China anyway, but at a more gradual pace. This acceleration is great for China in the short run, but some real adjustment problems loom ahead. Since joining the WTO in 2001, China's exports have grown at 29 per cent per year, and its imports at 26 per cent. Its real investment has increased at 14 per cent per year. These rates are clearly not sustainable. China is now a large player in the world market (the second-largest trader after the United States), and it would have to find huge new external markets every year to keep this up. And the United States cannot go on borrowing at its current rate forever. But getting out of this co-dependency is no simple matter.

The smooth adjustment in this situation requires an increase in savings in the United States, partly through slower growth of private consumption and partly through a lower fiscal deficit (probably through some combination of expenditure reduction and tax increases). On the Chinese side, there is a need to encourage consumption. Further real appreciation of the renminbi would push in this direction. Structural measures such as collecting dividends from state enterprises, better pension and health insurance schemes, and more public spending on health and education would meet human needs while directing the economy away from investment and exports.

It is quite possible, however, that this adjustment could go badly. On the US side, rising dollar interest rates and the end of the housing bubble could lead to a sharp contraction of consumption and a significant slowdown in global growth. The magnitude of interest rate rise will depend to some extent on the willingness of foreigners to continue to increase their holdings of US bonds. If the world loses confidence in US assets, then there could be the unpleasant combination of high interest rates and global recession.

On the Chinese side, considerable capital stock has been built up in this boom to export to the US market, and the growth of the capital stock in export industries continues to expand at a rapid rate. As US demand slows and the real exchange rate appreciates, however, a good chunk of that investment will turn out to be unprofitable. Those firms will not be able to service their loans, and non-performing loans will build up in the banking system. This happens in any boom in a market economy, and a robust financial system can deal with these problems pretty quickly. Unprofitable firms are forced into bankruptcy, their assets distributed and business goes on. But China has had a very big boom, and its banking system is still weak. There has been some reform of banking practices and regulatory supervision, and a small amount of private entry into the sector. We will only find out how deep this reform is when the economy experiences some kind of shock which requires the financial system to play this disciplining and restructuring role.

Natural Resource Scarcity

If China and the United States can successfully manage this structural adjustment and continue to grow well, China will need to confront natural resources constraints. The rate at which the Chinese economy has been using natural resources in recent years is unsustainable. This is clearest in the area of energy. While China is relatively well endowed with coal, it appears so far to be scarce in oil and natural gas. Over the past 15 years China's oil imports have been growing rapidly (at more than 30 per cent per year in volume terms), and it has emerged as the second-largest importer behind the United States. Before long it will emerge as the largest importer. Given the supply situation in the world and the fact that much oil and gas come from politically unstable countries, this is clearly a risk factor for the country's future.

While it is inevitable that energy use will grow with China's economy, much could be done to increase the energy efficiency of China's development. China uses more energy than OECD countries for several specific industrial processes. Its residential space heating is highly inefficient, using 50–100 per cent more energy than is used in OECD countries with comparable climates. Given the rapid pace of housing construction, enforcing strict standards now would make a big difference for future energy demand. The same is true with auto standards. Thirty percent of the buildings and 60 per cent of the cars which will be in use in five years have not been built yet. Energy use and air pollution could be dramatically reduced by enforcing strict energy efficiency standards for both buildings and vehicles. Air pollution has become a serious problem in China. Of the 30 most air-polluted cities in the world, 20 are in China. The air pollution results from the combination of coal use for power, industry and home heating plus growing motorization.

Despite its extreme scarcity, energy is often priced low in China. The retail price of gasoline (about 50 cents per liter) is below the US level and far behind other OECD members such as Japan or Western Europe, encouraging inefficient motorization. China's cheap gas policy is an important factor encouraging the development of a car culture. China in many ways is following the US policy of car-led development from the 1950s, a policy in which the United States built an impressive highway system and guaranteed cheap gas to consumers. Whether or not this has been a good policy for the United States is debatable, but in China's case the fact that the country is much more densely populated than the United States and that petroleum worldwide is increasingly scarce makes this a very questionable development choice.

China's leaders recognize the importance of energy scarcity. In recent years China's energy use has risen faster than GDP. For the next five-year plan the government has set an extremely ambitious target of increasing energy efficiency by 20 per cent. The key elements of an energy policy to meet this target are pricing and standards. A significant petroleum tax which raises the retail price of gasoline could lead to more conservation and also provide a source of funds for urban planning and for public transportation investments.

China is already the second-largest emitter of greenhouse gases, after the United States, and is projected to become the largest emitter by 2010. So, an important question for the world will be whether China and the United States, together with the other major industrial producers, can cooperate on energy efficiency and control of greenhouse gases. Under any scenario, demand for oil and gas (and hence prices) are likely to remain high, and the global climate is likely to become warmer. With sound energy policies and new technologies, the world can achieve a result of high – but stable – energy prices and mitigation of climate change. Without better cooperation and policies, however, the world could face some bad scenarios of climate change and competition over ever-scarcer oil and gas resources.

Can the Transformation be Harmonious?

China should be praised for achieving the most rapid poverty reduction in history. The World Bank estimates that the number of people living on $1 per day (measured at PPP) declined from over 600 million at the beginning of economic reform to 135 million in 2004 (World Bank 2007). The country is on track to eliminate $1 per day poverty by 2015. While poverty has been reduced, however, there has been mounting inequality in recent years which has generated social tension. Roughly speaking, urban real incomes have been growing at about 12 per cent per year, while rural real incomes have grown at 5–6 per cent. The rural–urban income gap in China is one of the largest observed in the world, fueling massive migration from the countryside to cities. Already, about 200 million people have relocated. In the next 10–15 years it is likely that another 200 million will move from countryside to city.

China's Gini coefficient has risen from 0.25 at the beginning of reform to 0.41 today. Some increase in inequality was inevitable, starting from the 1978 situation, and 0.41 is not high compared with Gini measures of inequality in large Latin American countries, for example, Brazil (0.58) or Mexico (0.50). But still, the rapid recent increase is a real worry. China's recent growth is also having surprisingly little effect on social welfare. Infant mortality declined at a rate of 2.5 per cent per year since 1990. This rate is higher than in Pakistan (1.5 per cent) or India (1.7 per cent), but slower than in other Asian countries that have not grown as well as China: Philippines (3.0 per cent rate of decline), Thailand (3.6 per cent), Bangladesh (3.8 per cent), Indonesia (4.7 per cent) or Vietnam (5.2 per cent). High-income countries with pre-existing low infant mortality have also managed to continue high rates of decline (3.6 per cent per annum). In this sense China's growth in the last 15 years has brought less social improvement than expected. The top leadership in China has recognized this slow social improvement and rising inequality and focuses now on developing a more 'harmonious society'.

The lack of social progress partly reflects the pattern of growth noted above. Many resources have gone into investment, especially for export. This has created many jobs and helped many poor families increase their income and move out of poverty. But government spending has grown less rapidly, and that is reflected in the low share of GDP which is accounted for by public health expenditure. China spends 2 per cent of GDP on public health, compared with 3 per cent for other middle-income countries and much higher levels in rich countries. Similarly, it spends 2 per cent of GDP on public education, compared with 4 per cent in other middle-income developing countries. China, ironically, has one of the most privatized health care and education systems in the world in which the majority of expenditure is paid for privately, out of peoples' pockets.

Increasing the social benefit of further growth in China will require a number of measures. One important issue concerns rights over agricultural land. The ongoing process of urbanization requires alienating some land out of agriculture to urban uses. At the moment this is handled in an administrative way, with relatively little benefit accruing to the farmers who are displaced. There are reasons why the country may not want the full market value of the land to go to individual peasant families, but there is considerable scope to increase the compensation to rural families. This would ease their adjustment to urban life and reduce inequalities. Also, newspaper reports suggest that the current, non-transparent system is often a source of abuse, leading to unhappiness and growing protest.

To be fair to local governments, currently they have few sources of revenue to finance their infrastructure needs and social expenditure. There is a need to overhaul the inter-governmental fiscal system, to ensure that every community can pay for basic health and education and to devise sustainable funding sources for local infrastructure. Adequate financing of local services and a more market-based system of land transfer would greatly ease the inevitable process of rural–urban migration.

While rural–urban differences are the most striking aspect of inequality in China, another important dimension is the large gap which has opened up between coastal cities in the southeast and cities in the interior and northeast of China. The difference in per capita GDP between coastal cities and interior cities is eight-fold. There are a number of factors at work here; coastal locations have inherent advantages from being closer to the global market. But the inherent advantages are magnified because many coastal cities have created good investment climates for private investors. Interior cities still tend to be dominated by state enterprises, that have about one-third the rate of return as private enterprises (Dollar and Wei 2007). The mindset of local government in the interior and northeast is different from along the coast, less investor friendly and more focused on protecting local firms.

As noted earlier, wages in coastal cities have risen sharply. There is some ongoing labor migration into these cities, but there is not a huge scope for relocation of populations to the existing production centers. A key issue for China is whether more cities in the interior and northeast can reform their investment climates and attract labor-intensive production. Many of these cities have 3–5 million people and thus are of scale for efficient production; most have good transport links as well. Creating a better investment climate in these cities is critical if China's growth is to continue smoothly and if the whole population is to benefit from that growth.

These many challenges are all inter-related. China's current level of urbanization – about 40 per cent of the population – is low for its level of income, especially given the scarcity of arable land and water. Rural–urban migration is a source of growth, as people move from low productivity agriculture to higher productivity urban employment and also leave the remaining rural population with a better ratio of land-to-people. But for this rural–urban migration to proceed relatively smoothly, it is important that the still-large rural population has good public health and education and some assets which they can bring to the city. Reform of interior cities is important, otherwise too many people will try to move to the coast and create congestion problems. Urbanization is much more energy-intensive than rural life, hence the explosive growth of energy demand. Standards for buildings and cars, gasoline prices and investments in urban mass transit are critical if the growth of energy demand and its environmental consequences are to be handled well. When preparing its most recent urban plan, for 2006–2010, Beijing took the unprecedented step of polling citizens about priorities, and the two most important issues on peoples' minds are pollution and traffic. Redirecting Chinese production to meet these diverse domestic needs will be good for China and also a necessary adjustment in the world economy. But if the financial system does not handle this adjustment well, then considerable potential output could easily be lost in financial crisis and its aftermath.

THE RISE OF CHINA AND IMPLICATIONS FOR THE DEVELOPING WORLD

So far, I have argued that the 'rise of Asia' is something of a myth, whereas the rise of China is real. For a long time, the health of developing economies depended to a considerable extent on growth in the largest economy, the United States. The United States will continue to be important, but as China moves quickly toward becoming the largest economy in the world, the health of China's economy will be at least as important to the developing world as the health of the US economy. China's continued success will pose challenges for the rest of the developing world, but also great opportunities. On the other hand, if China manages its challenges poorly, the consequences for much of the developing world will be negative.

There is an entire continuum of potential outcomes for China, but here I will focus on a scenario in which China handles all of its challenges poorly and another in which it handles its challenges well. The 'bad scenario' starts with a sharp global contraction sometime in the next few years. It will be a contraction with high US dollar interest rates, because the United States has not contained its demand for overseas capital, while the world has diminished interest in purchasing additional US assets. A sharp slowdown in the world economy would most likely lead to falls in many commodity prices. So, the contraction could have some similarity to the one in the early 1980s, when the combination of high interest rates and falling commodity prices led to debt crises in a range of developing countries, particularly ones which had been dependent on commodity exports and had prospered in the prior boom.[6]

In the bad scenario China is likely to have a growth recession as it finds that it can no longer increase exports at the same rate, but the financial and corporate sectors do a poor job of reorienting the economy toward domestic demand. There may well be some significant losses in the banking sector which have to be covered by the government, but the reservoir of US $1 trillion in reserves means that there is virtually no chance of a serious crisis. To restore growth the government can resort to fiscal expansion, both social spending and infrastructure investment, so China is likely to grow fairly well even in the bad scenario.

A second aspect of the bad scenario is that China does not succeed in increasing energy efficiency and resource efficiency more generally. Once the global recession ends, China will continue to generate large demand for commodities, benefiting commodity exporters. But without significant increases in energy efficiency, China's growth is likely to lead to competition over ever-scarcer energy supplies. By the middle of the century global warming will be a serious issue for the world. The specific numbers in the Stern report on the economics of climate change can be debated, but there is certainly a very serious risk that climate change will impose large costs on the developing world (UK Treasury 2006).

The third aspect of the bad scenario is that issues of inequality and social harmony in China are not addressed very successfully. A somewhat reduced growth rate in China makes it difficult to generate all the jobs needed to absorb surplus rural labor. If interior cities fail to improve their investment climates, then they will continue to lag behind, and the population will try to cluster in coastal cities, creating self-defeating congestion. The high level of inequality may well generate rising crime and social conflict.

Hopefully the dire specter of the bad scenario will convince everyone of the importance of achieving the 'good scenario'. The good scenario depends not just on China's management, but also on cooperation between China and the rest of the world, especially the United States. Resolving the current global economic imbalance requires coordinated effort between China and the United States, in which the United States takes fiscal steps to increase public savings and policy measures to encourage private savings. China, in turn, needs to encourage greater consumption through expansion of its pension and health safety net to reduce household insecurity, increase public spending on education and health and further exchange rate appreciation. Managing this well would be the most important contribution that China and the United States can make to healthy growth in the developing world in the next five years. In the good scenario, more and more of the developing world's trading opportunities would be in China, rather than the United States or other developed markets.

Looking longer term, the good scenario also has China and the United States cooperating on energy efficiency and curbing greenhouse gases. Some kind of global limits on greenhouse gas emissions with a trading system will almost certainly be required, and China and the United States will be the keys to reaching this kind of agreement. The right incentives and subsidies could well usher in a period of technological advance which addresses energy efficiency but also has all kinds of unpredictable spillover benefits.

The final piece of the good scenario is that China successfully improves the investment climate in a range of interior cities, while at the same time providing the rural population with better education, health, water and other services. The better rural services equip some people for the successful transition to urban life, while at the same time making a better life for the large rural population which will remain in agriculture. These kinds of reforms will tend to keep China in labor-intensive production longer, posing competition for the labor-abundant parts of the developing world (e.g., nearby Vietnam and Bangladesh). At the same time, these reforms would keep China's aggregate growth rate higher and make for larger overall demand, creating greater opportunities in the aggregate for the developing world.

CONCLUSION: A MULTIPOLAR CENTURY?

The 'Asian century' is something of a myth. Looking at the past 15 years, only China has risen strongly in the global economy. Looking ahead, China has the potential to continue to grow well and to provide an ever-greater market for products from other developing countries. If India sustains its rapid growth of the past five years it will also become a large player in the global economy. But it would be premature to write off the rich world. The United States in particular, with a relatively dynamic economy and population growth higher than China's, is likely to be an important part of global growth in the next few decades. Successful growth of the global economy in the near future requires that China and the United States smoothly resolve the unsustainable trade imbalance; if they do a poor job of this, it will have negative repercussions for the developing world.

Looking further down the road, China and the United States are the two largest users of energy and the two largest emitters of greenhouse gases, and India is coming up strongly. If these big economies do not reach some accommodation on capping global emissions and distributing the costs fairly, the best estimates suggest that there will be disastrous economic consequences for the developing world. Hence the label 'multipolar century' seems more appropriate than 'Asian century'. If things go badly, it will most likely be because China, India and the United States have cooperated poorly on short-term and long-term challenges. On the other hand, good collaboration among the existing superpower and the emerging powers could usher in a long period of harmony and successful development.

NOTES

Views expressed are those of the author and do not necessarily reflect official views of the World Bank or its member countries. I thank Pieter Bottelier, Lant Pritchett, Wang Shuilin, Xue Lan and Ernesto Zedillo for helpful comments on an earlier draft.

1. Early stages of China's reform are described in Lin (1988) and Lin (1992). See Rawski (1994) on the industrial reforms in the 1990s.
2. Lardy (2002) analyzes the importance of liberalizing foreign trade and investment for China's modern development.
3. Dollar, Hallward-Driemeier and Mengistae (2005) show that these investment climate

indicators affect firm productivity and profitability in a study covering Bangladesh, China, India and Pakistan.
4. India's reform efforts are described in Acharya et al. (2003) and Srinivasan (2001).
5. Freedom House ranks political freedom on a scale of 1–7, with 1 most democratic and 7 most authoritarian. ICRG ranks countries' property rights/rule of law strength on a scale of 1–5, with 1 as poor property rights and 5 as strong property rights. Figure 3.2 has 79 developing countries for which both data sources are available; some countries have identical data points and thus there are only 34 different combinations in the figure. There is a very slight tendency for more authoritarian countries to have weaker property rights, but the slope is not statistically different from zero and the R^2 of the relationship is 0.02, indicating no correlation.
6. For more analysis of how a hard landing may unfold, see Roubini and Setser (2005) and Williamson (2005).

BIBLIOGRAPHY

Acharya, Shankar, Isher Ahluwalia, K.L. Krishna and Ila Patnaik (2003), 'India: Economic Growth, 1950–2000', Global Development Network project, 'Explaining Growth'.

Barro, Robert J. and Jong-Wha Lee (2000), 'International Data on Educational Attainment: Updates and Implications', Cambridge, MA, National Bureau of Economic Research (NBER) Working Paper No. 7911.

Deolalikar, Anil, Rana Hasan, Haider Khan and M.G. Haider (1997), 'Competitiveness and Human Resource Development in Asia', *Asian Development Review*, **15** (2), 131–63.

Dollar, David R., Mary Hallward-Driemeier and Taye Mengistae (2005), 'Investment Climate and Firm Performance in Developing Economies', *Economic Development and Cultural Change*, **54** (1), 1–31.

Dollar, David R. and Shang-Jin Wei (2007), 'Das Wasted Kapital: Firm Ownership and Investment Efficiency in China', Cambridge, MA, National Bureau of Economic Research (NBER) Working Paper No. 13103.

Felipe, Jesus and Joseph Anthony Lim (2005), 'Export or Domestic-led Growth in Asia?', *Asian Development Review*, **22** (2), 35–75.

Freedom House (2006), 'Civil Liberties Index Data', at http://earthtrends.wri.org/text/environmental-governance/variable-508.html.

International Country Risks Guide (ICRG) (2006), 'Rule of Law Index Data', at http://www.icrgonline.com.

Lardy, Nicholas R. (2002), 'The Economic Future of China', presentation for the Asia Society, Houston, TX, 29 April. Available at http://www.asiasociety.org/speeches/lardy.html.

Lin, Justin Yifu (1988), 'The Household Responsibility System in China's Agricultural Reform: A Theoretical and Empirical Study', *Economic Development and Cultural Change*, **36** (3), S199–S224.

—— (1992), 'Rural Reforms and Agricultural Growth in China', *American Economic Review*, **82** (1), 34–51.

—— (2004), 'Development Strategies for Inclusive Growth in Developing Asia', *Asian Development Review*, **21** (2), 1–27.

Morrisson, Christian and Fabrice Murtin (2005), 'The World Distribution of Human Capital, Life Expectancy, and Income: a Multi-Dimensional Approach'. Available at http://www.paris-jourdan.ens.fr/ydepot/semin/texte0506/MUR2005WOR.pdf.

Rawski, Thomas G. (1994), 'Chinese Industrial Reform: Accomplishments, Prospects and Implications', *American Economic Review*, **84** (2), 271–75.

Roland-Holst, David, Jean-Pierre Verbiest and Fan Zhai (2005), 'Growth and Trade Horizons for Asia: Long-term Forecasts for Regional Integration', *Asian Development Review*, **22** (2), 76–107.

Roubini, Nouriel and Brad Setser (2005), 'Will the Bretton Woods 2 Regime Unravel Soon? The Risk of a Hard Landing in 2005–2006', paper presented at the Federal Reserve Bank of San Francisco and University of California – Berkeley symposium 'Revived Bretton Woods System: A New Paradigm for Asian Development?', San Francisco, CA, 4 February.

Srinivasan, T.N. (2001), 'Indian Economic Reforms: Background, Rationale, Achievements, and Future Prospects', in N.S.S. Narayana, (ed.) *Economic Policy and State Intervention: Selected Papers of T.N. Srinivasan*, New York: Oxford University Press, pp. 230–70.

United Kingdom, Treasury of, (2006), 'Stern Review on the Economics of Climate Change', London, UK: HM Treasury.

Williamson, John (2005), 'The Potential of International Policy Coordination', Washington, DC, Peterson Institute for International Economics Working Paper.

World Bank (2006), 'Governance, Investment Climate and the Harmonious Society: Competitiveness Enhancements for 120 Cities in China', Washington, DC, Report No. 37759–CN.

PART TWO

Drivers and Limitations of Development

4. Specialization Patterns under Trade Liberalization: Evidence from India and China

Choorikkadan Veeramani

India and China, like many developing countries, have rejected development strategies based on import substitution in favor of international openness. China started the trade liberalization process in earnest in 1978, while India introduced 'cautious liberalization' during the 1980s, focusing on internal deregulation rather than on trade liberalization. Until 1991 India's trade regime was considered one of the most restrictive in the world, due to its complexity and the wide number of tools used as policy instruments. The most pronounced overhaul of India's trade policy regime occurred during the early 1990s in response to a severe balance of payments crisis.

The domestic firms in India and China which had been operating under protective umbrellas were forced to respond to the competitive pressures from imports. Decision makers hoped that the policy changes would improve export competitiveness through efficient resource allocation, greater specialization, diffusion of international knowledge and heightened competition. The commodity structure of the country's trade is also expected to undergo changes. The conventional wisdom is that competition will induce a process of resource reallocation from the import-competing industries to those industries where the country has comparative advantages. It follows that a natural consequence of trade liberalization is the expansion of inter-industry trade – that is, exports increase in one set of industries, while imports increase in another. Further, trade liberalization invariably involves adjustment costs, as some domestic industries may go out of business.

However, many studies suggest that trade liberalization biases a country's trade expansion toward intra-industry trade rather than inter-industry trade. Intra-industry trade (IIT) refers to the simultaneous presence of imports and exports of products of a given industry. Verdoorn (1960), writing about the Benelux union, and Balassa (1966), focusing on the European Economic

Community, discovered that trade liberalization had led to a higher incidence of IIT. More recent studies also find a positive relationship between trade liberalization and IIT. For example, following the demise of central planning, an increasing share of the trade between many Central and Eastern European countries and the European Union was found to be intra-industry in nature (Hoekman and Djankov 1997). Fontagne and Freudenberg (2002) showed considerable growth of IIT in intra-EU trade between 1980 and 1999, and Fukao, Ishido and Ito (2003) reported the growing significance of IIT in East Asia.

According to these studies, in a liberalized environment, different countries will specialize in different types of products, and exports from practically every manufacturing industry could increase. Fears that import liberalization might lead to the demise of domestic industries in the developing countries – de-industrialization – will subside if the intensity of IIT increases with the reduction of trade barriers. The widely held 'smooth adjustment hypothesis' states that a high share of IIT will be associated with relatively low adjustment costs, since workers move within industries rather than between them.[1]

Intra-industry trade grows due to greater specialization in the manufacturing of unique varieties or product lines by individual plants in different countries. Because there are fixed costs associated with the production of each variety, it is imperative that each plant specializes in a unique variety, if economies of scale in production are to be exploited. Therefore, the firms in each country would manufacture a subset of the varieties within an industry to meet domestic demand and to export. At the same time, firms and individuals will import varieties which are not produced within the country in order to meet domestic demand. The result is IIT in final consumer goods (Helpman and Krugman 1985). Further, greater specialization at the level of distinct components used in an industry will promote IIT in intermediate goods (Ethier 1982).

There are two distinct types of IIT – horizontal and vertical. Horizontal IIT refers to the simultaneous export and import of differentiated products within an industry which are of a similar quality. Vertical IIT refers to the exchange of differentiated products of different qualities. Horizontal IIT arises when countries with similar factor endowment ratios specialize in unique varieties to exploit internal-scale economies. Vertical IIT, however, arises when countries with different factor endowment ratios specialize in varieties that are differentiated by quality: capital-abundant countries would specialize in the production of higher quality varieties, while labor-abundant countries would specialize in low-quality varieties. Vertical IIT will arise between two countries when there is an overlap in the demand for different qualities, particularly when there is a large gap in factor endowments (Falvey 1981; Falvey and Kierzkowski 1987). In practice, the trade which emerges from specialization at different production stages of a particular good may also be treated as vertical IIT (for example,

China imports components and exports the finished product). The extent of adjustment cost associated with trade liberalization can differ depending upon whether IIT is horizontal or vertical. While any type of IIT entails relatively lower adjustment costs than inter-industry trade, the adjustment cost will be the least when IIT is horizontal in nature.

This chapter analyzes IIT trends and patterns in the merchandise trade of India and China. Following an overview of the main features of liberalization in India and China and their implications for IIT in the two countries, I will compare the merchandise trade performance of India and China and identify any patterns of IIT in India and China.

LIBERALIZATION IN INDIA AND CHINA

Prior to their market-oriented reforms, both India and China followed a relatively autarkic trade policy accompanied by a battery of trade and exchange controls which severed the link between domestic and world relative prices (Lal 1995). Exchange rates were overvalued in both countries, creating a bias against exports. In China, a handful of centrally controlled foreign trade corporations monopolized trade activities. India instituted an elaborate system of exchange controls and allocation to ensure that any foreign exchange profits earnings were used to import only those commodities which conformed to the priorities set in the five-year plans (Srinivasan 1990).

Beijing decentralized foreign trade rights, allowing hundreds of thousands of firms to participate in trade activities. China also created special economic zones and actively promoted foreign direct investment (FDI) in joint ventures. Imports of intermediate inputs for use in the production of exports and capital goods for use in joint ventures were completely liberalized. Quantitative restrictions (QRs) on imports were removed and tariffs rates were gradually reduced. Processing trade and foreign investments enjoyed major tariff exemptions. After 14 years of arduous negotiations, China became a member of the World Trade Organization (WTO) in 2001.[2]

Until the reforms, China had severe distortions in all its factor and commodity markets (Lal 1995). The Chinese labor market was characterized by direct allocation of jobs and administrative control of wages. Beijing has gradually liberalized the labor market, particularly in the non-state sector, providing greater flexibility in the allocation of resources (Meng 2000; Brooks and Tao 2003). A flexible factor market will facilitate changes in the structure of production on the basis of comparative advantage and exploit the allocative efficiency gains from trade liberalization.

Disillusioned with the import-substitution policy, India cautiously began to reorient its policy framework in the early 1980s. The policy reforms included deregulation of state controls in selected industries, softening restrictions on monopolies, liberalizing capital goods imports with a view toward upgrading technology and modernizing industry, some shifts from QRs to tariffs, greater subsidies for exports and a policy of active exchange-rate depreciation.

The reforms became far more comprehensive and systemic after a severe balance-of-payments crisis in 1991. Significant progress has been made in dismantling the industrial licensing system, price controls and trade and exchange controls. The QRs on importing capital goods and intermediates were completely removed in 1992, although the ban on importing consumer goods continued, with some exceptions, until the late 1990s. Alongside the removal of QRs, customs duties in the manufacturing industries were gradually reduced. In 1993 the government adopted full convertibility of the rupee for the current account, making the exchange rate dependent on the demand for and supply of foreign exchange in the market. FDI has been encouraged in all manufacturing industries (except those of strategic or environmental concern) and the approval process has been made simple and transparent. The list of industries reserved for the public sector has been reduced considerably and the amount of government equity holdings in the portfolio of public sector enterprises has been gradually reduced.

However, although policy changes have gone a long way toward easing the entry barriers, the multiple barriers to exit for non-viable production units still remain, due to India's rigid labor and bankruptcy laws (Ahluwalia 2002). Labor market rigidities and other exit barriers can hobble the process of resource reallocation on the basis of comparative advantage.

IMPLICATIONS OF THE POLICY REGIMES FOR INTRA-INDUSTRY TRADE

The nature and bias of protection policies shape the patterns of industrial specialization under import substitution. In general, import substitution provides no compulsion for product rationalization, as the domestic producers are protected irrespective of the considerations of efficiency and comparative advantage. Under such circumstances, there is limited potential for intra-industry specialization and IIT. The criterion of 'indigenous non-availability' which had been followed in granting import licenses in India virtually ruled out the possibility of recording 'competing imports' (Bhagwati and Desai 1970). However, opening up the economies of India and China changed the rules of the game.

The transition from a controlled to a market-based economy can result in three types of allocative efficiency gains. First, productive resources could shift from inefficient to efficient industries (inter-industry resource reallocation). Second, resources may shift from inefficient to efficient firms within an industry (intra-industry resource reallocation). Third, resources could shift from inefficient to efficient activities and product lines within the firm (intra-firm resource reallocation). Which scenario best describes the situation in India and China?

As already pointed out, factor-market rigidities might stand in the way of resource reallocation. Labor market reforms have not yet been undertaken in India, due to political concerns and opposition from organized labor unions.[3] China's labor market, in comparison, is far more flexible. Therefore, it might be easier to reallocate productive resources from one industry to the other (inter-industry) in China than in India. The industrial composition of Chinese exports might also show greater degree of structural change than India's.

The second channel – reallocation of resources from inefficient to efficient firms within the industry – would also be slower to operate in India, as the barriers to exit continue to be high due to legislation preventing retrenchment. Labor-market rigidities, however, need not necessarily block the third channel – intra-firm resource reallocation from inefficient to efficient activities and product lines. Firms are likely to restructure their operation whereby individual plants tend to specialize in fewer product lines to exploit economies of scale.[4]

While it is plausible that all three allocative efficiency channels operate in China, in general, Indian manufacturing firms could realistically exploit only the third channel, due to the rigidities in the organized labor market. Despite these unused channels in India's liberalization, IIT can grow as a result of the rationalization in the choice of product lines by the individual plants and intra-firm resource reallocation. While IIT may grow in both India and China, the industry composition of the latter's exports may undergo a greater degree of structural change due to the higher flexibility of China's labor market.

COMPARATIVE TRADE PERFORMANCE, 1950–2005

Several studies argue that economic liberalization leads to rapid growth of exports through efficient resource allocation, greater specialization, diffusion of international knowledge and heightened competition. In order to assess the impact of liberalization on export growth, however, it is important to keep in mind that the growth is determined by external as well as internal factors. Among the external factors, the most crucial is the growth of world demand.

The internal and external factors combine to determine the export performance of a country. A country may fail to exploit the buoyancy of world demand if the domestic policy environment is highly restrictive. Similarly, even with policy reforms, a country's exports may not grow faster if world demand happens to decelerate in the post-reform period. Clearly, a simple before and after comparison, without taking into account the world demand (or world export) conditions, can be misleading. It is therefore appropriate to compare the country's export performance in the pre- and post-liberalization periods, keeping in mind the world demand conditions in the two periods.

The next section provides a brief overview of the merchandise trade performance of India and China from 1950 to 2005. (Analysis of trade in services is beyond the scope of this study.) The decade of the 1980s is divided into two sub-periods: 1980–85 (a period which witnessed major deceleration in world demand following the second oil price hike) and 1986–1990 (a period of recovery and faster growth of world demand). India's post-liberalization period (1992–2005) is divided into three sub-periods: 1992–97 (before the East Asian financial crisis); 1999–2001 (immediately after the crisis) and 2002–2005 (a period of rapid export growth in India, China and the world as a whole).

Growth of Trade

Exports were largely neglected during the first (1950–56) and second (1956–61) five-year plans in India, a stance based on the argument that demand for Indian exports was inelastic. While global exports were growing at 6.3 per cent per annum during the 1950s, exports from India stagnated (see Table 4.1). In China, exports were perceived mainly as a means of financing planned imports for 'socialist industrialization' (Lardy 1992). Thus, China's exports and imports both grew rapidly during the 1950s.

As global exports expanded relatively faster during the the 1960s, growth of China's exports and imports decelerated sharply while the growth rate of India's exports improved marginally compared with the 1950s. Clearly, both countries failed to make the best use of the trade possibilities available during the 1960s. World exports registered a hefty annual growth rate of 20.4 per cent during the 1970s. Buoyant world demand and a relatively favorable domestic policy in both India and China provided an atmosphere conducive to the rapid growth of exports. As industrialization progressed, imports also grew rapidly in both countries.

The export boom of the 1970s, however, could not be maintained during the first half of the 1980s. As the growth rate of world exports turned negative in the aftermath of the second oil price hike, exports decelerated in both India and China. The world economy, however, recovered during the second half of the

Table 4.1   *Comparative Trade Performance, India and China (US$ Millions)*

| Period[b] | Average annual growth rates[a] | | | | | Share of world exports | |
| | Exports | | | Imports | | exports | |
	India	China	World	India	China	India	China
1950–59	0.22	20.91	6.30	4.73	15.18	1.39	1.55
1960–69	3.58	1.75	8.77	1.36	1.49	0.90	1.29
1970–79	17.97	19.24	20.41	19.52	23.07	0.54	0.81
1980–85	2.39	7.64	–0.86	0.79	13.77	0.47	1.19
1986–90	17.76	18.29	12.36	11.15	7.78	0.48	1.63
1992–97	13.33	17.13	9.64	14.06	11.62	0.60	2.74
1999–01	10.26	16.84	4.09	3.57	21.24	0.66	3.86
2002–05	25.29	30.02	17.58	35.25	31.27	0.81	6.14

Notes:
a. Growth rates are calculated using semi-logarithmic regressions.
b. The year 1991 is excluded due to a major balance-of-payments crisis in India; the year 1998 is excluded due to the East Asian crisis.

1980s, and exports from both countries grew at a healthy pace, driven by the buoyancy of world demand and domestic economic reforms.[5]

India's economic reforms became far more comprehensive and systemic after a severe balance of payments crisis in 1991. During 1992–97, India's exports recorded a growth rate of about 13 per cent per annum and China's about 17 per cent. As a result of the slow-down in world demand triggered by the financial crisis that swept East Asia in 1997–98, India's exports declined in absolute value from 1997 to 1998. While China's exports continued to grow at a rate of about 17 per cent, India's exports showed signs of recovery during 1999–2001, growing by about 10 per cent annually. As the world economy fully recovered from the Asian crisis, India and China showed exceptional export performance, growing at an annual rate of about 25 per cent and 30 per cent, respectively, during 2002–2005.

A separate growth-decomposition exercise established that the actual export growth of India had been far below the potential offered by the growth of world demand in the pre-reform period (Veeramani 2007). The lack of competitiveness and specialization in the 'wrong' commodities were the major factors constraining export growth in the pre-reform period. In contrast, throughout the post-reform period, India's actual export growth has been above the potential offered by the growth of world demand, and the gap between the actual and the potential comes from an improvement in the overall competitiveness of India's exports. While the competitive surge of China since

1980 is well known, the growth-decomposition exercise also shows a major improvement in the competitiveness of India's exports since 1991.

Structure of Exports

The combined share of primary products (SITC 0–4) and textiles (SITC 65) in India's total exports declined from 90 per cent in 1962 to 70 per cent in 1970 and 33 per cent in 1980.[6] Lardy (1992, 32) noted, 'The share of primary product exports in China's total exports did fall sharply from almost 80 per cent in 1953 to 64 per cent in 1957, and then 56 per cent in 1965–66'. The share of primary goods in China's exports remained fairly constant at around 53–54 per cent throughout the 1970s. The share of manufactured goods in India's total exports showed a consistent increase from about 54 per cent during 1980–84 to about 76 per cent during 2000–2003, and it has increased from 64 per cent to almost 90 per cent in China (Veeramani 2008). Much of China's increase in the share of manufactured exports can be attributed to machinery and transport equipment; the total export share of these sectors increased from 7 per cent to 38 per cent between 1980–84 and 2000–2003. Detailed analysis by Schott (2006) showed that China's export basket contains more 'sophisticated' items than countries with similar relative endowments.

The industry structure of India's export basket shows a high degree of persistence during the post-reform period. Spearman's rank correlation coefficients are estimated to gauge the extent of structural changes over time in India's exports. Between 1993 and 2005, the correlation coefficient of the shares of various commodities (at the two-digit level of SITC) in India's total exports is 0.92. The correlation coefficient between 2002 and 2005 is as high as 0.98. The high positive correlations (both significant at the 1 per cent level) suggest that there have been no major structural changes (at the two-digit level) in India's merchandise exports during the post-reform period. A plausible explanation for the high degree of persistence in the structure of India's export profile during the post-reform period is the rigidities in the labor market, that might have discouraged resource reallocation across industries.

Using disaggregated trade data, I have shown elsewhere (Veeramani 2008) that the industry structure of China's exports had undergone a greater degree of structural change over the years than has India's. In addition, China's gain of market share (or comparative advantage) in a given product did not necessarily mean India's loss of market share (or comparative advantage) in the same product and vice versa. The fear of a 'Chinese invasion' of India's export markets is just a popular myth; the two countries have been expanding their exports by specializing in different product lines within each of the product categories.

TRENDS AND PATTERNS OF INTRA-INDUSTRY TRADE

Having established the positive impact of trade liberalization on export growth in India and China, I now investigate the hypothesis that liberalization increases IIT. My previous studies provided estimates of India's IIT in selected sections of commodities during the 1990s (Veeramani 2002, 2004). These estimates showed a significant increase in the intensity of IIT in India's trade flows. The present study makes some important departures from the previous analysis. First, it disaggregates IIT into its horizontal and vertical components. Second, it uses a different data set (COMTRADE–WITS), plus it covers a longer time period (1962–2005) and the entire spectrum of commodities. Third, I compare the trends and patterns of India's IIT with those of China.

Measurement and Data

I use the Grubel and Lloyd (1975) index to measure the intensity of IIT in a particular industry. The index of IIT (GL_{jt}) in industry j and year t in the multilateral trade of the country under consideration (India or China) is defined as:

$$GL_{jt} = \frac{(X_{jt} + M_{jt}) - \left| X_{jt} - M_{jt} \right|}{(X_{jt} + M_{jt})} \times 100 \qquad (4.1)$$

where: X_{jt} = value of exports from India or China in industry j and year t and M_{jt} = value of imports to India or China in industry j and year t.

The numerator of the ratio in (4.1) represents the value of IIT in industry j, which is the difference between total trade ($X_{jt} + M_{jt}$), and the absolute value of net trade $\left| X_{jt} - M_{jt} \right|$. The index, therefore, measures the percentage share of IIT in the total trade (the denominator is total trade) between the two trading partners in industry j. As the degree of IIT increases, this measure approaches 100 (GL_{jt} becomes 100 when $X_{jt} = M_{jt}$), as either exports or imports dominate trade in the industry (inter-industry trade), GL_{jt} approaches zero (GL_{jt} becomes zero when one of X_{jt} or M_{jt} is zero). While GL_{jt} measures IIT in a specific industry, its trade-weighted average could be used to measure IIT in the aggregate groups of industries and the economy as a whole.

As the GL_{jt} refers to the pattern of trade in one year, it is often referred as a 'static' measure of IIT. Hamilton and Kniest (1991) pointed out certain problems encountered in comparing the Grubel–Lloyd indexes for different time periods. In order to overcome such problems, they proposed the use of an index of 'marginal IIT' which measures the share of IIT in the *change* in trade flows between the two years under consideration. One such index (B_j), suggested by Brülhart (1994), is a transposition of the GL_{jt} formula to first-differenced trade flows:

$$B_j = \frac{(|\Delta X_j| + |\Delta M_j|) - |\Delta X_j - \Delta M_j|}{(|\Delta X_j| + |\Delta M_j|)} \times 100 \qquad (4.2)$$

where Δ is the difference operator. The value of B_j like the Grubel–Lloyd index, varies from 0 to 100; the closer the value to 100, the greater the share of IIT in the change in trade flows between the two years under consideration. The trade-weighted average of B_j could be used to measure the marginal IIT in the aggregate groups of industries and the economy as a whole. The above indexes are measured here assuming that the products grouped under the four-digit level of SITC constitute an industry j.[7] Trade data for India and China at the four-digit level of SITC are taken from COMTRADE–WITS.

Following Abed-el-Rahman (1991) and Greenaway, Hine and Milner (1995), I separate total IIT into its two components – horizontal and vertical – using relative unit values of export and imports. The rationale for using unit value is that a variety sold at a higher price must be of higher quality than a variety sold more cheaply (Stiglitz 1987). In the case of India, I use the unit value data from the Directorate General of Commercial Intelligence and Statistics (DGCI&S) supplied in electronic form by the Centre for Monitoring the Indian Economy (CMIE). As far as China is concerned, I rely on the estimates available in Zhang, Witteloostuin and Zhou (2005) to assess the relative importance of horizontal and vertical IIT.

Horizontal IIT (HIIT) was defined as the simultaneous export and import of a product where the ratio of export unit value to import unit value was within the range of 0.85 to 1.15. When the ratios were outside that range, any IIT was considered to be vertical in nature (VIIT). I have disentangled the total IIT in each four-digit industry into its horizontal and vertical components. First, I computed the ratio of export unit value to import unit value at the six-digit level of the Indian trade classification system (ITC).[8] Then for each four-digit ITC industry, I isolated those six-digit items with ratios within the specified range (0.85 – 1.15) from those outside the range. Export and import values of those six-digit items within the specified range (0.85 – 1.15) and within a given four-digit ITC industry are aggregated to measure horizontal IIT in that industry. Similarly, the export and import values of the six-digit items which are outside the range are aggregated to measure vertical IIT in a given four-digit ITC industry. Specifically, HIIT in given industry j is measured using equation 4.3.

$$HIIT_{jt} = \frac{\sum_i^h \left[\left(X_{ijt}^h + M_{ijt}^h \right) - \left| X_{ijt}^h - M_{ijt}^h \right| \right]}{\sum_i^h \left(X_{ijt}^h + M_{ijt}^h \right)} \times 100 \qquad (4.3)$$

where i^h refers to the six-digit ITC item within the four-digit ITC industry j with the ratio of the unit values within the range of 0.85 – 1.15. Similarly, VIIT in a given industry j is measured using equation 4.4.

$$VIIT_{jt} = \frac{\sum_i^V \left[\left(X_{ijt}^V + M_{ijt}^V \right) - \left| X_{ijt}^V - M_{ijt}^V \right| \right]}{\sum_i^V \left(X_{ijt}^V + M_{ijt}^V \right)} \times 100, \tag{4.4}$$

where i^V refers to the six-digit ITC item within the four-digit ITC industry j with the ratio of the unit values outside the range of 0.85 – 1.15. Unit values of either exports or imports or both are not available for a few six-digit items in the sample. Exports and imports of these items within a given four-digit industry are also aggregated separately in the above manner to measure IIT, but without categorizing these as either horizontal or vertical (treated as 'residual'). Thus, the total IIT in a given four-digit ITC industry (IIT_{jt}) is split into three categories: $IIT_{jt} = HIIT_{jt} + VIIT_{jt} + residual$. The trade-weighted averages of IIT_{jt}, $HIIT_{jt}$, and $VIIT_{jt}$ are computed for aggregate groups of industries and the economy as a whole. Finally, VIIT is further subdivided into high-quality VIIT (HVIIT) and low-quality VIIT (LVIIT). If the ratio of the unit value of export to import is greater than 1.15, then the quality of exports is higher than the quality of imports (HVIIT), while ratios below 0.85 indicate higher quality imports compared with exports (LVIIT).

Trends and Patterns of IIT

Table 4.2 provides estimates of IIT in India and China for primary and manufactured goods for selected years. As expected, manufactured products generally show higher IIT intensity compared with primary products, a logical result since the opportunities for specialization based on product differentiation and scale economies are greater for manufactured goods than for primary goods. Further, a steady increase in IIT intensity can be observed in India's manufacturing trade, while the primary products do not show any particular trend in either India or China. The increase in the Grubel–Lloyd index in India's manufacturing industries has been accompanied by a marked decline of the coefficient of variations, indicating the growing convergence of IIT intensity in the individual industries within the manufacturing sector.

China's IIT in manufactured products showed some decline in the early 1990s followed by a slight increase. It may be surprising that the share of IIT in India's manufacturing trade has been higher than that of China since 1993. Careful examination of the data, however, suggests that the difference is attributable to just two commodities – SITC 6672 (diamonds, not industrial,

Table 4.2   Intra–Industry Trade in India and China, Weighted Averages of GL_{jt}, Selected Years*

Groups[a]	1962	1970	1980	1986	1990	1993	1997	2000	2002	2005
					India					
Primary products	11.8	10.7	3.7	6.7	6.2	9.4	10.0	7.1	7.5	7.6
	(1.6)	(1.6)	(1.9)	(1.8)	(1.8)	(1.5)	(1.3)	(1.3)	(1.1)	(1.1)
	6.5	17.6	25.5	27.7	36.8	38.0	40.9	46.3	47.9	48.3
	(1.3)	(1.2)	(1.1)	(1.1)	(0.9)	(0.9)	(0.7)	(0.7)	(0.6)	(0.6)
Manufactured products[b]	6.5	15.3	16.7	16.8	25.4	25.6	32.4	36.6	38.3	42.0
	9.3	14.5	14.0	20.8	27.4	30.2	32.5	33.4	35.2	34.9
Total	(1.4)	(1.3)	(1.3)	(1.3)	(1.1)	(1.1)	(0.9)	(0.9)	(0.8)	(0.7)
Total[b]	9.3	13.2	9.5	13.1	18.7	20.4	25.5	25.5	27.1	29.5
					China					
Primary Products	–	–	–	–	21.3	32.1	30.5	22.2	22	17.2
	–	–	–	–	(1.3)	(1.1)	(1.0)	(1.1)	(1.1)	(1.1)
Manufactured products	–	–	–	–	42.2	31.3	39.3	44.7	42.8	43.9
	–	–	–	–	(0.8)	(0.7)	(0.7)	(0.7)	(0.7)	(0.7)
Manufactured products[b]	–	–	–	–	42	31.2	39.2	44.5	42.6	43.8
	–	–	–	–	37.8	31.4	37.9	41.5	40.4	40.5
Total	–	–	–	–	(0.9)	(0.9)	(0.8)	(0.9)	(0.9)	(0.9)
Total[b]	–	–	–	–	37.6	31.4	37.8	41.4	40.2	40.4

Notes:

a. 'Primary products' comprises SITC 0–4 and 'Manufactured products' comprises SITC 5–8.

b. Excluding SITC 6672 ('Diamonds, not industrial, not set') and SITC 6673 ('Other precious and semi–precious stone').

c. Values in parentheses are coefficient of variations of GL_{jt}.

* The years are chosen keeping in mind the periodization used in Table 4.1 and the availability of data. COMTRADE data are available since 1962 for India and since 1984 for China. China's IIT estimates are provided since 1990 as there is considerable missing data pertaining to China for the earlier years. In order to deal with the 1991 balance-of-payment crisis, the Indian government took some temporary measures of import compression during the early 1990s. Import compression, however, was temporary and withdrawn by 1993. The year 1993 has been chosen (instead of 1992) keeping in mind the possibility that import compression might bias the estimates of India's IIT.

not set) and SITC 6673 (other precious and semi-precious stones). Due to their extremely high export (and import) values in India's trade, these commodities exert an undue influence on the overall index, that is a weighted average. Thus, when these commodities are excluded, China's manufacturing trade shows a higher level of IIT than India's although the difference has narrowed considerably over the years. By 2005 the manufacturing industries of the two countries showed roughly similar values on the IIT index: 42 per cent in India and 44 per cent in China. However, the overall level of IIT (primary and manufactured products combined) remains considerably higher in China than in India, due to the higher IIT in the primary products of China.

Since the trend analysis of two aggregated sectors might mask the differential performances at a more detailed level of the industry classification, I present the Grubel–Lloyd index at the one- and two-digit levels of SITC (see Table 4.3). There is a significant increase in the levels of IIT in the case of various food items in both India and China. In particular, processed food items show significant levels of IIT. As many as 21 primary product groups (out of 28) at the two-digit level showed a higher IIT index in 2005 compared with 1990 in India. In the case of China, 17 groups showed higher indexes in 2005 compared with 1990, while 11 groups showed a decline. Among the primary products, India's IIT is found to be the highest in 'fruits and vegetables' (SITC 05), 'miscellaneous food preparations' (SITC 09) and 'beverages' (SITC 11), while China shows significant levels of IIT in 'fish and fish preparations' (SITC 03), 'miscellaneous food preparations' (SITC 09) and 'tobacco and tobacco manufactures' (SITC 12).

India's manufacturing industries show steadily increasing levels of IIT. As many as 22 manufacturing industry groups (out of 28) at the two-digit level showed higher IIT index in 2005 compared with 1990 in India. Since the mid-1970s India has made periodic efforts at trade liberalization in selected industries, such as machinery. Thus, groups like machinery and transport equipment (SITC 7) attained relatively high IIT indexes as early as 1980 and increased further since then.

China's manufacturing trade recorded relatively high IIT intensity as early as 1990 and no consistent trend can be observed since then. This is expected, since China's trade liberalization was initiated a decade before India's. There are several important differences in the IIT industry pattern of the two countries. India's IIT is generally higher than China's in 'chemicals', 'non-metallic mineral manufactures', 'iron and steel', 'manufactures of metal', 'wood', 'furniture' and 'sanitary, plumbing, heating items'. China's IIT is higher than India's in 'machinery and transport equipments' 'leather products' 'textile yarn, fabrics, and made-up articles' and 'scientific and control instruments'. India's textile and leather industries were reserved for small-scale production (Ahluwalia

2002) and overly protected from imports until the early 2000s (Das 2003). These would have hobbled the rationalization process in these industries, therefore their low IIT intensity in India's trade until recently is not surprising.

In the year 2005, the Spearman rank correlation coefficient between the IIT indices of India and China at the four-digit level is only 0.27 in manufactures and 0.32 in primary products. The relatively small value of the correlations, although statistically significant, indicates considerable dissimilarities in the industry structure of IIT in India and China. This is consistent with the observation that China's export items are more 'sophisticated' than countries with similar relative endowments (Schott 2006) and that China sells products which are associated with a productivity level which is much higher than a country at China's level of income (Rodrik 2006).

A different way of addressing the temporal changes of IIT is by analyzing marginal IIT, that measures the share of IIT in the *change* in trade flows between the two years under consideration. The indexes of marginal IIT computed for the different time intervals are shown in Tables 4.4 and 4.5. These tables reinforce the findings discussed above based on the Grubel–Lloyd index. The value of the marginal IIT index in India's manufacturing sector is the highest for the time interval '2000 (over 1990)', a period which witnessed significant trade liberalization in India, compared with previous time intervals. The value of the index in India's manufacturing sector shows further growth in the more recent periods – specifically, '2005 (over 2000)' and '2005 (over 2002)'. In the case of China, the value of the marginal IIT index has remained above 40 per cent since 1990 and no particular trend can be observed. The pattern of marginal IIT at the two-digit level of SITC (Table 4.5) largely conforms to the general pattern here.

Apart from the evidence shown here, econometric analysis, using panel data from Indian industries, shows that the reduction of trade barriers contributed significantly to the increase in IIT intensity (Veeramani 2008). Similarly, the econometric analysis of China's bilateral IIT by Zhang, Witteloostuin and Zhou (2005) established the negative relationship between trade barriers and IIT. In short, both descriptive evidence and available econometric studies indicate that trade liberalization has had a positive effect on IIT in India and China.

While it is clear that trade liberalization causes higher levels of IIT, the effect of FDI inflows on IIT may differ depending upon the nature of the multinational activity in the host country. The relationship between FDI and IIT can be positive if the multinational activity is export-promoting in nature (vertical FDI), while it can be negative if the multinational activity is primarily targeted toward the domestic market (horizontal FDI).[9] According to the 2003 *World Investment Report* (UNCTAD 2003), FDI has contributed to the rapid growth of China's merchandise exports at an annual rate of 15 per cent

Table 4.3   *Intra-Industry Trade in India and China, Weighted Averages of GL$_{jt}$, Selected Years*

		India						China		
Code	Description	1962	1970	1980	1990	2000	2005	1990	2000	2005
0	Food & Live Animals	7	12	11	13	22	26	16	33	34
00	Live animals	0	4	4	0	0	22	6	9	30
01	Meat & meat preparations	1	0	0	0	0	0	13	60	23
02	Dairy products & eggs	2	2	3	26	26	7	7	27	21
03	Fish & fish preparations	5	0	4	0	1	3	14	50	56
04	Cereals & cereal preparations	0	4	22	25	5	3	17	14	19
05	Fruit & vegetables	53	56	18	30	65	61	9	15	23
06	Sugar, sugar preparations & honey	0	1	47	5	23	36	21	30	28
07	Coffee, tea, cocoa, & spices	3	1	4	3	12	32	5	13	21
08	Feed.-stuff for animals	0	1	1	1	8	6	37	40	24
09	Miscellaneous food preparations	64	80	0	46	43	50	58	39	45
1	Beverages & Tobacco	13	0	1	7	12	24	63	50	51
11	Beverages	3	2	66	78	57	60	27	28	33
12	Tobacco & tobacco manufactures	13	0	0	1	5	11	87	76	71
2	Crude Materials, inedible, except fuels	23	12	5	7	12	15	18	12	11
21	Hides, skins & fur skins	7	8	9	1	1	24	23	4	2
22	Oil-seeds, oil nuts & oil kernels	0	7	3	4	3	11	6	11	8
23	Crude rubber	0	0	0	1	9	35	10	8	9
24	Wood, lumber & cork	63	4	22	0	1	2	23	20	30
25	Pulp & paper	1	0	4	0	1	0	1	1	1
26	Textile fibers, not manufactured	37	22	1	10	18	35	23	13	15
27	Crude fertilizers & crude mineral	8	8	6	10	16	21	10	24	27
28	Metalliferous ores & metal scrap	8	5	6	4	9	10	17	4	7
29	Crude animal & vegetable materials	22	12	11	28	25	30	18	41	42
3	Mineral Fuels, lubricants	7	5	1	0	1	1	30	23	15
32	Coal, coke & briquettes	18	10	18	2	7	4	18	6	35
33	Petroleum & petroleum products	7	5	1	0	0	0	32	26	12
34	Gas, natural & manufactured	0	20	0	0	0	9	18	25	15
35	Electric energy	0	0	0	0	0	0	12	28	53
4	Animal & vegetable oils & fats	9	1	1	7	4	5	14	14	6
41	Animal oils & fats	3	0	4	52	78	36	3	13	19
42	Fixed vegetable oils & fats	4	1	1	2	1	2	14	14	4
43	Oils & fats, processed	31	16	8	62	31	24	11	15	26
5	Chemicals	7	23	17	33	52	58	40	36	42
51	Chemical elements & compounds	32	18	15	45	59	64	68	53	49
52	Crude chemicals	65	38	0	9	0	84	7	29	26
53	Dyeing, tanning & colouring materials	5	48	41	28	26	37	65	50	62
54	Medicinal & pharmaceutical products	9	48	72	49	45	42	71	39	37
55	Perfume materials, toilet & cleansing	32	40	21	43	56	59	34	56	55
56	Fertilizers, manufactured	0	0	1	0	4	1	2	14	22
57	Explosives & pyrotechnic products	0	28	7	40	37	65	1	1	2
58	Plastic materials, etc.	1	49	5	15	97	87	27	15	29
59	Chemical materials & products, nes	10	16	16	29	57	55	37	40	48
6	Manufs. classified chiefly by material	7	16	29	49	55	64	42	47	46
61	Leather & products & dressed fur skins	1	0	1	18	32	45	61	47	59
62	Rubber manufactures, nes	52	37	49	28	37	47	41	41	35
63	Wood & cork prodts excluding furniture	28	9	11	62	58	58	10	27	20

Table 4.3   (continued)

Code	Description	India						China		
		1962	1970	1980	1990	2000	2005	1990	2000	2005
64	Paper, paperboard & manufactures	5	14	4	10	49	42	49	36	44
65	Textile yarn, fabrics, made-up articles	9	2	2	11	15	31	47	65	53
66	Non-metallic mineral manufactures	18	69	82	84	82	83	36	43	45
67	Iron & steel	4	20	9	31	58	69	31	36	46
68	Non-ferrous metals	1	13	7	18	28	53	56	37	50
69	Manufactures of metal, nes	16	48	47	58	48	58	38	40	38
7	Machinery & Transport Equipments	3	21	32	37	50	38	54	60	52
71	Machinery, other than electric	4	19	34	40	49	45	38	61	56
72	Electrical machinery & apparatus	1	28	40	35	55	37	51	64	51
73	Transport equipment	3	22	22	29	45	30	78	31	41
8	Miscellaneous Manufactured Articles	14	8	8	8	18	19	25	23	26
81	Sanitary, plumbing, & heating	38	7	3	63	38	55	58	11	13
82	Furniture	49	31	28	82	80	81	37	8	8
83	Travel goods, h&bags & similar	6	0	0	0	3	10	3	2	4
84	Clothing	5	2	1	0	1	2	1	7	4
85	Footwear	0	0	0	0	4	11	1	1	2
86	Scientific & control instruments	8	9	19	22	36	34	74	70	57
89	Miscellaneous manufactured articles	21	14	28	31	49	30	53	30	28
9	Commodities & transactions not classified according to kind	3	2	38	10	2	4	24	53	50
94	Animals, nes, incl. zoo animals	9	3	58	37	0	11	24	52	52
95	Firearms of war & ammunition	0	0	0	48	20	12	0	68	35
96	Coin, other than gold coin	0	0	0	0	0	0	13	4	45

between 1989 and 2001. In 1989 foreign affiliates accounted for less than 9 per cent of total Chinese exports, but by 2002 they provided 50 per cent. In contrast, FDI has been much less important in driving India's export growth, except in information technology. FDI accounted for only 3 per cent of India's exports in early 1990s, and in the 2000s it is estimated to account for less than 10 per cent of India's manufacturing exports. In short, while the multinationals mostly engage in export activities in China, they target the domestic markets in India (Wei 2005). This differential behavior of multinationals may be the result of the relatively high trade barriers in India (which encourage market-seeking FDI) and the rigidities in India's labor market (which discourage export- promoting FDI).

The econometric analysis by Zhang, Witteloostuin and Zhou (2005) established the positive impact of FDI on China's IIT, which is consistent with the evidence that China's inward FDI is mostly vertical (export-promoting) in nature. But another econometric analysis (Veeramani 2008) suggests that horizontal (market-seeking) multinational activities in the domestic industries of India exert a negative influence on IIT. This conforms to the consensus that India's inward FDI is mostly horizontal in nature and that the horizontal multinationals displace direct exports to the host country.

Table 4.4   Marginal IIT in India and China, Weighted Averages of Bj, at Selected Time Intervals

Groups[a]	India						China		
	1970 (over 1962)	1980 (over 1970)	1990 (over 1980)	2000 (over 1990)	2005 (over 2000)	2005 (over 2002)	2000 (over 1990)	2005 (over 2000)	2005 (over 2002)
Primary products	7.7	2.5	6.0	5.2	5.5	4.9	12.4	13.5	13.2
Manufactured products	14.3	25.0	31.0	37.5	45.2	44.4	42.8	41.0	41.8
Manufactured products[b]	11.6	14.7	21.4	27.0	40.3	40.5	42.6	40.8	41.8
Total	12.0	12.4	24.5	26.0	32.0	30.7	38.5	37.6	37.9
Total[b]	10.2	7.5	15.8	18.2	27.9	27.3	38.4	37.4	37.9

Notes:
a. 'Primary products' comprises SITC 0 – 4 and 'Manufactured products' comprises SITC 5–8.
b. Excluding SITC 6672 ('Diamonds, not industrial, not set') and SITC 6673 ('Other precious & semi-precious stone').

Table 4.5 Marginal Intra-Industry Trade in India and China, Weighted Averages of B_j

		India					China	
		1970 (over 1962)	1980 (over 1970)	1990 (over 1980)	2000 (over 1990)	2005 (over 2000)	2000 (over 1990)	2005 (over 2000)
Code	Description							
0	Food & live animals	13	8	17	19	17	28	33
00	Live animals	1	3	3	0	13	1	0
01	Meat & meat preparations	0	0	0	0	0	54	21
02	Dairy products & eggs	3	3	2	19	5	37	18
03	Fish & fish preparations	0	5	0	2	7	40	61
04	Cereals & cereal preparations	8	2	29	4	2	14	11
05	Fruit & vegetables	57	12	30	51	35	11	24
06	Sugar, sugar preparations, honey	0	37	49	22	6	24	18
07	Coffee, tea, cocoa, & spices	0	6	7	16	34	19	27
08	Feed.-stuff for animals	5	2	0	16	5	7	0
09	Miscellaneous food preparations	82	65	46	0	42	36	40
1	Beverages & tobacco	0	0	13	19	23	39	44
11	Beverages	7	8	75	42	43	24	30
12	Tobacco & tobacco manufactures	0	0	3	12	10	60	65
2	Crude materials, inedible, except fuels	3	3	3	7	12	9	9
21	Hides, skins & fur skins	9	5	0	1	37	0	1
22	Oil-seeds, oil nuts & oil kernels	0	4	6	2	19	2	3
23	Crude rubber	0	0	1	6	44	7	10
24	Wood, lumber & cork	3	42	0	1	3	20	28
25	Pulp & paper	0	6	0	3	0	1	1
26	Textile fibers, not manufactured	2	0	3	3	6	8	13
27	Crude fertilizers & crude mineral	2	1	5	20	27	26	26
28	Metalliferous ores & metal scrap	5	5	4	4	10	1	7
29	Crude animal & vegetable materials	4	10	16	18	22	48	43
3	Mineral fuels, lubricants	3	1	2	1	1	6	11
32	Coal, coke & briquettes	21	3	1	9	3	0	47
33	Petroleum & petroleum products	2	1	2	0	0	5	5
34	Gas, natural & manufactured	20	0	0	0	10	25	2
35	Electric energy	0	0	0	0	0	0	88
4	Animal & vegetable oils & fats	4	1	1	3	4	9	3
41	Animal oils & fats	0	15	0	69	14	16	58
42	Fixed vegetable oils & fats	2	1	0	1	2	7	2
43	Oils & fats, processed	29	6	25	23	11	15	36
5	Chemicals	19	13	27	31	53	30	44
51	Chemical elements & compounds	17	13	42	36	59	47	45
52	Crude chemicals	37	38	9	0	0	0	25
53	Dyeing, tanning & colouring materials	6	26	22	22	49	46	73
54	Medicinal & pharmaceutical products	39	60	38	32	36	23	35
55	Perfume materials, toilet & cleansing	1	18	53	29	55	48	53
56	Fertilizers, manufactured	0	1	1	5	0	8	18
57	Explosives & pyrotechnic products	0	6	11	31	44	1	5
58	Plastic materials, etc.	27	3	17	31	83	13	39
59	Chemical materials & products, nes	19	15	14	60	53	35	52
6	Manufs. classified chiefly by material	17	31	45	44	63	38	35
61	Leather & products, dressed fur skins	0	1	17	0	35	36	59

Table 4.5   *(continued)*

	India					China	
	1970	1980	1990	2000	2005	2000	2005
	(over	(over	(over	(over	(over	(over	(over
Code Description	1962)	1970)	1980)	1990)	2000)	1990)	2000)
62 Rubber manufactures, nes	9	51	19	44	51	35	33
Wood & cork prodts excluding							
63 furniture	1	11	4	22	57	12	3
64 Paper, paperboard & manufactures	10	2	10	49	35	31	19
65 Textile yarn, fabrics, made-up articles	8	2	13	11	35	50	24
66 Non-metallic mineral manufactures	69	82	78	80	82	42	37
67 Iron & steel	16	7	20	8	67	28	47
68 Non-ferrous metals	4	3	1	15	47	35	37
69 Manufactures of metal, nes	18	48	59	39	63	37	37
7 Machinery & Transport Equipments	10	30	34	44	34	59	48
71 Machinery, other than electric	8	33	42	44	43	63	51
72 Electrical machinery & apparatus	23	44	30	56	31	62	46
73 Transport equipment	10	15	25	18	26	28	39
8 Miscellaneous Manufactured Articles	3	7	7	23	19	24	27
81 Sanitary, plumbing, & heating	4	2	64	32	53	7	13
82 Furniture	0	27	0	80	81	5	8
83 Travel goods, h&bags & similar	0	0	0	5	22	2	7
84 Clothing	2	1	0	1	3	9	3
85 Footwear	0	0	0	7	16	1	4
86 Scientific & control instruments	4	22	20	45	30	70	52
89 Miscellaneous manufactured articles	4	22	26	52	20	29	27
Commodities & transactions not							
9 classified according to kind	2	0	4	2	0	11	8
94 Animals, nes, incl. zoo animals	47	0	19	16	0	0	0
95 Firearms of war & ammunition	0	0	53	14	4	68	68
96 Coin, other than gold coin	0	0	0	0	0	4	54

Having established the growing significance of IIT in India and China, the next section examines the relative shares of horizontal and vertical IIT (see Table 4.6). The results suggest that vertical IIT constituted the major share of India's total IIT across all the commodity sections in 1990–91 as well as in 2005–06. However, the growing significance of HIIT in India's trade is evident. The increased intensity of total IIT in 2005–06 over 1990–91 is shared by both HIIT and VIIT indexes in all the commodity sections. It is also evident that in most of the commodity sections VIIT arises in India's trade primarily due to the exports of low-quality varieties from India and simultaneous imports of high-quality varieties from other countries (LVIIT). Nevertheless, the share of the high-quality VIIT (in total VIIT) seemed to have increased in 2005–06 (compared with 1990–91) in many commodity sections, including: 'chemicals', 'plastics and rubber', 'textiles', 'footwear and umbrellas', 'base metals',

Table 4.6   HIIT and VIIT in India's Trade, 1990–91 and 2005–06

		1990–91				2005–06			
Code	Sections	HIIT	VIIT	Total IIT	LVIIT (%of VIIT)	HIIT	VIIT	Total IIT	LVIIT (%of VIIT)
I	Live animals, products	0.0	0.5	0.6	22.7	0.7	2.4	3.1	47.2
II	Vegetable products	0.1	19.5	21.7	11.5	0.2	33.1	33.3	11.2
III	Fats & oils	0.0	5.8	6.2	7.6	1.0	3.4	4.4	1.8
IV	Beverages & tobacco	0.1	8.5	8.8	34.5	3.1	12.2	16.1	66.7
V	Mineral Products	0.0	0.5	0.6	98.9	0.0	1.8	16.2	61.1
VI	Chemicals	1.2	25.9	29.4	68.2	10.1	31.1	41.2	49.4
VII	Plastics & rubber	0.6	12.6	13.3	79.5	18.5	40.4	59.0	65.2
VIII	Hides, skins & leather	3.3	10.5	13.8	0.3	1.8	14.5	16.3	21.7
IX	Wood & cork	0.3	0.9	2.0	0.3	2.0	8.7	10.8	41.7
X	Paper	0.4	7.9	8.3	65.9	2.7	30.3	33.1	88.5
XI	Textiles	0.7	1.9	4.9	65.9	2.4	8.3	14.9	58.8
XII	Footwear, umbrellas etc	1.0	2.6	3.6	89.5	0.2	14.9	15.2	7.0
XIII	Stone & cement	0.2	19.7	23.7	41.9	3.7	33.4	38.8	82.0
XIV	Gems & Jewelry	0.0	1.3	47.1	9.6	2.5	16.1	18.6	1.6
XV	Base Metals	2.9	19.0	22.7	96.9	12.8	29.4	42.2	85.2
XVI	Machinery	0.5	26.9	27.5	82.4	1.8	36.5	38.6	74.4
XVII	Transport equipments	0.4	25.9	26.9	79.0	0.9	31.5	32.3	97.1
XVIII	Instruments, apparatus	0.2	10.9	12.3	96.8	1.7	31.7	38.3	70.0
XIX	Arms & ammunition	0.0	23.3	30.9	95.2	0.0	29.6	29.6	42.4
XX	Misc. Manufactures	2.0	10.4	25.2	99.5	4.5	50.0	58.4	58.7
XXI	Works of art etc	0.0	0.1	4.6	97.4	19.3	2.9	22.2	82.3

Note: Total IIT differs from the sum of HIIT and VIIT due to the residual.

'machinery', 'instruments and apparatus' and 'miscellaneous manufactures'. In short, it is clear that while VIIT dominates the IIT of India, HIIT seems to be gaining importance. Further, low-quality VIIT accounts for the major share of India's VIIT, although the share of high-quality VIIT is clearly on the increase.

The predominance of VIIT over HIIT in China's trade has been established in Hu and Ma (1999) and Zhang, Witteloostuin and Zhou (2005). While the VIIT index in China's total trade increased from 19.4 per cent during 1992–94 to 32.4 per cent during 1999–2001, the HIIT index declined from 11.4 per cent in the first period to 7.6 percent in the second period (Zhang, Witteloostuin and Zhou 2005). By comparison, HIIT in India's total trade increased from 0.7 per cent in 1990–91 to 4 per cent in 2005–06, while VIIT increased from 9.7 per cent to 18 per cent.[10] In short, VIIT dominates the IIT of both India and China; therefore comparative advantage, on the basis of factor endowment differences, has an important role in explaining the IIT in both the countries.

The analysis used in this chapter has a multilateral context – that is, IIT has been measured with respect to the trade relation of each country (India and

China) with the rest of the world. A detailed analysis of IIT in the bilateral trade of India and China is beyond the scope of this chapter. My previous studies have established that, unlike industrialized countries, India tends to have relatively less IIT with countries at a similar stage of development: India's IIT is more intense with high-income countries than with low- and middle-income countries (Veeramani 2002). The intensity of India's IIT showed considerable variation across the trading partners. The econometric analysis, carried out to explain the cross-country variation of India's IIT, provided support to the hypotheses drawn from the theoretical models of VIIT. For example, greater factor endowment dissimilarity between India and her trading partners promotes IIT intensity. Further, IIT is higher if the trading partner is larger in size and is closer geographically (Veeramani 2002).

Hu and Ma (1999) and Zhang, Witteloostuin and Zhou (2005) established significant variation in the intensity of China's bilateral IIT across the developing and developed countries. Their econometric analysis provided support to the various hypotheses drawn from the theoretical models of IIT. For example, *similarity* between China and its trading partners was found to be important in explaining HIIT, while China's *difference* from her trading partners is important in explaining VIIT. Further, trading partners with a larger market size tend to display higher HIIT and VIIT, while greater geographical distance between China and her trading partners discourages both types of IIT.

CONCLUSION

While both India and China failed to take advantage of opportunities offered by growing world trade under import substitution, the export levels of both the countries have been growing faster than the growth rate of world exports since they began economic reforms. India's share of world exports has been increasing since the 1990s, yet she contributed only 1 per cent of total world exports in 2006. The export performance of China, in comparison, has been spectacular, accounting for nearly 8 per cent of world exports in 2006. Several factors might have contributed to the superior export performance of China, such as a favorable exchange rate, large domestic market, flexible labor market and the huge volume of vertical FDI inflows.[11] The analysis in this chapter showed that China's rapid export growth has been accompanied by significant changes in the commodity composition of China's exports. India's export structure, in comparison, has been more persistent over time. This observation underlines the imperative of achieving structural changes, on the basis of a country's comparative advantage, for rapid export growth. Rapid structural changes in production and exports, in turn, are facilitated, *inter alia*, by a flexible labor market. Rigidities in India's labor market stand in the way of maximizing the allocative efficiency gains from trade liberalization. A flexible labor market, low trade barriers and adequate physical infrastructure are imperative for attracting vertical (export-promoting) FDI. All these factors make China an attractive destination for vertical FDI compared with India. Viewed from this perspective, China's rapid export growth of labor-intensive products, compared with India's, is not surprising.

While labor-market rigidities might have discouraged vertical FDI and the inter-industry reallocation of productive resources in India, the Indian firms could survive competition from imports, *inter alia*, by rationalizing the choice of their product line and by reallocating resources within the firm. Thus, the significant growth of intra-industry trade (IIT) in India's manufacturing sector is not surprising. By 2005, the manufacturing industries of India and China show a roughly similar intensity of IIT. Growing IIT reflects greater specialization in unique varities and product lines by the individual plants in India and China. The apprehension that import liberalization might lead to the large-scale demise of domestic industries in developing countries (the fear of de-industrialization) is unwarranted. The majority of domestic manufacturing industries and firms in both India and China could compete and survive by specializing in narrow product lines.

The analysis showed that vertical IIT (VIIT) dominates the IIT of both India and China. Further, low-quality VIIT accounts for the major share of India's VIIT, although the share of high-quality VIIT and horizontal IIT (HIIT) show some increase in the recent years. Low-quality VIIT refers to the export of low-quality varieties and the simultaneous import of high-quality varieties within the same industry. Though IIT has been growing in both India and China under trade liberalization, the dominance of VIIT (rather than HIIT) implies that trade liberalization may entail some adjustment costs in both countries. Nevertheless, growth of any type of IIT generally implies relatively lower adjustment costs compared with the adjustment costs associated with the growth of inter-industry trade. The primary sector, however, might have faced and may continue to face greater adjustment difficulties under trade liberalization, since the scope for intra-industry specialization is much more limited in the primary sector.

New policy measures are needed to attract vertical FDI into India, if multinationals have to augment the process of integrating Indian industry with the fragmented structure of global production activities. A flexible labor market, with appropriate social safety nets, would stimulate the ongoing process of resource reallocation and would lead to a rapid growth of labor-intensive exports from India.

NOTES

1. Empirical tests of this hypothesis can be seen, for example, in Greenaway, Hayes and Milner (2002) and Brülhart (2000).
2. For details of China's trade reforms, see Lardy (1992, 2002).
3. 'Any firm wishing to close down a plant or to retrench labor in any unit employing more than 100 workers can only do so with the permission of the state government, and this permission is rarely granted' (Ahluwalia 2002, 76). Besley and Burgess (2004) establish the deleterious effect of labor market rigidities in India's manufacturing production.
4. In a review of economic policy reforms in developing countries, Krueger (1992,104) noted that '[i]n some instances, firms that held monopoly or quasi-monopoly positions in the domestic market and that were high-cost have been able to make sharp reductions in their cost structure once incentives have been changed. This can come about because of increased specialization within individual plants in fewer lines of output, because of rationalization or for other reasons'.
5. It is well known that China has witnessed major reforms since the late 1970s. As far as India is concerned, a major depreciation of the real effective exchange rate (REER) of the rupee and increased export subsidies led to an improvement in export competitiveness during the second half of the 1980s (Joshi and Little 1994). This period also witnessed some doses of industrial deregulation and liberalization of capital goods imports in India.
6. Estimated from COMTRADE-WITS.
7. Use of a more detailed system of classification is not necessarily better, as it might separate commodities which are good substitutes in production and consumption (Balassa 1979).
8. As the unit values are more reliable at the finer level of data disaggregation, I use the data at the six-digit level rather than at the four-digit level.
9. Horizontal FDI refers to the situation where the multinational performs essentially the same range of production activities in both its plants located in their home and the host country. Vertical FDI represents the international fragmentation of production process by multinationals, locating each stage of production in the country where it can be done at the least cost (Markusen 1995).
10. Note that Zhang, Witteloostuin and Zhou (2005) used the unit value data at the four-digit level of SITC which is substantially more aggregated than six-digit ITC data used here. Further, Zhang, Witteloostuin and Zhou used a unit value dispersion of 25 per cent to disentangle HIIT and VIIT, while I used a dispersion of 15 per cent, that is used more frequently in the literature. Thus, my estimates for India are not strictly comparable with the ones for China provided in Zhang et al. It may also be noted that the criterion of 25 per cent unit value dispersion would lead to higher estimates of HIIT than the criterion of 15 per cent unit value dispersion. In fact Zhang, Witteloostuin and Zhou noted that using the criterion of 15 per cent results in very low HIIT indices for China. Thus, based on the HIIT indices reported above for India and China, it cannot be concluded that Beijing has a higher HIIT intensity than New Delhi.
11. Even after adjusting for the 'round tripping' of capital and other definitional problems, the gap in the volume of FDI into China and India remains very high (Wei 2005).

BIBLIOGRAPHY

Abed-el-Rahman, Kamel (1991), 'Firms' Competitive and National Comparative Advantages as Joint Determinants of Trade Composition', *Weltwirtschaftliches Archiv*, **127** (1), 83–97.

Ahluwalia, Montek S. (2002), 'Economic Reforms in India since 1991: Has Gradualism Worked?', *Journal of Economic Perspectives*, **16** (3), 67–88.

Balassa, Bala (1966), 'Tariff Reductions and Trade in Manufactures among the Industrial

Countries', *American Economic Review*, **56** (3), 466–73.

——— (1979), 'Intra-Industry Trade and the Integration of the Developing Countries in the World Economy', in Herbert Giersch (ed.), *On the Economics of Intra-Industry Trade,* Tübingen: J.C.B. Mohr.

Bhagwati, Jagdish and Padma Desai (1970), *India: Planning for Industrialization*, New York: Oxford University Press.

Besley, Timothy and Robin Burgess (2004), 'Can Labor Regulation Hinder Economic Performance?: Evidence from India', *Quarterly Journal of Economics*, **119** (1), 91–134.

Brooks, Ray and Ran Tao (2003), 'China's Labor Market Performance and Challenges', Washington, DC, International Monetary Fund Working Paper No. 03/210.

Brülhart, Marius (1994), 'Marginal Intra-Industry Trade: Measurement and the Relevance for the Pattern of Industrial Adjustment', *Weltwirtschaftliches Archiv*, **130** (3), 600–13.

——— (2000) 'Dynamics of Intra-Industry Trade and Labour-Market Adjustment', *Review of International Economics*, **8** (3), 420–35.

Das, Deb Kusum (2003), 'Quantifying Trade Barriers: Has Protection Declined Substantially in Indian Manufacturing?', Indian Council for Research on International Economic Relations Working Paper No 105.

Ethier, Wilfred J. (1982), 'National and International Returns to Scale in the Modern Theory of International Trade', *American Economic Review*, **72** (3), 389–405.

Falvey, Rodney E. (1981), 'Commercial Policy and Intra-Industry Trade', *Journal International Economics*, **11** (3), 495–511.

Falvey, Rodney E. and Henryk Kierzkowski (1987), 'Product Quality, Intra-industry Trade and Imperfect Competition', in Henryk Kierzkowski (ed.), *Protection and Competition in International Trade*, New York: Blackwell.

Fontagne, Lionel and Michael Freudenberg (2002), 'Long-term Trends in Intra-Industry Trade', in P.J. Lloyd and Hyun-Hoon Lee (eds), *Frontiers of Research on Intra-Industry Trade*, New York: Palgrave Macmillan, pp. 131–58.

Fukao, Kyoji, Hikari Ishido and Keiko Ito (2003), 'Vertical Intra-Industry Trade and Foreign Direct Investment in East Asia', *Journal of the Japanese and International Economies*, **17** (4), 468–506.

Greenaway, David, Robert C. Hine and Chris Milner (1995), 'Vertical and Horizontal Intra-Industry Trade: A Cross Industry Analysis for the United Kingdom', *Economic Journal*, **105** (433), 1505–18.

Greenaway, David, Michelle Haynes and Chris Milner (2002), 'Adjustment, Employment Characteristics and Intra-Industry Trade', *Weltwirtschaftliches Archiv*, **138** (2), 254–76.

Grubel, Herbert G. and Peter J. Lloyd (1975), *Intra-Industry Trade: The Theory and Measurement of International Trade in Differentiated Products*, London: Macmillan.

Hamilton, Clive and Paul Kniest (1991), 'Trade Liberalisation, Structural Adjustment and Intra-Industry Trade: A Note', *Weltwirtschaftliches Archiv*, **127** (2), 356–67.

Helpman, Elhanan and Paul Krugman (1985), *Market Structure and Foreign Trade: Increasing Returns, Imperfect Competition, and the International Economy*, Cambridge, MA: MIT Press.

Hoekman, Bernard and Simeon Djankov (1997), 'Determinants of the Export Structure of Countries in Central and Eastern Europe', *World Bank Economic Review*, **11** (3), 471–87.

Hu, Xiaoling and Yue Ma (1999), 'International Intra-Industry Trade of China', *Weltwirtschaftliches Archiv*, **135** (1), 82–101.

Joshi, Vijay and I.M.D. Little (1994), *India: Macroeconomics and Political Economy, 1964–1991*, New York: Oxford University Press.

Krueger, Anne O. (1992), *Economic Policy Reform in Developing Countries*, Cambridge, MA: Blackwell.

Lal, Deepak (1995), 'India and China: Contrasts in Economic Liberalization?', *World Development*, **23** (9), 1475–94.

Lardy, Nicholas (1992), *Foreign Trade and Economic Reform in China, 1978–90*, New York: Cambridge University Press.

—— (2002), *Integrating China into the Global Economy*, Washington, DC: Brookings Institution Press.

Markusen, James R. (1995), 'The Boundaries of Multinational Enterprises and the Theory of International Trade', *Journal of Economic Perspectives*, **9** (2), 169–89.

Meng, Xin (2000), *Labour Market Reform in China*, New York: Cambridge University Press.

Rodrik, Dani (2006), 'What's So Special about China's Exports?', *China and World Economy*, **14** (5), 1–19.

Schott, Peter K. (2006), 'The Relative Sophistication of Chinese Exports', Cambridge, MA, National Bureau of Economic Research (NBER) Working Paper No. 12173.

Srinivasan, T.N. (1990), 'External Sector in Development: China and India, 1950–89', *American Economic Review*, **80** (2), 113–17.

Stiglitz, Joseph E. (1987), 'The Causes and Consequences of the Dependence of Quality on Price', *Journal of Economic Literature*, **25** (1), 1–48.

UNCTAD (2003), *World Investment Report, 2003*, New York: United Nations Conference on Trade and Development.

Veeramani, Choorikkadan (2002), 'Intra-Industry Trade of India: Trends and Country-Specific Factors', *Weltwirtschaftliches Archiv*, **138** (3), 509–33.

—— (2004), 'Growing Intra-Industry Trade in Manufacturing: Implications for Policy', *Economic and Political Weekly*, **39** (41), 4556–9.

—— (2007), 'Sources of India's Export Growth in Pre- and Post-Reform Periods', *Economic and Political Weekly*, **42** (25), 2419–27.

—— (2008), 'India and China: Changing Patterns of Comparative Advantage?', in R. Radhakrishna (ed.), *India Development Report 2008*, New York: Oxford University Press.

—— (2008), 'Trade Barriers, Multinational Involvement and Intra-Industry Trade: Panel Data Evidence from India', *Applied Economics* (forthcoming).

Verdoorn, P.J. (1960), 'The Intra-block Trade of Benelux', in Edward Robinson (ed.), *Economic Consequences of the Size of Nations*, London: Macmillan, pp. 291–321.

Wei, Wenhui (2005), 'China and India: Any Difference in their FDI Performances?', *Journal of Asian Economics*, **16** (4), 719–36.

Zhang, Jianhong, Arjen van Witteloostuijn and Chaohong Zhou (2005), 'Chinese Bilateral Intra-Industry Trade: A Panel Data Study for 50 Countries in the 1992–2001 Period', *Weltwirtschaftliches Archiv*, **141** (3), 510–40.

5. Sources of China's Export Growth

Roberto Álvarez and Sebastián Claro

After decades of autarky, Chinese exports have grown vigorously – especially since the 1990s – making China one of the most important trading partners in the world. This phenomenon has generated a growing literature which analyzes the potential impact of Chinese competition on third countries, especially in labor-intensive industries where China's exports are dominant. Although there are some descriptive and illustrative works discussing the potential impact of China (Devlin, Estevadeordal and Rodriguéz 2006; Blásquez-Lidoy, Rodriguéz and Santiso 2006), only a few works have studied this phenomenon in detail. Some papers have focused on the impact on other Asian countries' exports (Eichengreen, Rhee and Tong 2004) while others have analyzed the relative effects on Latin American exports to a third market (López-Córdova, Micco and Molina 2008). There are also some recent works on the potential effects Chinese imports could have on competition among domestic industries. Alvarez and Claro (2008) study whether Chilean manufacturing plants have been negatively affected by Chinese competition or if they have been able to adjust through changes in the product mix and exports.[1] Contrary to the evidence of Bernard, Jensen and Schott (2006), who show that US manufacturing firms have escaped import competition from low-wage countries by improving quality, the evidence for Chile suggests that the potential for upgrading is much smaller, meaning that domestic firms have shrunk in response to low-wage import competition.

However, a detailed study of the impact of Chinese competition on other economies requires an analysis of the characteristics of Chinese products. In other words, we do not have a complete and broad view of the characteristics of China's exports, data which is crucial to a good understanding of the potential effects of Chinese exports on world markets. There is evidence that China's exports are higher in labor-intensive sectors, that is consistent with traditional endowment-based trade theory (Leamer 1995). There is, however, much less information regarding product heterogeneity within industries, like price and quality differences. Recently, the trade literature has emphasized that factor-endowment differences can lead not only to cross-industry specialization, but also to within-product specialization. For example, using import data from the United States, Rodrik (2006) and Schott (2006) have shown that China's exports may be relatively higher and less sophisticated compared with exports of other countries with similar factor endowments, depending on the standard used to compare export sophistication. Branstetter and Lardy (2006) argue that the evidence of relatively sophisticated Chinese exports, as in Rodrik (2006), does not take into account that China imports high-value-added parts and components, suggesting that after controlling for the structure of intermediate inputs, China's export structure reflects the low costs of labor-intensive assembly. Our study is an effort to analyze the characteristics of Chinese competition in developing countries, using highly disaggregated data for Chilean imports between 1990 and 2005. We focus on within-industry heterogeneity in order to distinguish the characteristics of Chinese products vis-à-vis the rest of the world.

This chapter uses the methodology developed by Hummels and Klenow (2005) to decompose import growth into two different margins: imports in common product categories from China and the rest of the world (intensive margin) and imports in different product categories (extensive margin). This distinction allows us to study how much of China's import penetration in Chile, relative to the rest of the world, is due to higher penetration in common product categories or due to an increase in the set of products produced and exported from China. We also decompose the intensive margin into price and quantity margins to distinguish whether within-industry import differences are due to price differences and/or quantity differences. Next, we analyze the relative sophistication of Chinese exports by comparing cross-country differences in export prices. Following the idea that prices may reflect – albeit imperfectly – the quality of goods, we estimate price differentials between China and the rest of the world and analyze whether there are systematic differences in export prices. Finally, we analyze quality differences more deeply. We compare China's export basket to Chile with that of other exporters – especially OECD countries – and we report some results regarding quality differentials between Chinese varieties and those from the rest of the world.

INTENSIVE AND EXTENSIVE MARGINS OF CHINESE EXPORTS

Data

Our data were obtained from Chile's Customs Office and consists of all import entries at the eight-digit Harmonized System (HS) level (4,815 categories in

Table 5.1   *Chilean Imports, 1990–2005*

	Imports (Millions of Dollars)			Number of Products (8-Digit HS)		
	Total	China	Partici- pation	Total	China	Partici- pation
1990	7,023	57	0.8	4,815	1,035	21.5
1991	7,515	95	1.3	4,874	1,065	21.9
1992	9,542	147	1.5	4,969	1,252	25.2
1993	10,641	212	2.0	4,949	1,445	29.2
1994	11,291	281	2.5	4,950	1,478	29.9
1995	15,061	390	2.6	5,037	1,665	33.1
1996	16,975	515	3.0	5,429	1,803	33.2
1997	18,330	659	3.6	5,163	1,944	37.7
1998	17,155	753	4.4	5,142	2,103	40.9
1999	13,703	647	4.7	5,197	2,090	40.2
2000	16,790	949	5.7	5,215	2,276	43.6
2001	16,134	1,014	6.3	5,151	2,346	45.5
2002	15,639	1,102	7.0	6,724	3,182	47.3
2003	17,549	1,290	7.4	6,670	3,470	52.0
2004	22,483	1,848	8.2	6,745	3,759	55.7
2005	29,932	2,541	8.5	6,702	3,994	59.6

Source: Chilean Customs data.

1990 and 6,702 in 2005).[2] For each product, we have data for China and all other exporting countries on the cost, insurance and freight (CIF) dollar value of imports and the quantity imported. We denote China with the subscript c, and the rest of the world by subscript r. Therefore, unitary import prices from country c in product j, defined at the eight-digit level, are computed as $P_{ctj} = M_{cjt} / X_{cjt}$, where M_{cjt} is the CIF value of imports (in current US dollars) from country c in product j in year t, and X_{cjt} is the quantity imported (i.e., pairs of shoes, pounds of folic acid, meters of carpets, etc.) Table 5.1 summarizes the data.

We observe a significant increase not only in Chile's imports from China, but also in China's market share. In 1990 China accounted for only 0.8 per cent of total Chilean imports, but by 2005 this number had climbed to 8.5 per cent, representing an annual growth rate of 16.9 per cent. These numbers coincide with the increase in China's total export growth in the same period (18 per cent annually). The increase in the value of imports from China is accompanied by an increase in the number of eight-digit-level products imported from China.

The share of products which Chile imports from China rose from 21.5 per cent in 1990 to 59.6 per cent in 2005.

Export Margins

Based upon the work of Hummels and Klenow (2005), we analyze the structure of imports coming from China (c) and the rest of the world (r). Import penetration of country c relative to country r is expressed as the S_t Overall Share S, that is the ratio of total imports from c and r:

$$S_t = \frac{M_{ct}}{M_{rt}} = \frac{\sum_{j \in N_{ct}} M_{cjt}}{\sum_{j \in N_{rt}} M_{rjt}} \tag{5.1}$$

where M_{ct} denotes total imports from country c in period t, and M_{rt} represents total imports from r. M_{ct} is equal to the sum of imports across all eight-digit product categories j in which c is present, denoted by N_{ct}. Likewise, N_{rt} stands for eight-digit products with positive imports from r in period t.

The Overall Share S_t can be expressed as the product of two components: the Extensive Margin and the Intensive Margin. Intuitively, the ratio of imports from c to r depends on the number of products j imported from each country and the average value of imports within common product categories. For example, c's imports could be lower than r's either because c exports fewer product categories than r or because imports from c are lower than imports from r within common categories. Analytically, the overall share in period t can be written as:

$$S_t = \frac{\sum_{j \in N_{ct}} M_{rjt}}{\sum_{j \in N_{rt}} M_{rjt}} \times \frac{\sum_{j \in N_{ct}} M_{cjt}}{\sum_{j \in N_{ct}} M_{rjt}} = E_t \times I_t \tag{5.2}$$

The Extensive Margin E_t measures the percentage of imports from r which is subject to direct competition from Chinese products; that is, the ratio of total imports from r in categories where c is present to total imports from r. The Intensive Margin I_t compares imports from c and r within common product categories; those imported from c (i.e., N_{ct}), and it can be further decomposed into a Quantity Index and a Price Index. Within the common set of products, the value of imports from c and r may differ because of differences in unit prices or because of differences in quantities imported. The Price Index measures the (weighted) average ratio of c to r unit prices at each eight-digit level product j, where the weights are the shares of each product category in total imports of common categories. The Quantity Index also weights the ratio of import quantities within each product according to their share in total imports. Analytically:

$$I_t = P_t \cdot X_t \qquad (5.3)$$

where $\displaystyle P_t = \prod_{j \in N_{ct}} \left(\frac{P_{cjt}}{P_{rjt}}\right)^{\omega_{jt}}$ and $\displaystyle X_t = \prod_{j \in N_{ct}} \left(\frac{X_{cjt}}{X_{rjt}}\right)^{\omega_{jt}} \times P_{cjt}$

and P_{rjt} are CIF unit prices and X_{cjt} and X_{rjt} are imported quantities of product j from c and r, respectively, and

$$\omega_{jt} = \left(\frac{\phi_{cjt} - \phi_{rjt}}{\ln \phi_{cjt} - \ln \phi_{rjt}}\right) \Bigg/ \sum_{j \in N_{ct}} \frac{\phi_{cjt} - \phi_{rjt}}{\ln \phi_{cjt} - \ln \phi_{rjt}}$$

is the logarithmic mean of ϕ_{cjt} and ϕ_{rjt} (the share of product $j \in N_{ct}$ in total imports from c and r, respectively).[3] At the eight-digit level, P_{ct} is the ratio of c to r unit prices, and X_{ct} is the ratio of import quantities. At the aggregate level, P_{ct} and X_{ct} are weighted averages of eight-digit-level price and quantity ratios.

Table 5.2 reports the Overall Share S_t, the Extensive Margin E_t, the Intensive Margin I_t, the Price Index P_i and the Quantity Index X_t computed for each year between 1990 and 2005. The Overall Share increased from 0.8 per cent in 1990 to 9.3 per cent in 2005, with an annual growth rate of 17.6 per cent. In 2005, S_t is the product of an Extensive Margin of 47.8 per cent and an Intensive Margin of 19.4 per cent, meaning that almost 50 per cent of r's imports were subject to direct competition from Chinese products and that the value of imports from China was almost 20 per cent that of r's within common categories. The Intensive Margin results from an average ratio of unit prices of 53 per cent and an average ratio of import quantities of 36.5 per cent. These margins are relatively similar to those computed by Hummels and Klenow (2005) for China's penetration in the US market in 1995: $S = 9.3$ per cent, $E = 70.4$ per cent, $I = 13.3$ per cent, $P = 56.3$ per cent and $X = 23.6$ per cent.

Several elements of the evolution of these margins are interesting. First, the Overall Share increases continuously throughout the period. Second, the Extensive Margin grows in the 1990s, but it stagnates in 2000 at about 48 per cent. In contrast, there is a continuous increase in the Intensive Margin (see Figure 5.1). Figure 5.2 shows that the rise in the intensive margin results mainly from an increase in the Quantity Index – with an average annual rate

Table 5.2   *China's Export Margins Relative to the Rest of the World: Chile, 1990–2005 (per cent)*

	Overall	Extensive	Intensive	Price	Quantity
1990	0.8	33.1	2.5	59.4	4.1
1991	1.3	28.4	4.5	54.7	8.2
1992	1.6	30.8	5.1	55.3	9.1
1993	2.0	37.8	5.4	57.1	9.4
1994	2.5	35.9	7.1	61.0	11.6
1995	2.7	40.2	6.6	61.1	10.8
1996	3.1	38.8	8.1	59.0	13.7
1997	3.7	45.6	8.2	57.5	14.2
1998	4.6	46.4	9.9	49.9	19.7
1999	5.0	50.1	9.9	57.5	17.2
2000	6.0	47.1	12.7	56.8	22.4
2001	6.7	49.6	13.5	55.3	24.4
2002	7.6	45.6	16.6	58.6	28.3
2003	7.9	43.0	18.5	54.9	33.6
2004	9.0	45.7	19.6	56.6	34.6
2005	9.3	47.8	19.4	53.0	36.5
Annualized Growth (%)	17.6	2.5	14.7	−0.8	15.6

Source: Authors' elaboration using Chilean Customs data.

of growth of 15.6 per cent – and a fall in the Price Index, which fluctuates between 59.4 per cent and 53.0 per cent with an average rate of growth of –0.8 per cent. Overall, these numbers are similar to those for the United States in the same period. For example, data from the US Census Bureau reveals that the Overall Share of China's exports to the United States grew at an annual rate of 12 per cent between 1990 and 2005. Also, data on US imports from Feenstra, Romalis and Schott (2002) at the two-digit level reveals that the largest part of the growth in China's import penetration in the United States is explained by the growth in the Intensive Margin. This data also shows that the price index of Chinese imports fell at an annual rate of 1.3 per cent between 1990 and 2001.

These figures suggest two puzzles. First, while Chinese varieties are significantly cheaper than those from the rest of world, consumption of Chinese products is relatively small. Therefore, elements other than – or in addition to – relative prices explain consumption patterns. Second, the evidence that the increase in China's quantity penetration has been achieved without a significant drop in its relative product prices also points to the hypothesis that features

China, India and Beyond

Figure 5.1   Evolution of Chinese Export Margins, 1990–2005

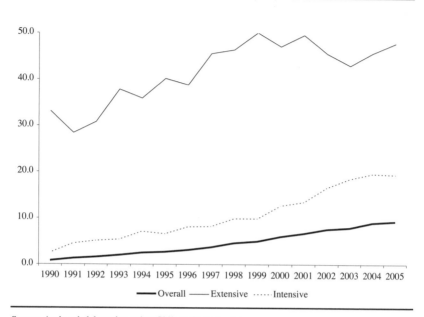

Source: Authors' elaboration using Chilean Customs data.

other than the evolution of relative prices explain the growth in imports from China. There are at least two possible explanations for these phenomena. One possibility is that there is heterogeneity across products even within highly disaggregated product categories (i.e., eight-digit HS level), meaning that countries produce different numbers of varieties of each product. If consumers have preferences for varieties, imports are higher from countries which produce more varieties. Alternatively, there might be differences in the quality of varieties or in the willingness to pay for varieties from different sources, that would explain the different demand for products within the same eight-digit category. In other words, it is possible that China offers a low number of varieties of each product or that the quality of its products is relatively low compared with products from the rest of the world. At the same time, it is possible that the increase in quantity penetration is due to more varieties being produced in China or to quality improvements. Alvarez and Claro (2006a) address this issue in detail.

Figure 5.2   Evolution of Quantity and Price Margins, 1990–2005

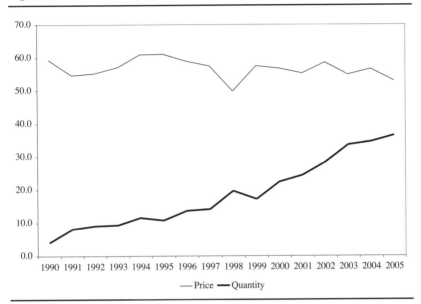

Source: Authors' elaboration using Chilean Customs data.

PRICING AND WITHIN-PRODUCT SPECIALIZATION

The empirical literature dealing with international trade has typically used broad industry aggregates to study the determinants of international specialization (see, for example, Leamer 1987; Harrigan 1997). In two recent studies, however, Schott (2003, 2004) has shown that traditional industry classification hides significant differences in the way countries specialize. Consistent with the factor-endowment-based theory of comparative advantage, we expect China to specialize in labor-intensive industries. Nevertheless, specialization could not only occur across industries, but also within industries and even within narrowly defined products. Using disaggregated information for products defined to ten-digits in the Harmonized System, Schott (2004) shows that product prices differ significantly according to income and factor endowments. Rich countries (relatively more abundant in physical and human capital) specialize in high-priced products which use their abundant factors more intensively.

We test this hypothesis using Chilean import data. In particular, we first show evidence of a systematic relationship between import prices and the exporter's income and analyze how Chinese product prices compare with those of countries with similar income per capita. We use highly disaggregated eight-digit HS import data from all importing countries during the period 1990–2005 as provided by Chilean Customs. We compute the price for each product as unit value: imports in dollars over imported quantity.

We first estimate the following equation:[4]

$$LogP_{jit} = \alpha_{jt} + \delta \times LogI_{it} + \varepsilon_{jit} \qquad (5.4)$$

where P_{jit} is unit value (in dollars) of imports from country i in eight-digit product j in year and I_{it} is per capita GDP in PPP for the exporter country i. Product-year fixed effects are denoted by α_{jt}. The parameter δ of interest is expected to be positive, consistent with the idea that richer countries specialize in high-priced goods. The results confirm the hypothesis of within-product specialization (Table 5.3). The parameter δ in column (1) is estimated to be 0.24, meaning that a 10 per cent increase in per capita income is associated with a 2.4 per cent increase in product prices. In column (2) we get a similar result using a restricted sample of products imported from both low- and high-income countries.[5]

In Alvarez and Claro (2006b), using a sample of 44 exporting countries for the period 1990–2003, we estimate equation (1) for each of 80 manufacturing industries at four-digit International Standard Industrial Classification (ISIC) to check whether the estimated coefficient varies across industries. The results are fairly consistent with the idea that richer countries receive higher prices for their exports across all sectors. In 65 out of 80 industries (81.3 per cent of the manufacturing industries) the estimated parameter is positive and significant (at 5 per cent), and the parameter is negative but not significant only for one industry.

We estimate a different version of equation (5.1) to analyze whether Chinese import prices differ from those of other countries after controlling for income per capita. The specification used is:

$$LogP_{jit} = \alpha_{jt} + \beta \times CHN + \delta \times LogI_{it} + \varepsilon_{jit} \qquad (5.5)$$

In equation (5.2), CHN is a dummy variable for products imported from China. We are particularly interested in testing if β is negative or positive. If β is negative, we conclude that China's products are cheaper than those of countries with similar per capita income. The results are shown in the third and fourth columns of Table 5.3. We find that imports from China receive a price which is – on average – between 28.6 per cent and 31.9 per cent lower than that of countries at similar development stages. The evidence that Chinese products are relatively cheap, even compared with countries having similar income, is

Table 5.3   *Import Prices and Per Capita GDP*

	(1)	(2)	(3)	(4)	(5)	(6)
Per capita GDP (in logs)	0.238	0.242	0.219	0.222	0.220	0.222
	(9.93)**	(9.77)**	(8.37)**	(8.32)**	(8.36)**	(8.32)**
China	–	–	–0.286	–0.319	–	–
	–	–	(2.13)*	(2.32)*	–	–
China 1990–1995	–	–	–	–	–0.111	–0.361
	–	–	–	–	(–0.79)	(–0.94)
China 1996–2000	–	–	–	–	–0.227	–0.263
	–	–	–	–	(1.72)	(1.94)
China 2001–2005	–	–	–	–	–0.398	–0.442
	–	–	–	–	(2.93)**	(3.20)**
Constant	5.105	5.207	4.961	5.056	4.962	5.057
	(17.06)**	(16.08)**	(16.26)**	(15.76)**	(16.25)**	(15.76)**
Observations	757,397	649,074	757,397	649,074	757,397	649,074
R^2	0.73	0.72	0.73	0.72	0.73	0.72

Notes: Robust t-statistics in italics. Standard errors adjusted at the country level.
*significant at 5 per cent level** significant at 1 per cent level.
Columns (1), (3) and (5) include all products. Columns (2), (4), and (6) include products imported from at least one low and high income country. Low income countries are those with income per capita lower than the 30 per cent of countries in the sample, and high-income countries are those with income per capita higher than the 70 per cent of countries in the sample. Per capita GDP in PPP is from World Development Indicators.

consistent with that from Schott (2006), who shows that, during the 1990s, Chinese products on average sold in the United States for a discount relative to products of countries with similar GDP per capita.[6]

We also analyze how the China coefficient has changed over time. Columns (5) and (6) report the evidence of estimating equation (5.5), including an interaction term between the dummy for China and period-specific dummy variables for the periods 1990–1995, 1996–2000 and 2001–2005. Our results show no evidence of a statistical price difference, after controlling for income, for the period 1990–1995, and weak evidence for the period 1996–2000. However, there is significant evidence that Chinese prices have declined relative to countries with similar income per capita in the period 2001–2005.

This evidence is robust if we restrict the sample to include only products imported from low- and high-income economies.[7]

In sum, we have found evidence of within-product specialization, in the sense that income per capita differences are associated with differences in product prices within highly disaggregated product categories, presumably reflecting cross-country differences in the types of varieties produced in response to differences in technology and factor abundance. In particular, price differences are highly correlated with the per capita income of the exporter's country, and products imported from China are low priced compared with those from countries with similar income per capita. Finally, we also find that the prices of Chinese products have declined relative to those from the rest of the world since the mid-1990s. However, this decline is relatively small, suggesting that elements other than relative prices explain China's export growth.

CHINESE EXPORT QUALITY

In this section, we analyze the relative sophistication (or quality) of Chinese exports in two dimensions. First, we look at China's export basket compared with that of developed economies. Second, we present some evidence regarding quality differences between Chinese varieties and the rest of the world. The idea is to search for direct or indirect evidence supporting the hypothesis that there has been an increase in quality or a willingness to pay for Chinese products relative to those from the rest of the world.

Similarity of Export Baskets

A first measure of an increase in the quality of Chinese products is obtained by comparing China's export basket with that of other countries, especially developed economies. Following Rodrik (2006) and Schott (2006), we conclude that China's export mix has become more sophisticated over time if it has become more similar to that of developed countries. We measure the similarity of export baskets using an index developed by Finger and Kreinin (1979). For any two exporters, say China (c) and other country (i), the Export Similarity Index in Chile is given by:

$$SIM_{cit} = \sum_{j} \min(s_{jct}, s_{jit}) \qquad (5.6)$$

where j is an eight-digit level product category, s_{jct} is the share of product j in total Chinese exports to Chile in year t, and s_{jit} is the share of product j in total exports of country i to Chile in year t. This bilateral measure is bounded by zero

Figure 5.3   Export Similarity Index

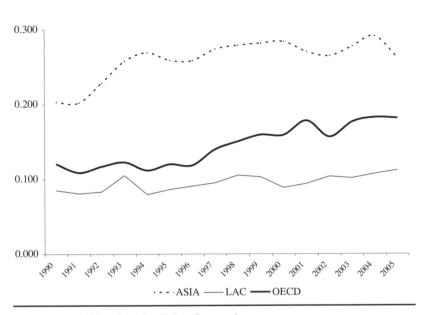

Source: Authors' elaboration using Chilean Customs data.

(if there are no common product categories between China and country i) and one (if the share of each product in total exports is identical in both countries). To illustrate how Chinese exports perform relative to countries at different development stages, we compare the export similarity of China with three groups of countries: Asia, Latin America, and members of the Organization for Economic Cooperation and Development (OECD).[8]

The results are shown in Figure 5.3. Comparing the three groups of countries, we find that China's export bundle resembles more that of other Asian countries than those of Latin American and OECD countries. This is true at the beginning and at the end of the period under study. Interestingly, there is convergence in the Export Similarity Index between China and OECD countries over time. In fact, the index went from 0.121 in 1990 to 0.182 in 2005. Although there is also some convergence with the export structure of Asian and Latin American economies, this trend is significantly higher with OECD countries. In fact, the increase in the similarity index with OECD is 50.4 per cent between 1990 and 2005, while it is only 31.5 per cent with Latin American countries, and 29.6 per cent with Asian countries. In sum, over time

Table 5.4   *Countries with the Highest Export Similarity to OECD Exports in Chile*

Country	1990	Country	2005
Brazil	0.602	South Korea	0.700
Taiwan	0.540	Brazil	0.568
Mexico	0.467	Taiwan	0.544
Argentina	0.398	Mexico	0.484
China	*0.388*	*China*	*0.434*
South Korea	0.370	Colombia	0.384
Indonesia	0.368	Uruguay	0.382
Panama	0.240	India	0.360
Peru	0.224	Singapore	0.353
Colombia	0.215	Thailand	0.343
Uruguay	0.176	Argentina	0.276
Singapore	0.162	Panama	0.242
Thailand	0.151	Malaysia	0.230
India	0.118	Indonesia	0.227
Venezuela	0.118	Venezuela	0.225
Malaysia	0.114	Costa Rica	0.216
Trinidad and Tobago	0.109	Philippines	0.199
Philippines	0.095	Peru	0.078
Guatemala	0.084	Vietnam	0.070
Jamaica	0.073	Bolivia	0.062

Source: Authors' elaboration using Chilean Customs data.

Chinese exports have tended to be more similar to high-income countries than to countries in Latin America and Asia.

We also compare China's export similarity in relation to individual developing countries. Table 5.4 shows a sample of 20 Asian and Latin American countries with the highest export similarity to the OECD countries. China has been one of the top five countries in this ranking in both 1990 and 2005, meaning that it has a high degree of similarity with OECD countries among developing economies. Figure 5.4 shows the performance of China for the entire sample. With the exception of 2002, where it was ranked seventh, China has typically been between fifth and sixth place among countries with higher export similarity to OECD. This result corroborates Rodrik's (2006) evidence that China has a sophisticated export mix given its level of income

Figure 5.4   Ranking of Export Similarity Compared with OECD

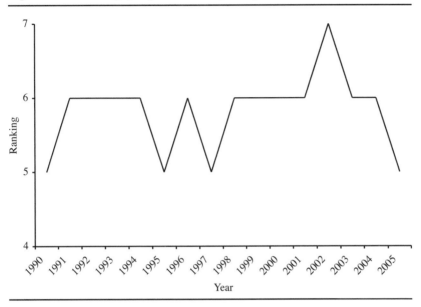

Source: Authors' elaboration using Chilean Customs data.

per capita, because a high share of its exports corresponds to products mainly exported by high-income countries.

The evidence that China's export similarity with OECD countries is one of the highest among developing countries, and that the similarity has increased significantly in the last 15 years, suggests some kind of increasing sophistication of Chinese exports.[9] This can be understood as indirect evidence that the quality of Chinese varieties has improved over time. This link is weak in several dimensions, however. First, as discussed by Branstetter and Lardy (2006), the Chinese export mix does not take into account that China imports high-value-added intermediate inputs, meaning that China should be judged in terms of the value added to an export basket which is highly labor intensive. Another issue is that the link between export sophistication and the export similarity index with OECD countries implicitly assumes that products are homogeneous. In other words, it assumes that varieties within each product category have similar quality or price. For instance, if both China and Italy only export 'pants', the Export Similarity Index will take the maximum value of one, and we will conclude that Chinese exports are as sophisticated as Italian exports. However, as shown above, even within narrowly defined products there are large differences in prices across countries. Unless we take into

Table 5.5 China's Relative Exports Quality Growth, 1990–2005

Sample[a]	Trade barriers[b]	Mean[c]	95% Confidence interval	
Panel A: ROW comprises countries with positive imports in the corresponding eight-digit product category.				
	Yes	9.8	8.3	11.3
	No	10.7	8.9	12.4
Panel B: ROW comprises countries with positive imports in at least one eight-digit product category within the two-digit level group.				
	Yes	11.2	8.8	13.5
	No	11.5	9.4	13.6

Notes:
a. Includes product-year observations with $0.05 < p_{jt} < 20$.
b. Yes means that the regression includes nominal average tariffs.
c. Compound annualized rate of growth of the quality gap.

account these price (and quality) differentials, the comparison of the Export Similarity Index may not be an adequate measure for export sophistication. In the next subsection, we explore a more direct measure of product quality.

Estimation of Quality Differences

The results in the last section illustrate how Chinese exports tend to be relatively sophisticated in comparison with those from other developing countries. This becomes clear from comparing its export similarity to that of OECD countries. However, more specific measures of sophistication are required to strengthen the hypothesis that elements other than relative product prices explain China's export growth. Yet it can be assumed that product prices reflect product quality, and price differences also reflect several other features.[10] Product quality is unobservable, and we need some methodology for inferring quality measures from trade statistics. In an earlier study we developed a theoretical model to distinguish the impact of prices and unobserved variety and quality on import penetration (Alvarez and Claro 2006a). Under traditional assumptions of monopolistic competition in a three-region setup (Chile, China and the rest of the world), we demonstrated that the ratio of consumption in z- (Chile) of some product variety j imported from countries c (China) and r (rest of the world) can be expressed as:

$$\ln X_{jt}^z = \alpha_{0j} + \alpha_1 \times t + \alpha_2 \times \ln p_{jt}^z + \alpha_3 \times \ln \phi_{jt} +$$
$$\alpha_4 \ln \omega_{cjt} + \alpha_5 \ln \omega_{zjt} + \alpha_6 \ln \tau_{jt} + \upsilon_{jt} \tag{5.7}$$

where X_{jt} is the China/rest of the world ratio of imported quantities of product j, p_{jt} is the China/rest of the world relative price of product j, ϕ_{jt} is relative size of China and the rest of the world, ϕ_{cjt} and ϕ_{zjt} are relative factor prices between China and the rest of the world and between Chile and the rest of the world,[11] respectively, and ϕ_{jt} are trade costs measured as average nominal tariffs in Chile. The variable t is a time trend resulting from the assumption that relative export quality is given by:

$$q_{jt} = e^{\delta_{oj} + \delta} \tag{5.8}$$

where q_{jt} is the China/ROW quality ratio in product j. The annual growth in the quality ratio between imports from China and the rest of the world is recovered, after estimating equation (5.4), as

$$\delta_1 = \frac{-\alpha_1}{\left(\alpha_2 + \alpha_4 + 1\right)} \tag{5.9}$$

Table 5.5 reports results for the exports quality growth obtained by Alvarez and Claro (2006a). Under different specifications, we found that the relative export quality growth of Chinese products is positive and statistically significant. Moreover, the point estimate is very similar for each specification. In Panel A, results refer to GDP and income variables measured for all importers at eight-digit products and Panel B corresponds to these variables measured for all importers at two-digit products.[12] For both cases, the model is estimated with and without tariffs. The results show that the annualized rate of growth of the quality ratio is between 9.8 and 11.5 per cent.

Alvarez and Claro (2006a) explore the causes of cross-product differences in quantity penetration, estimating differences in the rate of growth of the quality ratio across products, depending on their degree of differentiation. If quality growth matters for the growing importance of China, we should observe that an increase in quality is more relevant for products in which product differentiation is more important. In the case of homogeneous products, we should not expect significant differences in price and quality at very detailed product classifications. In such a case, perfect competition would imply that a country imports only from the cheapest source.

We show here the estimates of quality growth for different product groups according to the classification provided by Rauch (1999). Table 5.6 presents the

Table 5.6   *Across-Product Differences in Quality Growth*

Type of Product	Panel A eight-digit income variables	Panel B two-digit income variables
Differentiated	11.2	12.9
	(1.2)	(1.8)
Reference priced	4.8	4.8
	(0.3)	(0.9)
Homogeneous	2.8	4.3
	(0.8)	(1.4)
Test (Probability > F)		
q(Diff) = q(Ref)	0.00	0.00
q(Diff) = q(Hom)	0.00	0.00
q(Ref) = q(Hom)	0.02	0.77

Notes:
Product conservative classification from Rauch (1999).
Standard errors in parentheses. All regressions include product-year observations in which $0.05 < p_{jt} < 20$ and control for trade barriers.

average rate of quality growth for differentiated goods, reference-priced goods and homogeneous goods. There is strong evidence that quality growth is much higher for differentiated products than for reference-priced and homogeneous products. Note, for example, in column (1), that the annual rate of growth of the quality of Chinese varieties relative to the rest of the world is 11.2 per cent (12.9 per cent) for differentiated products, and only 4.8 per cent (4.8 per cent) and 2.8 per cent (4.3 per cent) for reference priced and homogeneous products, respectively.[13]

The bottom part of Table 5.6 reports tests for the equality of quality growth across these three groups of products. In general, the null hypotheses – that quality growth is the same for differentiated and reference priced products – can be rejected for all the cases analyzed. The same is true for the test of equality of growth between differentiated and homogenous products. In sum, the evidence seems to favor the idea that the quality of Chinese exports has grown more rapidly in more differentiated products. Interestingly, these products are those with a deepest fall in the relative price of Chinese varieties (see Alvarez and Claro 2006a), revealing that the fall in prices is associated with an increase in quality. The first culprit for this association is productivity growth: a high rate of growth of productivity in differentiated products may explain an increase in their quality together with a fall in their price. This process coincides with the increasingly dominant position of productivity-advanced foreign firms in China's exports. A formal test of this link is far beyond the scope of this study, but we think it constitutes a very important avenue for future research.

CONCLUSION

The impact of Chinese competition is commonly thought to be transmitted through prices. In particular, based upon traditional endowment-based trade theory, the main impact of China's competition is expected to be associated with a fall in the relative price of labor-intensive products and high penetration in labor-intensive sectors. Although there is some evidence supporting this view, we find that a large part of the action takes place within sectors. The literature has provided strong evidence that there is also differentiation within products, that presumably reflects factor endowment and technological differences. As expected, rich countries export high-priced products while poor countries export low-priced products.

In this context, this study analyzed the sources of China's export growth. Using highly disaggregated data on Chilean imports between 1990 and 2005, we first show that China's strong export penetration relative to other countries is mainly explained by an increase in the intensive margin; that is, an increase in the volume of exports in product categories which are also exported by other countries. Surprisingly, the main source of growth in the intensive margin is explained by an increase in exported quantities, without a significant fall in the relative price of Chinese products. One explanation for this apparent paradox is an increase in the willingness to pay for quality Chinese products relative to the rest of the world. The study provides detailed evidence showing that the fall in Chinese prices is relatively small to explain the huge increase in export quantities. We also show direct and indirect evidence of growing sophistication of China's export mix. In particular, we show that exports from China have increased their similarity with exports from rich countries, and we also show that the quality of Chinese exports has improved over time. This is consistent with the idea that product quality is an important dimension of Chinese export growth.

NOTES

We thank Alvaro Garcia for assistance and Consuelo Edwards for editing this article. Sebastián Claro acknowledges the financial support from Fundación Andes through grant 14-060-9. This article does not necessarily reflect the views of the Board of the Central Bank of Chile.

1. See also Castro, Olarreaga and Saslavsky (2007) for an empirical study of how Chinese and Indian imports affect manufacturing employment in Argentina.
2. Throughout this chapter, we refer to a product as an eight-digit level category.
3. See Feenstra (1994), Hummels and Klenow (2005) and Broda and Weinstein (2006).
4. We also include year-fixed effects to control for shocks, that are common across products imported from different countries.
5. Low-income countries are those with per capita income lower than that of 30 per cent of countries in the sample, and high-income countries are those with per capita income higher than that of 70 per cent of countries in the sample. Per capita GDP in PPP is taken from World Development Indicators.
6. He also provides evidence that the number of product categories exported from China to the United States is significantly larger than those of countries at similar stages of development. This explains why he argues that China's exports are relatively sophisticated compared to those of countries with similar income.
7. For both specifications, the null hypothesis that China's coefficient is the same in 1995–2000 and 2001–2005 is rejected at 1 per cent significance.
8. While grouping countries, we sum exports over countries in the group and then use group-level rather than individual export shares for computing the similarity index.
9. Claro (2007) presents a model where FDI liberalization in China generates a shift in the export structure toward labor-intensive products. In this context, exports are dominated by productivity-advanced foreign-owned firms rather than productivity-backward domestically-owned enterprises. Therefore, the increase in the willingness to pay for Chinese products relative to those from other countries may depend upon an increase in the relative 'sophistication' of exporting firms.
10. See Hallak and Schott (2005) for a discussion of how prices are an imperfect measure of product quality.
11. Relative size is measured as the PPP-adjusted GDP ratio and relative productivities as the PPP-adjusted per capita GDP ratio. Both variables are obtained from the World Bank World Development Indicators dataset.
12. The relevant rest of the world may be assumed to be all exporters of the same product (eight-digit HS) or some lower level of aggregation (two-digit HS).
13. The results are similar, albeit somewhat weaker, when products are differentiated according to the elasticity of substitution across varieties within each product computed by Broda and Weinstein (2006).

BIBLIOGRAPHY

Álvarez, Roberto and Sebastián Claro (2008), 'David versus Goliath: The Impact of Chinese Competition of Developing Countries', *World Development*, (forthcoming).
—— (2006a), 'The China Phenomenon: Price, Quality or Variety?', Santiago, Central Bank of Chile, Working Paper No. 411.
—— (2006b), 'The China Price: Evidence and Some Implications', *Estudios de Economía*, **33** (2),117–39.
Bernard, Andrew, J. Bradford Jensen and Peter K. Schott (2006), 'Survival of the Best Fit: Exposure to Low-Wage Countries and the (Uneven) Growth of U.S. Manufacturing Plants', *Journal of International Economics*, **68** (1), 219–37.
Blázquez-Lidoy, Jorge, Javier Rodríguez and Javier Santiso (2006), 'Angel or Devil? China's Trade Impact on Latin American Emerging Markets', Paris, OECD Development Centre Working Paper No. 252.

Branstetter, Lee and Nicholas Lardy (2006), 'China's Embrace of Globalization', Cambridge, MA, National Bureau of Economic Research (NBER) Working Paper No. 12373.

Broda, Christian and David Weinstein (2006), 'Globalization and the Gains from Varieties', *Quarterly Journal of Economics*, **121** (2), 541–85.

Castro, Lucio, Marcelo Olarreaga and David Saslavsky (2007), 'The Impact of Trade with China and India on Argentina's Manufacturing Employment', Washington, DC, World Bank Policy Research Working Paper No. 4153.

Claro, Sebastián (2007), 'FDI Liberalization as a Source of Comparative Advantage in China', Santiago, Instituto de Economía, Pontificia Universidad Católica de Chile, unpublished paper.

Devlin, Robert, Antoni Estevadeordal and Andrés Rodríguez (2006), *The Emergence of China: Opportunities and Challenges for Latin America and the Caribbean*, Washington, DC: Inter-American Development Bank.

Eichengreen, Barry, Yeongseop Rhee and Hui Tong (2004), 'The Impact of China on the Exports of Other Asian Countries', Cambridge, MA, National Bureau of Economic Research (NBER) Working Paper No. 10768.

Feenstra, Robert (1994), 'New Product Varieties and the Measurement of International Prices', *American Economic Review*, **84** (1),157–77.

Feenstra, Robert, John Romalis and Peter Schott (2002), 'U.S. Imports, Exports and Tariff Data, 1989-2001', Cambridge, MA, National Bureau of Economic Research (NBER) Working Paper No. 9387.

Finger, J. Michael and M.E. Kreinin (1979), 'A Measure of "Export Similarity" and Its Possible Uses', *Economic Journal*, **89** (356), 905–12.

Hallak, Juan Carlos and Peter K. Schott (2005), 'Estimating Cross-country Differences in Product Quality', New Haven, CT, Yale School of Management, unpublished paper.

Harrigan, James (1997), 'Technology, Factor Supplies, and International Specialization: Estimating the Neoclassical Model', *American Economic Review*, **87** (4), 475–94.

Hummels, David and Peter Klenow (2005), 'The Variety and Quality of a Nation's Exports', *American Economic Review*, **95** (3), 704–23.

Leamer, Edward E. (1987), 'Paths of Development in the Three- Factor, n-Good General Equilibrium Model, *Journal of Political Economy*, **95** (5), 961–99.

——(1995), 'The Heckscher-Ohlin Model in Theory and Practice', Princeton Studies in International Finance, 77.

López Córdova, J. Ernesto, Alejandro Micco and Danielken Molina (2008), 'Competing with the Dragon: Latin America and Chinese Exports to the US Market', Washington, DC, World Bank Policy Research Working Paper No. 4497.

Nicita, Alessandro and Marcela Olarreaga (2006), 'Trade, Production and Protection 1976–2004', *World Bank Economic Review*, **21** (1), 165–71.

Rauch, James (1999), 'Networks versus Markets in International Trade', *Journal of International Economics*, **48** (1), 7–35.

Rodrik, Dani (2006), 'What's So Special about China's Exports?', Cambridge, MA: Harvard University, John Kennedy School of Government, Working Paper 06–001.

Schott, Peter K. (2003), 'One Size Fits All? Heckscher-Ohlin Specialization in Global Production', *American Economic Review*, **93** (3), 686–708.

——(2004), 'Across-Product versus Within-Product Specialization in International Trade', *Quarterly Journal of Economics*, **119** (2), 647–78.

—— (2006), 'The Relative Sophistication of Chinese Exports', Cambridge, MA, National Bureau of Economic Research (NBER) Working Paper No. 12173.

6. Trade Liberalization and R&D Investment: Evidence from Manufacturing Firms in India

Mavannoor Parameswaran

The issue of whether a more open trade policy regime accelerates technological progress and economic growth is highly debated in the economics literature. It has attracted even wider intellectual attention not only because of the increasing importance of trade in an economy, but also due to the ambiguity regarding which trade policy will generate faster technological progress. The theoretical models examining various ways trade can affect technological progress are informative, but they are not unanimous in their predictions. There are sound theoretical arguments supporting more liberalized trade, but there are also equally sound theoretical arguments for protecting some industries from international competition. Thus trade liberalization merits further empirical analysis (Hallak and Levinsohn 2004).

A number of empirical studies have examined how trade openness affects technological progress and economic growth. This literature attempts to identify the empirical relationship between the degree of openness to international trade and a country's economic performance, using standard econometric methods on country-level measures of specific variables. Although the preferred choice of variables and the exact econometric techniques employed have improved considerably over time, this literature has not produced a set of results which provides informed and convincing recommendations for trade policy. The indicators of openness used by these studies are either problematic as a measure of trade barriers or are highly correlated with other sources of poor economic performance. Furthermore, a liberal trade policy regime affects technological progress through a variety of channels which are also contingent upon the particular economic environment, making it almost impossible for an econometric framework consisting of cross-country regressions to uncover the relevant mechanism and its conditional nature. However, studies focusing on a particular channel and uncovering its conditional nature using micro-level information seem to be quite fruitful (Hallak and Levinsohn 2004; Rodriguez and Rodrik 2000; Edwards 1993).

Building on these studies, this chapter examines the impact of trade liberalization on the firms' investment in research and development (R&D) in the context of India's manufacturing sector. In the modern industrial world, a firm's investment in R&D is an important source of technological progress. R&D investment is required not only for introducing innovations, but also for adapting and absorbing technology from outside sources (Cohen and Levinthal 1989). Further, policymakers are usually told that if trade is liberalized, firms would have no choice but to modernize their techniques and cut their costs in order to compete with foreign producers (Rodrik 1992; Ahluwalia 1996). Empirical verification of this argument seems to be quite interesting in the context of trade liberalization in India.

Since 1991 the Indian economy has experienced dramatic changes in the country's policy framework. India is moving from an import-substituting and inward-oriented trade policy regime toward a more open and liberal regime. Along with trade liberalization, the government also introduced major changes in industrial policy. The important external-sector policy changes include a reduction in tariff and non-tariff barriers to trade, exchange rate reform, measures to promote foreign direct investment and a liberalization of technology imports. With the initiation of liberal trade policy regime, the mean tariff rate dropped from 79 per cent in 1990 to 32.5 per cent in 1999. Similarly, while 39 per cent of the tariff lines at the ten-digit level were subjected to non-tariff barriers as of 1 April 1996, this was reduced to 5.3 per cent as of 1 April 2001 (Srinivasan and Tendulkar 2003). These reform measures are intended to improve the productivity of Indian industry by creating a more competitive market structure.

LIBERALIZATION AND R&D INVESTMENT IN THEORY

Trade liberalization can affect a firm's investment in R&D through increased import competition, greater export opportunities and technology imports.[1] Each channel is briefly reviewed below.

Import Competition

A number of theoretical models have analyzed the impact of import competition on firms' R&D investment. For example, Rodrik (1992) examines this relationship by assuming monopoly and oligopoly structures for the domestic market. Under monopoly, the incentive to invest in R&D increases with the scale of output.[2] In the monopoly model, therefore, import competition shrinks the market share of the domestic producer and reduces the incentive to invest in innovation. In the second case, where domestic industry is an oligopoly behaving according to the Bertrand assumption, import competition stimulates R&D efforts. Indeed the predictions, as in any oligopoly model, depend on the particular behavioral assumptions about the conduct of firms in the market. According to Smulders and Klundert (1995), firms have greater incentive to invest in R&D when there is greater market concentration and lower market power. Import competition can generate this conducive situation through a simultaneous reduction in mark-up and an increase in the market concentration through the exit of inefficient firms and absorption of their market share by the extant ones.

Aghion et al. (2001) and Aghion (2003) consider the effect of product market competition on innovation effort. These models, assuming duopoly with Bertrand price competition, predict an inverted U-shaped relationship between product market competition and innovation efforts.[3] In the extreme case of monopoly, profit is independent of the monopolist's technological leadership and therefore, it has no incentive to invest in technological progress. But at greater levels of competition, firms find it more difficult to appropriate rents from innovation and, therefore, have a lower incentive to be innovative.[4] In this framework, firms have greater incentive to invest in R&D when there is higher market concentration along with intense competition. Extending this logic to import competition, it would encourage R&D investment only in those industries where domestic competition is very low (or concentration is very high). For industries where competition is already high, import competition may discourage R&D efforts.

Exports

Exports allow firms to produce on a large scale and thereby exploit the increasing returns to scale made possible by fixed investments like R&D. Hughes (1986) argues that exports can have a positive effect on innovation efforts, because the elasticity of foreign demand with respect to R&D is likely to be greater than that of the domestic demand. There are several explanations for this argument. First, since the export market usually consists of several segmented markets and each sub-market varies in terms of consumer preferences, entry barriers and elasticities, the likelihood that R&D will increase demand in some of these markets is higher than that in the domestic market. Second, if R&D leads to product differentiation or to the development of a new product which likely to be preferred by a small group of consumers, then exporting enables the firm to realize economies of scale in the production of this differentiated commodity. In this case, export possibilities allow the firm to make required the R&D investment.

Technology Imports

Under a liberal trade policy regime firms can import technology from abroad. This can be either in the form of capital goods embodying better technology or in disembodied form, such as blueprints and design schematics. Technology imports can affect the incentive of the firm to fund in in-house R&D. The relationship between the two, however, has been a subject of intense debate in the development literature (see Evenson and Westphal 1995). One view suggests substitutability between the two, implying that importing technology would reduce R&D investment (Pillai 1979). The other view considers them as complementary (Cohen and Levinthal 1989; Bell and Pavitt 1997). It argues that, since most technologies contain a portion of tacit knowledge, absorption of imported technology requires a degree of technological capability on the part of the firm. Investment in in-house R&D is one source of such capability (Cohen and Levinthal 1989). Similarly, imported plants and machinery may also require adaptations and modifications to suit local conditions, raw materials and usage patterns. This may also require investment in R&D[5] (Mani 1995 and Basant 1997).

DATA AND RESEARCH DESIGN

I use an econometric approach to analyze the impact of trade liberalization on a firm's investment in R&D. The R&D intensity (RDINS) of the firm, defined as the ratio of R&D expenditure to sales, is regressed on a set of explanatory variables. The explanatory variables include variables related to trade and other determinants. The trade-related determinants are import penetration rate (IPR), export intensity (EXPOIN), disembodied technology import intensity (TECHIN) and capital goods import intensity (CGOOD). The other determinants include size of the firm (SIZE), age of the firm (AGE), advertising intensity (ADVTIN), rate of profit (ROP), share of value added in sales (VAS), domestic market concentration (MCON) and a dummy variable (D_FEP) which takes a value of one if the firm has foreign equity participation; otherwise it is zero. The choice of other determinants is based on previous studies in the context of the Indian manufacturing industry.

The regression model for firm i in industry j in year t is given in equation (6.1):

$$RDINS_{ijt} = \beta_0 + \beta_1 SIZE_{ijt} + \beta_2 EXPOIN_{ijt} + \beta_3 TECHIN_{ijt} + \beta_4 ADVTIN_{ijt} + \beta_5 ROP_{ijt} +$$
$$\beta_6 IPR_{jt} + \beta_7 MCON_{jt} + \beta_8 AGE_{ijt} + \beta_9 D\_FEP_{ijt} + \beta_{10} IPR_{jt} * MCON_{jt} +$$
$$\beta_{11} CGOOD_{ijt} + \beta_{12} VAS_{ijt} + \delta Z_{ijt} + \varepsilon_{it}$$

$$(6.1)$$

where Z is a matrix of industry-specific dummy variables to capture the inter-industry variation in innovation, adaptation opportunities and appropriability conditions and δ is its coefficient vector.

The study uses firm-level panel data, covering the whole manufacturing industry for the period 1994–95 to 1999–2000, obtained from the Centre for Monitoring the Indian Economy's electronic database, PROWESS. During this period Indian industry was operating under a more liberal trade policy regime than in prior years. The panel is unbalanced and consists of 15,181 observations on 3,675 firms, organized into 92 four-digit industries of National Industrial Classification (NIC 1998) scheme. The dataset provides information on a number of variables such as a firm's expenditure on R&D, technology imports, capital goods imports and advertising, value of exports, foreign equity participation and value of sales. I also use industry-level output data collected from the Annual Survey of Industries (ASI) and import and export data for manufactured products collected from the World Bank-compiled Trade and Production Database.[6] The classification in different datasets have been harmonized using two concordance tables; one is between NIC 1986 and 1998 and the second is between NIC 1998 and ISIC revision 2. This harmonization process necessitated the merging of some of the four-digit industries into one group to get proper matching. The final dataset for estimation consists of 59 industry groups.[7]

The method for constructing variables and their expected relationship with R&D intensity are explained below.

Import-Penetration Rate (IPR)

Import competition in an industry is measured using the import-penetration rate. It is an industry-level variable. The import penetration rate of industry j in year t is defined in equation (6.2):

$$IPR_{jt} = \left(\frac{IMPORT_{jt}}{OUTPUT_{jt} + IMPORT_{jt} - EXPORT_{jt}} \right)$$

(6.2)

where export and output denote the export and output of industry j and import denotes the import of industry j's product.[8] The output figures are taken from the Annual Survey of Industries (ASI), while trade data are from World Bank's Trade and Production Database.

Market Concentration (MCON)

The relationship between market concentration and innovation effort has been extensively analyzed in the theoretical and empirical literature.[9] Previous studies suggest that a concentrated market might encourage innovation by allowing firms to differentiate their products as well as by improving the appropriability conditions. It is also possible that greater market concentration may discourage R&D, as it allows firms to exercise monopoly power. Concentration in the domestic market is measured using the Herfindahl Index (HI^D). The Herfindahl Index of domestic concentration of industry j in year t is shown in equation (6.3):

$$HI_{jt}^{D} = \sum_{i}^{n} S_{ijt}^{2}$$

(6.3)

where S_{ijt} is the share of firm i's domestic sales in the total domestic sales of n firms in industry j in year t. Sales in the domestic market are calculated by subtracting exports from total firm sales.[10]

I chose the Herfindahl Index over other alternative measures of concentration for several reasons.[11] First, it satisfies all the desirable properties required for a concentration index (see Chakravarty 1995). Second, its statistical distribution properties allow its estimation from a sample of firms. Hart (1975) shows that, when the size distribution of firms follows log normal distribution, the Herfindahl Index is a function of the moments of the original and first moment distributions of the log of the size variable. Third, it can be directly linked with oligopoly theory. For example, for a given elasticity of demand, the divergence between marginal cost and price (mark up) is lower when the Herfindahl Index is low (Chakravarty 1995). Indeed, in an open economy context, the Herfindahl Index of domestic concentration does not indicate the true market power of firms, for they are subjected to import competition. Here, the price-marginal cost ratio, reflecting both domestic and foreign competition, is recommended as a better measure of market power (Aghion 2003). I use this measure because one of my objectives is to examine how domestic market structure conditions the impact of import competition; the two sources of competitive pressure on domestic firms, namely other domestic firms and imports, need to be identified separately.

Interaction of IPR and MCON (IPR*MCON)

I hypothesize that import competition encourages investment in R&D in more concentrated industries. In the regression framework, this means that IPR and MCON not only have separate effects, but also have an interactive effect. An interaction variable between these two variables is included in the regression model to test this hypothesis. If it is valid, the interaction variable will have a significant positive sign.

Firm Size (SIZE)

I expect firm size to have a positive effect on R&D investment for several reasons.[12] Since R&D cost is fixed, big firms can spread this cost over a greater amount of output than small ones. Firm size, therefore, is likely to exert a positive influence on innovation effort. Large firms are also in a favorable position regarding the financing of R&D. They usually have more internal resources at their disposal, and they can more easily mobilize funds from the capital market. Further, large firms often produce a variety of products, so they benefit more from their innovation activities, if these involve economies of scope. Following the earlier studies, firm size is proxied by its sales.[13]

Rate of Profit (ROP)

One important source of finance for R&D expenditure is firm profits. Therefore, profit should have a positive effect on R&D investment. Kumar and Saqib (1996) and Pamukcu (2003), however, note that a negative effect is possible if lower profits, that firms might view as a threat to their survival, force them to be innovative to improve their competitiveness.[14] The rate of profit (ROP) is defined as the ratio of a firm's net profit after tax to its sales.

Advertising Intensity (ADVTIN)

Firms usually advertise their products to increase their market share. The effect of advertisement on R&D investment is ambiguous. It promotes R&D if it enables the firm to increase its market share and thereby enhance the rate of return on R&D. On the other hand, it can discourage investment in R&D if the firm opts to use advertisements rather than R&D to increase its market share.

Advertisement intensity is defined as the ratio of advertisement expenditure to sales.

Firm Age (AGE)

If learning by doing exists in production and R&D activity, more experienced firms have an accumulated knowledge stock which gives them an edge in research compared with younger firms. Hence, firm experience should affect investment in R&D positively. A firm's experience is proxied by its age, calculated from the year of incorporation. Of course, for some firms the year of incorporation and the year of starting production may not coincide; however, this proxy has been used for want of a better alternative.

Value-Added Share (VAS)

Since information is a commodity having an imperfect market, firms might better appropriate the returns from knowledge production by internalizing its use rather than selling it (Arrow 1962). Therefore, firms occupying the majority of the production chain of a product (higher vertical integration) should have better opportunities for the internal application of knowledge and, therefore, have greater incentive to invest in R&D. I measure the extent of vertical integration by the share of value added in sales.[15]

Foreign Equity Participation (D_FEP)

The effect of foreign equity participation on innovation effort is ambiguous. It can have a negative impact, if foreign participation allows firms to have access to technological knowledge from the parent firm abroad and thus avoid the need to do in-house R&D. On the other hand, it can have a positive effect, if the technology sourced from the parent firm needs to be adapted to suit local factor prices, usage patterns and so on. Such innovation and adaptation activities are more likely to take place in joint ventures, as they need not incur huge costs to search for suitable technology in the world market (Pack 1982). Further, Dahlman, Larsson and Westphal (1987) argue that if the local partner has the motivation and the ability to learn from the technological competence of the foreign partner, it is quite possible to have a positive effect from foreign equity participation in R&D investment. Further, in the context of global research activities of multinational firms, there is a higher probability that subsidiaries of foreign companies would start research units in India to take advantage of the low-cost R&D personnel available there. In the regression model, D_FEP is a dummy variable which takes value one if the firm has foreign equity participation, otherwise zero.

Export Intensity (EXPOIN)

The extent of a firm's involvement in exporting is measured by its export intensity. This is defined as the ratio of its exports to its sales. While exports can affect current year R&D through ways already noted above, current R&D investment can improve the future export potential of a firm by increasing its productivity.

Technology Import Intensity (TECHIN) and Capital Goods Import Intensity (CGOOD)

I use two variables to measure the technology import intensity of a firm. The first one, TECHIN, captures the intensity of disembodied technology imports through licensing, defined as the ratio of expenditure on disembodied technology imports to sales. The second variable, CGOOD, captures the intensity of capital goods imports, defined as the ratio of expenditure on capital goods imports to sales. These two variables are taken separately, as their effects on R&D investment are expected to be different.

Sectoral Classification of Industries

There is significant intersectoral variation in the process of innovation and technological progress, mainly due to the differences in incentive structures and opportunities for innovation. To accommodate this intersectoral variation in the extent of appropriability and opportunities for innovation, industries are classified into four sectors on the basis of the taxonomy developed by Pavitt (1984), one of the most widely used taxonomies in the innovation and R&D literature.[16] Pavitt classifies industries into four sectors on the basis of three criteria, namely sources of technology, the user's needs and means of appropriating the benefits.[17] The four sectors are (1) supplier dominated, (2) scale intensive, (3) specialized suppliers and (4) science based. The important features of these sectors and their constituent industries are briefly explained below.[18]

In the supplier-dominated sector, innovations are mainly process innovations through the use of improved capital equipment and intermediate inputs. Thus, in this sector, the process of innovation is primarily a process of diffusion of best-practice capital goods and innovative intermediate inputs, and R&D expenditure is limited due to the lack of endogenously generated opportunities.

The industries belonging to this sector include textiles, leather, wood and furniture, paper and printing. In the specialized suppliers sector, innovation activities relate primarily to product innovation which enters other sectors as capital inputs. Firms in this sector usually operate in close contact with their users and embody specialized and partly tacit knowledge in design and equipment building. Opportunities for innovation are generally abundant, but they are often exploited through 'informal' activities of design improvement, and formal R&D is often rather low. Idiosyncratic and cumulative skills make for a relatively high appropriability of innovation. This sector includes industries manufacturing machinery, instruments and optical goods. In the scale-intensive sector, innovation consists of both process and product innovation, and firms often devote a relatively high proportion of resources to innovation. Firms usually have well-equipped production and process engineering departments, and they form an important source of process technology. Firms maintain their technological lead through know-how secrecy around process innovation and through the inevitable technical lags in imitation as well as through patent protection. The scale-intensive sector include industries such as food, beverages and tobacco; oil, rubber and plastics; building materials; earthenware and glass; metal and metal products and transport equipment. In the science-based sector, innovation is directly linked to new technological paradigms made possible by advancements in the underlying science. Technological opportunities are higher, and innovation activities are formalized in R&D laboratories. Firms appropriate their innovation leads through a mix of methods, i.e. patents, secrecy, natural technical lags and firm-specific skills (Pavitt 1984; Dosi 1988). This sector includes chemicals and electrical and electronic goods.

RESULTS

The dependent variable in regression model (1) takes value zero for the majority of observations, and therefore its estimation using OLS methodology is not appropriate, as it leads to biased estimates (Amemiya 1984). Instead I use pooled tobit regressions for estimation, as discussed in Wooldridge (2002).[19] The estimated coefficients of the tobit regression are not the marginal effects of the explanatory variables as in the case of linear OLS regression. Hence, the marginal effects of explanatory variables are also estimated. The marginal effect of an explanatory variable gives change in the independent variable due to a small change in the explanatory variable. Further, it is important to base inference on marginal effects, as the sign and statistical significance of a variable having an interaction with another variable can differ from those of the corresponding coefficient, and they may also change from one observation

Table 6.1   Summary Measures of Variables

	Supplier dominated	Scale intensive	Specialized suppliers	Science based
RDINS	0.0007	0.0014	0.0034	0.0044
	(0.008)	(0.009)	(0.008)	(0.018)
IPR	0.0736	0.0909	0.3582	0.2249
	(0.143)	(0.131)	(0.158)	(0.239)
MCON	0.0950	0.1172	0.1932	0.0571
	(0.146)	(0.087)	(0.175)	(0.044)
SIZE	67.19	246.38	138.23	111.91
	(134.40)	(2044.35)	(462.78)	(258.28)
EXPOIN	0.223	0.0796	0.0835	0.1055
	(0.319)	(0.181)	(0.168)	(0.199)
TECHIN	0.0007	0.0015	0.0033	0.002
	(0.006)	(0.011)	(0.011)	(0.012)
CGOOD	0.0330	0.0176	0.014	0.0164
	(0.133)	(0.094)	(0.059)	(0.090)
ADVTIN	0.0045	0.0053	0.0078	0.0069
	(0.016)	(0.018)	(0.020)	(0.021)
ROP	–0.0656	–0.0370	–0.0095	–0.0185
	(0.382)	(0.322)	(0.309)	(0.305)
VAS	0.3097	0.2920	0.3974	0.3094
	(0.332)	(0.329)	(0.397)	(0.2856)
AGE	21.81	22.46	23.39	20.876
	(22.60)	(18.84)	(17.80)	(17.86)
Number of observations having R&D investment	390	1386	310	1706
Number of observations having foreign equity participation	311	1045	293	1005
Number of observations	2914	6407	903	4927

Note: All values except those in last three rows are mean over observations. Standard deviations are reported in parenthesis.

to another. The method of estimating the marginal effects and their standard errors is detailed in the appendix to this chapter.

Tables 6.2 and 6.3 respectively present the estimated tobit coefficients and the marginal effects of model (1) for the four sectors. The row LLF in Table 6.2 reports maximized value of the log likelihood function. LR Test reports the results of the likelihood ratio test of the null hypothesis that all the slope coefficients are equal to zero; that is, rejected in every case. Table 6.3 shows that the marginal effect of the size variable is significant and positive in all of the sectors. This implies that large firms have greater incentive to invest in R&D. Advertisement intensity has significant positive effect in every sector except specialized suppliers. This result may suggest a complementary relationship between R&D and advertisement. It may help firms to enhance their product market and thereby increasing the rate of return on innovation.

Rate of profit (ROF) has significant positive effect in two sectors, where investment in in-house R&D is important for technological progress, namely the scale-intensive and science-based sectors. The value-added share in output, a proxy for the extent of vertical integration at the firm level, is significant in all except the scale-intensive sector. However, in the specialized-supplier sector, it has a negative effect. Firm age, a proxy for its accumulated experience, has significant positive effect in all sectors. This result may indicate that firms' accumulated knowledge through production experience increases R&D productivity and thereby enhances the incentive to invest in R&D. The foreign equity participation dummy (D_FEP) is positive and significant in all but the supplier-dominated sector. One of the possible reasons for this positive effect is that multinational firms set up R&D centers in India in order to take advantage of the low-cost R&D personnel pool. The intersectoral variation in the effect of foreign-equity participation may be related to the importance of R&D in these sectors. For instance, in the supplier-dominated sector investment in R&D may not be as important to bring about technological progress as it is in the science-based sector.

The average marginal effect of market concentration is not significant in any of the sectors (see Table 6.3). Here, I also look at the distribution of the marginal effects and the test statistic, as the sign and statistical significance of the marginal effect can vary across observations; therefore, an average is not a good representative of their effect. Table 6.4 presents the distribution of marginal effects and t values of MCON, IPR and IPR*MCON. It shows that in supplier-dominated and science-based sectors, 69 and 66 per cent of the marginal effects, respectively, are negative and significant, indicating that in these two sectors, market concentration in general has a negative impact on R&D investment. This may suggest that in these two sectors, the negative

Table 6.2   Estimated Coefficients of Tobit Regression

	Supplier dominated	Scale intensive	Specialized suppliers	Science based
Constant	−0.041*	−0.034*	−0.006	−0.029*
	(−16.96)	(−19.30)	(−1.13)	(−5.07)
IPR	−0.034*	0.001	−0.021	−0.028*
	(−2.80)	(0.07)	(−1.92)	(−5.45)
MCON	−0.044*	0.008	−0.033*	−0.087*
	(−3.60)	(0.94)	(−1.98)	(−5.45)
IPR*MCON	0.214*	0.018	0.090*	0.248*
	(4.97)	(0.29)	(2.14)	(3.81)
SIZE	0.00003*	7.36e-07*	4.92e-06*	0.00001*
	(7.70)	(4.97)	(3.52)	(5.09)
EXPOIN	0.009*	0.005*	0.003	0.026*
	(3.39)	(2.23)	(0.53)	(8.64)
TECHIN	0.354*	0.062*	0.058	0.069
	(3.57)	(1.73)	(0.84)	(1.57)
CGOOD	0.011*	0.002	−0.031	−0.007
	(2.20)	(0.50)	(−1.59)	(−0.88)
ADVTIN	0.130*	0.067*	0.073*	0.134*
	(2.35)	(3.57)	(1.97)	(5.16)
ROP	0.001	0.005*	0.006	0.009*
	(0.39)	(2.97)	(1.69)	(3.59)
VAS	0.005*	−0.002	−0.009*	0.005*
	(2.55)	(−1.07)	(−2.74)	(2.13)
AGE	0.0001*	0.0003*	0.0003*	0.0003*
	(4.09)	(13.31)	(6.11)	(9.47)
D_FEP	0.002	0.009*	0.007*	0.013*
	(0.93)	(9.02)	(4.48)	(8.62)
LLF	371.53	1850.41	570.22	2037.32
LR test	5352*	9781*	788*	6313*
N	2914	6407	903	4927

Notes:
1. t-values are given in parentheses. For LR test Chi-square values are reported.
2. All regressions include industry dummies at two digit level of NIC 1998.
* Indicates significant at 5 per cent level.

Table 6.3   Estimated Marginal Effects of Tobit Regression

	Supplier dominated	Scale intensive	Specialized suppliers	Science based
IPR	−0.001	0.0005	−0.001	−0.004*
	(−0.95)	(0.47)	(−0.41)	(−3.21)
MCON	−0.002	0.002	−0.0003	−0.011
	(−1.55)	(1.08)	(−0.12)	(−1.83)
IPR*MCON	0.029*	0.004	0.027*	0.074*
	(2.93)	(0.32)	(1.96)	(3.92)
SIZE	3.70e-06*	1.29e-07*	1.54e-06*	3.06e-06*
	(5.35)	(4.91)	(2.84)	(4.58)
EXPOIN	0.001*	0.0009*	0.001	0.007*
	(2.88)	(2.17)	(0.52)	(7.44)
TECHIN	0.038*	0.011	0.018	0.019
	(2.94)	(1.70)	(0.83)	(1.56)
CGOOD	0.001*	0.0004	−0.009	−0.002
	(2.02)	(0.50)	(−1.53)	(−0.88)
ADVTIN	0.014*	0.012*	0.23	0.038*
	(2.15)	(3.34)	(1.88)	(4.87)
ROP	0.0001	0.0009*	0.002	0.003*
	(0.57)	(2.84)	(1.62)	(3.47)
VAS	0.0006*	−0.0003	−0.003*	0.001*
	(2.30)	(−1.07)	(−2.49)	(2.11)
AGE	0.00001*	0.00005*	0.0001*	0.0001*
	(3.31)	(8.41)	(4.45)	(8.15)
D_FEP	0.0002	0.002*	0.002*	0.004*
	(0.91)	(6.71)	(3.67)	(7.46)

Notes:
t-values are given in parentheses.
*Indicates significant at 5 per cent level.

effect of market concentration outweighs its positive effect through better appropriability conditions.

Export intensity has a significant positive effect on R&D investment in all the sectors, except specialized suppliers. This result, as argued in the theoretical literature, suggests that export-promotion policies encourage innovation and technological progress. Disembodied technology import intensity (TECHIN) and capital good import intensity (CGOOD) promote R&D investment only in

Table 6.4   *Distribution of Marginal Effects and Test Statistics*
               (as percentage of total observations in each sector)

Supplier dominated

Variable	Marginal effect		Test statistic	
	% of ME<0	% of ME>0	% of t<−1.96	% of t>1.96
IPR	83.63	16.37	60.22	10.50
MCON	87.13	12.87	68.84	2.30
IPR*MCON	3.67	96.33	0.00	83.77

Scale intensive

Variable	Marginal effect		Test statistic	
	% of ME<0	% of ME>0	% of t<−1.96	% of t>1.96
IPR	0.00	100.00	0.00	0.00
MCON	0.00	100.00	0.00	0.00
IPR*MCON	0.00	100.00	0.00	0.00

Specialized suppliers

Variable	Marginal effect		Test statistic	
	% of ME<0	% of ME<0	% of t<−1.96	% of t>1.96
IPR	78.63	21.37	0.00	4.98
MCON	52.16	47.84	4.54	0.55
IPR*MCON	0.44	99.56	0.00	61.35

Science based

Variable	Marginal effect		Test statistic	
	% of ME<0	% of ME<0	% of t<−1.96	% of t<1.96
IPR	84.96	15.04	77.69	2.44
MCON	78.16	21.83	65.90	1.73
IPR*MCON	0.00	100.00	0.00	98.32

supplier-dominated industries. The confinement of the R&D promoting effect of technology imports to supplier-dominated industries may be due to the lower technological and engineering capability of firms in this sector, so they must invest in R&D to absorb imported technology.

Table 6.3 shows that the average marginal effect of import competition on R&D investment is negative and significant only in the science-based sector. However, the distribution of its marginal effects, presented in Table 6.4, shows that in supplier-dominated and science-based sectors 60 and 78 per cent, respectively, are negative and significant.

Figure 6.1   Supplier Dominated

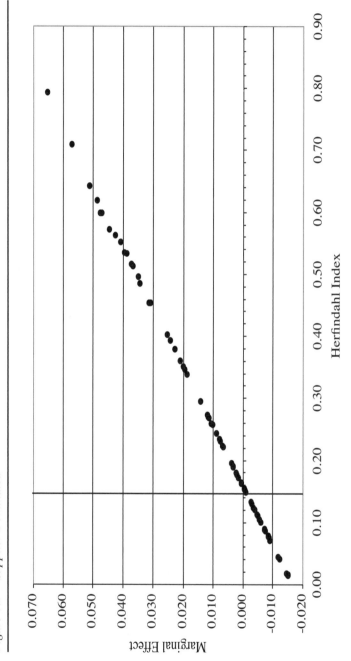

Figure 6.2   Specialized Suppliers

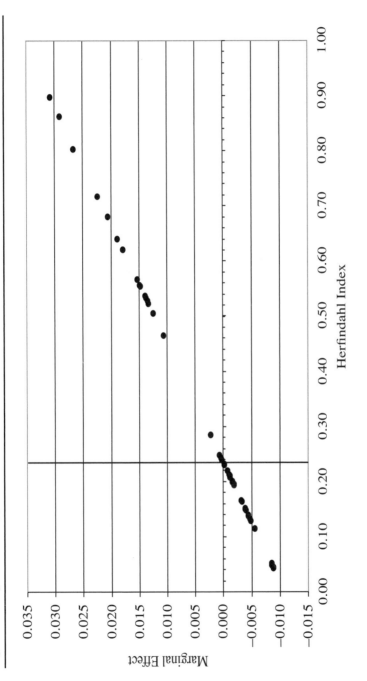

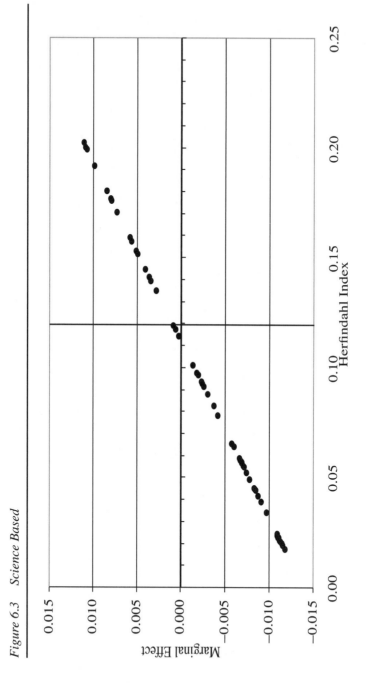

Figure 6.3   Science Based

One hypothesis of this study concerns the role of domestic market structure in shaping the impact of import competition. An interaction variable between IPR and MCON is included to test this hypothesis. Its average marginal effect is positive and significant in all sectors except the scale-intensive sector. The distribution shows that in the supplier-dominated sector 83.77 per cent of the cases are positive and significant and the corresponding figures for specialized suppliers and science-based sectors are 61.35 and 98.32 per cent, respectively. This result suggests that the effect of import competition depends on the domestic market structure. Import liberalization encourages investment in R&D in industries having greater market concentration.

The variation in the marginal effect of import competition with the level of market concentration in the three sectors where the interaction variable is significant is presented in Figures 6.1, 6.2 and 6.3. These marginal effects are computed by keeping all variables except IPR and MCON at their mean values. The figures show that at a lower level of concentration, more precisely for the Herfindahl Index below the vertical line, the marginal effect of import competition is negative.

The results show that the impact of import competition on R&D investment is shaped by the domestic market structure. Import competition encourages investment in R&D if the domestic market structure is highly concentrated. If the domestic market structure is already less concentrated, import competition has a negative effect on R&D investment. In a situation of greater market concentration, import competition may reduce the market power of firms, leaving them without any option other than making investment in productivity-enhancing activities like R&D. On the other hand, in industries which already have a competitive market structure, import competition may be further intensifying competitive pressure and thereby reducing the incentive of the firm to invest in R&D. The result seems to support the theoretical argument that both too much and too little competition are not conducive to innovation and technological progress. When there is too little competition in domestic industry, liberal import policies can be used to discipline the firms and thereby induce them to make productivity-enhancing investments.

CONCLUSION

The relationship between trade policy and technological progress is highly debated, both in the academic literature and in policy forums. The conventional wisdom holds that the impact of trade liberalization is contingent on many economic-, industry- and firm-specific factors. However, there are not many studies focusing on this aspect of trade liberalization. In this context the present study examined the impact of trade liberalization on firm investment in R&D and the role of domestic market structure in this process.

This chapter shows that exporting firms have greater incentive to invest in R&D. This implies that trade liberalization and the subsequent removal of any anti-export bias in the system can encourage innovation and technological progress within the given industry. Another important result is that the impact of import competition depends on the domestic market structure. Import competition promotes investment in R&D only in those industries where the market structure is highly concentrated. Import competition has a negative impact on R&D investment in industries having a less concentrated market structure. This result suggests that only the firms operating in highly concentrated market structures will have greater incentive to invest in R&D when they are subjected to international competition. One important policy implication of this result is that if the objective of the trade policy reform is to improve the innovation and technological progress of the domestic industry, then it needs to be accompanied with complementary policies to generate conducive domestic conditions. In the present context, the variation in the impact of import competition according to the domestic market structure implies the need for complementary industrial policy which helps firms to achieve a scale of operation which makes it possible to undertake various productivity-enhancing investment. So it should remove any legal barriers to entry and exit, restrictions on the scale of operation, mergers and amalgamation.[20] This will make sure that the industry can easily adjust itself to the pressures of import competition by upgrading their technological standards. Thus, trade policy must be aligned with suitable industrial policy.

NOTES

1. Trade liberalization can also affect R&D by changing the relative price of factors employed in research sector. The present study, however, does not consider this channel.
2. Since R&D investment is a fixed cost and its output, knowledge, is a non-rival commodity, the rate of return from research depends positively upon the scale of output across which the firm can spread the R&D cost.
3. Aghion (2003) extends the model to the case of three firms.
4. In these models, innovation effort is at its maximum when there is intense competition among a few firms having similar levels of productivity (neck-and-neck firms). In these situations, firms try to escape competition by innovating.
5. In this context, Kumar (1987) highlights the mode of technology import and Subrahmanian (1991) emphasizes the policy environment as factors determining the relationship between technology imports and in-house R&D efforts.
6. The World Bank Trade and Production database merges data on trade, production and tariffs available from different sources into a common classification: the International Standard Industrial Classification (ISIC) revision 2. More details on this database can be seen in Nicita and Olarreaga (2001).

7. In the 59 industry groups, a few are formed by aggregating two or three four-digit industries into one group and the rest are the four-digit industries of NIC 1998.
8. As the output figures are taken from ASI, that covers only the registered manufacturing sector, the denominator of this ratio provides only an approximate measure of domestic demand. Data on unregistered manufacturing output at this level of disaggregation are not available for the period of analysis.
9. For a review see Kumar and Siddharthan (1997) Chapter 5.
10. Domestic concentration is considered to be a good indicator of the extent of concentration and market power, if the industry in question is involved in export. If exports constitute a larger portion of sales, a concentration index based on firms' total sales is a misleading indicator of their actual market power, because sales in the foreign market and sales in the domestic market must be distinguished, since the corresponding relevant markets are distinct. Producers are usually price takers in foreign markets. Hence, for that part of the production which is exported, they are in a competitive market facing an elastic demand. So export value must be subtracted from the total sales to assess the market power of the producers in the domestic market (Jacquemin, de Ghellinck and Huveneers 1980).
11. Several alternative measures of concentration are available. For reviews of these measures see Hart (1975) and Chakravarty (1995).
12. For a review of the theoretical and empirical literature on firm size and innovation effort see Chapter 4 of Kumar and Siddharthan (1997).
13. Earlier studies using sales to proxy firms' size include Katrak (1997) and Basant (1997).
14. Current investment in R&D affects firms' future profitability, as successful innovation improves productivity and leads to higher profit. It is usually assumed that R&D investment takes time to produce results in terms of invention and innovation. Only at the stage of innovation does R&D shows up in profitability.
15. It is also argued that value-added-to-sales ratio tends to be higher in consumer goods industries. Firms in these industries are also more likely to invest in R&D because of the better appropriability and differentiability conditions (Kumar and Saqib 1996). As I use industry specific dummies to control for the industry characteristics, I expect that VAS would capture its intended meaning.
16. For example, see Greenhalgh and Rogers (2006) and Vossan (1998).
17. Pavitt's taxonomy has been recently updated by Tidd, Bessant and Pavitt (2001) by adding an 'information-intensive sector' which include firms in finance, retail and publishing. For a review of various taxonomies of patterns of innovation see de Jong and Marsili (2006).
18. My division of industries into various sectors is very similar to Vossan (1998).
19. Another method to estimate tobit regression using panel data is the random effect tobit model, that assumes strict exogeneity of regressors, while pooled tobit does not (see Wooldridge 2002). In the model used here some of the regressors are not strictly exogenous as the current year R&D affects future export and profit.
20. In India prior to the reform in 1991 restrictions were placed on capacity expansion, mergers, etc. in order to limit monopoly trade practices.

BIBLIOGRAPHY

Aghion, Philippe (2003), 'Empirical Estimates of the Relationship Between Product Market Competition and Innovation', in Jean-Philippe Touffut (ed.), *Institutions, Innovations and Growth: Selected Economic Papers*, Cheltenham, UK and Brookfield, VT: Edward Elgar, pp. 142–69.

Aghion, Philippe, Christopher Harris, Peter Howitt and John Vickers (2001), 'Competition, Imitation and Growth with Step-by-Step Innovation', *Review of Economic Studies*, **68** (3), 467–92.

Ahluwalia, Isher Judge (1996), 'India's Opening Up to Trade and Investment', in Isher Judge Ahluwalia, Rakesh Mohan and Okmar Goswami (eds), *Policy Reform in India*, Paris: OECD Development Centre, pp. 17–41.

Ai, Chunrong and Edward C. Norton (2003), 'Interaction Terms in Logit and Probit models', *Economics Letters*, **80** (1), 123–29.

Amemiya, Takeshi (1984), 'Tobit Models: A Survey', *Journal of Econometrics*, **24** (1–2), 3–61.

Arrow, Kenneth J. (1962), 'Economic welfare and allocation of resources for innovation', in Richard R. Nelson (ed.), *The Rate and Direction of Inventive Activity*, Princeton University Press for NBER, Princeton.

Basant, Rakesh (1997), 'Technology strategies of large enterprises in Indian industry: Some Explorations', *World Development*, **25** (10), 1683–1700.

Bell, Martin and Keith Pavitt (1997), 'Technological Accumulation and Industrial Growth: Contrasts between Developed and Developing Countries', in Danele Archibugi and Jonathan Michie (eds), *Technology, Globalisation and Economic Performance*, New York: Cambridge University Press, pp. 83–137.

Chakravarty, Sathya R. (1995), *Issues in Industrial Economics*, Brookfield, VT: Avebury.

Cohen, Wesley M. and Daniel A. Levinthal (1989), 'Innovation and Learning: The two faces of R&D', *Economic Journal*, **99** (397), 569–96.

Dahlman, Carl J., B. Ross Larsson and Larry E. Westphal (1987), 'Managing Technological Development: Lessons from the Newly Industrializing Countries', *World Development*, **15** (6), 759–75.

De Jong, Jeroen and Orietta Marsili (2006), 'The Fruit Flies of Innovations: A taxonomy of Innovative Small Firms', *Research Policy*, **35** (2), 213–29.

Dosi, Giovanni (1988), 'Sources, Procedures and Microeconomic Effects of Innovation', *Journal of Economic Literature*, **26** (3), 1120–71.

Edwards, Sebastian (1993), 'Openness, Trade Liberalization and Growth in Developing Countries', *Journal of Economic Literature*, **31** (3), 1358–93.

Evenson, Robert E. and Larry E. Westphal (1995), 'Technological Change and Technology Strategy', in Jere Behrman and T.N. Srinivasan (eds), *Handbook of Development Economics*, Volume 3a, Amsterdam: Elsevier, chapter 37.

Greene, William H. (2000), *Econometric Analysis*, 4th ed., Upper Saddle River, NJ: Prentice Hall.

Greenhalgh, Christine and Mark Rogers (2006), 'The Value of Innovation: The Interaction of Competition, R&D and IP', *Research Policy*, **35** (4), 562–80.

Hallack, Juan Carlos and James Levinsohn (2004), 'Fooling Ourselves: Evaluating the Globalization and Growth Debate', Cambridge, MA, National Bureau of Economic Research (NBER) Working Paper No. 10244.

Hart, P.E. (1975), 'Moment Distributions in Economics: An Exposition', *Journal of Royal Statistical Society – Series A*, **138** (3), 423–34.

Hughes, Kirsty (1986), *Exports and Technology*, New York: Cambridge University Press.

Jacquemin, Alexis, Elisabeth de Ghellinck and Christian Huveneers (1980), 'Concentration and Profitability in a Small Open Economy', *Journal of Industrial Economics*, **29** (2) 131–44.

Katrak, Homi (1997), 'Developing Countries' Imports of Technology, In-house Technological Capabilities and Efforts: An Analysis of the Indian Experience', *Journal of Development Economics*, **53** (1), 67–83.

Kumar, Nagesh (1987), 'Technology Imports and Local Research and Development in Indian Manufacturing', *The Developing Economies*, **25** (3), 220–33.

Kumar, Nagesh and Mohammed Saqib (1996), 'Firm Size, Opportunities for Adaptation and In-house R&D Activity in Developing Countries: The Case of Indian Manufacturing', *Research Policy*, **25** (5), 713–22.

Kumar, Nagesh and N.S. Siddharthan (1997), *Technology, Market Structure and Internationalization: Issues and Policies for Developing Countries*, New York: Routledge.

Mani, Sunil (1995), 'Technology Import and Skill Development in a Microelectronics Based Industry: The Case of India's Electronic Switching Systems', in Amiya Kumar Bagchi (ed.), *New Technology and the Worker's Response*, Sage Publication, New Delhi, pp. 98–122.

Nicita, Alessandro and Marcelo Olarreaga (2001), 'Trade and Production, 1976–1999', Washington, DC, World Bank Working Paper No. 2071.

Pack, Howard (1982), 'Aggregate Implications of Factor Substitution in Industrial Process', *Journal of Development Economics*, **11** (1), 1–37.

Pamukcu, Teoman (2003), 'Trade Liberalization and Innovation Decisions of Firms: Lessons from Post-1980 Turkey', *World Development*, **31** (8), 1443–58.

Pavitt, Keith (1984), 'Sectoral Patterns of Technical Change: Towards a Taxonomy and a Theory', *Research Policy*, **13** (6), 343–73.

Pillai, P. Mohanan (1979), 'Technology Transfer, Adaptation and Assimilation', *Economic and Political Weekly*, **14** (47), M121–M126.

Rodriguez, Francisco and Dani Rodrik (2000), 'Trade Policy and Economic Growth: A Skeptic's Guide to the Cross-national Evidence', in Ben S. Bernanke and Kenneth Rogoff (eds), *NBER Macroeconomics Annual 2000*, Cambridge: MA: MIT Press, pp. 261–234.

Rodrik, Dani (1992), 'Closing the Productivity Gap: Does Trade Liberalization Really Help?', in Gerald K. Helleiner (ed.), *Trade Policy, Industrialization and Development: New Perspectives*, New York: Oxford University Press, pp.155–75.

Smulders, Sjak and Theo van de Klundert (1995), 'Imperfect Competition, Concentration and Growth with Firm-specific R&D', *European Economic Review*, **39** (1), 139–60.

Srinivasan, T.N. and S.D. Tendulkar (2003), *Reintegrating India with the World Economy*, New York: Oxford University Press.

Subrahmanian, K.K. (1991), 'Technological Capability under Economic Liberalism: Experience of Indian Industry in Eighties', *Economic and Political Weekly*, **26** (31 August), M87–M89.

Tidd, Joe, John Bessant, Keith Pavitt (2001), *Managing Innovation*, Chichester, England: John Wiley and Sons.

Vossan, Robert. W. (1998), *R&D, Firm Size and Branch of Industry: Policy Implications*, Gronningen, Germany, University of Gronningen, SOM Research Institute Working Paper No. 98B43.

Wooldridge, Jeffrey (2002), *Econometric Analysis of Cross Section and Panel Data*, Cambridge, MA: MIT Press.

APPENDIX 6.1   COMPUTATION OF MARGINAL EFFECT IN TOBIT REGRESSION

Marginal effects (ME) of variables, except that of IPR, MCON, and IPR*MCON, are estimated as follows,[1]

$$\text{ME of } k^{th} \text{ variable} = F\left(\frac{\hat{\beta}'X}{\hat{\sigma}}\right)\hat{\beta}_k$$

Where $\hat{\beta}$ is the vector of estimated coefficients of tobit regression, β_k is the coefficient of kth explanatory variable, $\hat{\sigma}$ is the standard deviation of the random error term and $F(.)$ is the cumulative normal distribution function.

Marginal effects of IPR, MCON and the interaction between the two in model (1) are:

$$\text{ME of IPR} = F\left(\frac{\hat{\beta}'X}{\hat{\sigma}}\right)(\hat{\beta}_6 + \hat{\beta}_{10}MCON)$$

$$\text{ME of MCON} = F\left(\frac{\hat{\beta}'X}{\hat{\sigma}}\right)(\hat{\beta}_7 + \hat{\beta}_{10}IPR)$$

ME of IPR*MCON =

$$F\left(\frac{\hat{\beta}'X}{\hat{\sigma}}\right)\hat{\beta}_{10} + \frac{1}{\hat{\sigma}}\left[f\left(\frac{\hat{\beta}'X}{\hat{\sigma}}\right)(\hat{\beta}_6 + \hat{\beta}_{10}MCON)(\hat{\beta}_7 + \hat{\beta}_{10}IPR)\right]$$

Marginal effects and their standard errors are estimated for each observation and averages are reported.[2] The standard errors of the marginal effects are estimated using delta method[3] (see Ai and Norton 2003).

Notes:
1. See Greene (2000, 910).
2. One can compute marginal effects by evaluating the expression at the sample means or at every observation and use sample average of the individual marginal effects. Since the functions are continuous, the theorem of Convergence in Quadratic Means (the Slutsky theorem) applies and in large samples both approaches give same result. But in small or in moderate sized samples this is not applicable. Current practice favours averaging the individual marginal effects when it is possible to do so (Greene 2000, 816).
3. For delta method of computing standard errors of non-linear combination of parameters, see Greene (2000, 357–58).

7. Public–Private Partnership in the Provision of Health Care Services to the Poor in India

A. Venkat Raman and James Warner Björkman

Throughout the world, public–private partnerships have emerged as a promising model for health-sector reform. Change is needed partly due to resource constraints in the public sector (Mitchell-Weaver and Manning 1992) and partly due to a widespread belief that the public sector is endemically inefficient and unresponsive, while market mechanisms ensure good quality, cost-effective services (World Health Organization 2001; Bloom, Craig and Mitchell 2000). There is also a growing realization that, given their respective strengths and weaknesses, neither the public sector nor the private sector alone serves the best interests of the health system. Both the public and private health-care sectors can potentially gain from one another (Wang 2000). However, a partnership with the private sector will require the public sector to reorient its role in financing as well as delivering services.

In the Indian context, collaboration with the private sector to provide health services to poor and underserved sections of the population is critical, because approximately 29 per cent of India's population (almost 300 million people) live below the poverty line and depend on free public health services. But despite its extensive network of health centers and hospitals, India's public health-care system is unable to deliver health-care services at desirable levels of quality and efficiency due to inherent deficiencies in the system. Consequently, India's poor are forced to seek services from the private sector, often borrowing money or selling land, cattle and even children to pay for the services.

India has one of the world's highest levels of private, out-of-pocket health care financing; estimates range from 87 per cent (World Bank 2001) to 85 per cent (Kulkarni 2003). This mode of financing has debilitating effects on the poor. Over two-fifths of hospital patients must borrow money or sell assets to cover expenses, while one-third of hospitalized Indians fall below the poverty line because of hospital expenses. In any given year, out-of-pocket medical costs push more than two per cent of the population below the poverty line (Selvaraju and Annigeri 2001; Mahal et al. 2002).

Inequities in the health system are aggravated by the fact that public spending on health has stagnated at around one per cent of GDP (0.9 per cent), compared with a global average of 5.5 per cent. Even public health subsidies do not benefit the poor. The poorest quintile of the population uses only 10 per cent of subsidies, while the richest quintile receives over one-third of the benefits (Mahal et al. 2002).

The private health sector in India has grown rapidly for several reasons. First budgetary constraints have reduced services at public health facilities. Second, government subsidies and tax incentives have encouraged private investors to set up specialty facilities. Third, demand from middle-income groups is growing. Finally, India has a liberal regulatory environment (Baru 1998). Estimates indicate that at independence in 1947 India's private sector controlled only 8 per cent of the country's health care facilities (World Bank 2004). Today it accounts for 93 per cent of all hospitals, 64 per cent of patient beds, 80–85 per cent of doctors, 80 per cent of outpatients and 57 per cent of inpatients (World Bank 2001). In financial terms, the private sector market is estimated at around 710 billion rupees ($17.7 billion); by 2012, it will be over 1.5 trillion rupees ($37.5 billion), excluding the health insurance market (CII-McKinsey 2004). Commensurate expansion is expected in the number of private-sector health-provider facilities. Contrary to commonly held views, the primarily owner-operated private sector is relatively less urban-biased than public hospitals. Apart from providing clinical services, the private sector dominates all health submarkets, such as medical education and training, manufacturing medical technology and diagnostic instruments, and pharmaceuticals. The pervasiveness of the private sector offers both opportunities and challenges for the government.

Analysts have expressed serious concerns about the behavior of India's private health sector and its consequences. However, although the private health sector is among the most unregulated industries in India, it possesses great potential. While expensive, overly indulgent in clinical procedures and without quality standards or public disclosure of practices, the private sector is perceived to be more easily accessible, better managed and more efficient than its public counterpart. Advocates assume that collaboration with the private sector in the form of public–private partnership would improve the equity (by moderating economic impacts on the poor), accessibility, efficiency, accountability and quality of the entire health system. Furthermore, the public and private health-care sectors can benefit from shared resources, technology, knowledge and skills, cost-efficiency and even public image (Wang 2000).

Since the private sector is grossly underutilized due to its unplanned but rapid growth, such partnerships may actually benefit the private sector.

Several extensive studies of India's health care sector advocate harnessing the private sector's potential and countering its failures (India, Government of 2001, 2002, 2005b). Simultaneously, organizational and institutional reforms could help the public sector to improve its efficiency and adopt best practices from the private sector. Several state governments in India have been exploring the option of involving and creating partnerships with the private sector in order to meet the growing health care needs of the population.

PUBLIC VERSUS PRIVATE

The terms 'public' and 'private' can be defined in many ways (Wang 2000). Generally the public sector includes organizations and institutions which function under government budgets which are financed by state revenue and under state control. The private sector is less easy to characterize. It comprises individuals and organizations working outside direct control of the state (Bennett 1991). Broadly, the private sector includes all non-state actors, some explicitly seeking profits (for profit) and others operating on a non-profit or not-for-profit basis. The former are conventionally called private enterprise; the latter are labeled as non-governmental organizations (NGOs).

In the health sector, for-profit providers span individual doctors, diagnostic centers, ambulance operators, pathology labs, pharmacy shops, blood banks, commercial contractors, polyclinics, nursing homes and hospitals of various capacities. They also include community service extensions of industrial establishments, cooperative societies, community-based organizations, religious and philanthropic trusts, professional associations, self-help groups, citizen forums and other types of non-state organizations. The not-for-profit sector is likewise heterogeneous but significantly smaller in proportion. Apart from the motive, characteristics of the private sector also vary on the basis of geographical location, ownership and financing, systems of medicine and the scope of clinical services provided.

Partnerships

Defining the concept 'partnership' is difficult. Many definitions are either rhetorical or ambiguous and cover virtually any type of interaction between public and private actors. Yet the term usefully characterizes a range of inter-organizational relationships and collaborations. Some of the more common definitions of public–private partnership in the context of the health sector are:

- 'a means to bring together a set of actors for the common goal of improving the health of a population based on the mutually agreed roles and principles' (WHO 1999);
- 'a useful way of engaging a wide range of stakeholders and non-government organizations in achieving the complex set of development objectives in health' (Wang 2001);
- 'a dynamic relationship among diverse actors, based on mutually agreed objectives, pursued through a shared understanding of the most rational division of labor based on the competitive advantage of each partner' (Brinkerhoff 2002);
- 'a variety of co-operative arrangements between the government and private sector ... in delivering public goods or services ... provides a vehicle for coordinating with non-governmental actor[s] to undertake integrated, comprehensive efforts to meet community needs ... to take advantage of the expertise of each partner, so that resources, risks and rewards can be allocated in a way that best meets clearly defined public needs' (Axelsson, Bustreo and Harding 2003);
- 'a partnership means that both parties have agreed to work together in implementing a program, and that each party has a clear role and say in how that implementation happens' (Blagescu and Young 2005) and
- a 'form of agreement [which] entails reciprocal obligations and mutual accountability, voluntary or contractual relationships, the sharing of investment and reputational risks, and joint responsibility for design and execution' (World Economic Forum 2005).

Three themes emerge from these definitions: a sense of relative equality between the partners, a mutual commitment to agreed objectives and mutual benefits to the stakeholders involved. Partnerships are neither classical market-driven contractual transactions nor authority-based bureaucratic relationships. Rather, 'partnership' involves collaboration based on trust and a sense of equality. It is a collaborative effort and a reciprocal relationship between two or more parties with clear terms and conditions, clearly defined partnership structures and specified performance indicators to deliver a set of health services in a stipulated time period. A partnership entails beneficence (joint gains), autonomy (of each partner), joint-ness (shared decision-making and accountability), commitment (to public health goals) and equity (fair returns in proportion to investment and effort).

Challenges to Partnerships

Although the public–private partnership may be a judicious strategy, complexities arise in its design and implementation. While the health system as a whole has common objectives of equity, efficiency, quality and accessibility, the meaning of these objectives may be interpreted differently by public and private providers. The government seeks to provide health services to all at minimum – or no – cost and to develop policies and programs which ensure equity in access to such services. In contrast, the private for-profit sector focuses on cost-effectiveness and flexibility in the deployment of resources and services based on the capacity of patients to pay; equity and public good are not the main objectives.

The private for-profit sector can face image problems due to its perceived motives. Opinions range from outright distrust to strong support for closer cooperation. Those who oppose private-sector partnerships argue that the private for-profit sector is motivated only by money and has no concern for equity or access. There is a fear that any partnership with the private sector is an indirect attempt to privatize the public health system. Private, for-profit health services are often associated with the use of illegitimate or unethical means to maximize profit, a lack of concern about public health goals, a lack of interest in sharing clinical information, draining the public sector of qualified staff, a lack of regulatory control over practices and the 'commodification' of health services (Roemer 1984; Bennett et al. 1994; Rosenthal 2000).

However, Bloom, Craig and Mitchell (2000) suggest that the private sector is neither easy to characterize nor easy to neglect. Its strength is its innovation, efficiency and ability to learn from competition. Management standards are generally higher in the private sector. In addition, the private sector can play an important role in expanding coverage as well as transferring some of its resources, management skills and best practices to the public sector. In India, the for-profit sector is not only more diverse but also accounts for the largest proportion of services and resources in the health sector. Therefore, any strategy to improve public health should take its strengths into account (World Bank 2004). The private sector also has an incentive to work with the public sector in order to influence government policies on regulations, tax-exemptions, accreditation and tariffs (Wang 2000).

Non-profit organizations have a long history of reaching inaccessible areas and providing health services to the poor and the disadvantaged. However, in many states they account for less than 1 per cent of the health-care sector (India, Government of 2005b; World Bank 2004). They depend on philanthropic donations or external funding for sustenance. As a result, their interventions often remain ad hoc and their widespread dissemination is doubtful. But they

Table 7.1   Partnering with the Private Sector

Sub-sector	Advantages	Disadvantages
Informal	Easy access	Poor quality
	Client-centric	Difficult to mainstream
	Low cost	Poorly educated
Not-for-profit	Better quality	Low coverage
	Focus on the poor	Resource dependency
	Low cost	Problem of scale-up
	Community involvement	Ad hoc interventions
For profit	Efficient deployment of resources	Short-term orientation
		High cost
	High quality (in select disciplines)	Unregulated quality
		Clustered in cities
	Huge outreach/coverage	
	Innovative	

Source: Adapted from World Bank (2004).

have demonstrated an ability to provide good quality care at low cost, and they need little government regulation or oversight. They are also able to attract dedicated staff, willing to take on public health challenges which the for-profit sector is not willing or able to tackle, and they are generally more widely accepted at the community level. Their size and flexibility allow them to achieve notable successes where governments have failed. Given their non-profit motives and grassroots presence, NGOs are usually more acceptable partners than for-profit agents.

India has many indigenous medical practitioners from the Ayurveda, Unani, Sidhha and homeopathic schools who usually are sole practitioners in the private sector. There are also many non-licensed rural medical practitioners (faith healers, bonesetters, midwives, etc.) in the informal private sector. A conservative estimate puts the number of these practitioners at over 1.25 million. The private sector is very diverse in terms of size, composition and scope of service provision. Initiating partnership with such diverse actors is challenging. Table 7.1 lists the merits and drawbacks of partnering with each private-sector subgroup.

Notwithstanding these differences, the public and private sectors constantly interact with each other. The government of India (2005a) presupposes that partnership with the private sector in health care could improve service-delivery mechanisms and increase the mobilization of resources. Other presumed benefits of partnerships are improved service quality, reduced cost of care, due to either negotiated cost control or through economies of scale, reduction in the duplication of services, adoption of best practices, services targeted to the poor, redeployment of public resources to more critical areas and improved self-regulation and accountability.

Characteristics of Partnership

Partnerships are useful when the net benefits exceed those of independent activities and when the joint efforts result in more efficient or more effective services than would independent action (Bazzoli et al. 1997). Partnerships typically work with one side financing the services and the other side delivering the services (Wang 2000). Although partnerships are formed between organizations, they succeed because individuals who are strong leaders champion the partnership projects with vision, commitment and enthusiasm (Paoletto 2000). However, partnerships are no substitute for good governance. In fact, partnerships require strong governmental leadership. Wherever governance is weak, there is an unhealthy tendency to tout private-sector partnerships as a solution rather than improving governance per se.

Wang (2000) suggests several conditions which enable a partnership to be successful:

- Clear understanding among partners about mutual benefits;
- Clear understanding about the responsibilities and obligations of partners;
- Strong community support;
- Some catalyst to start the process of partnership (an individual, a donor, a compelling vision, even a political or economic crisis);
- Stability of the political (government) and legal climate (laws);
- A regulatory framework which is followed and enforced;
- Government capacity and expertise at different levels in designing and managing contracts;
- Appropriate organizational and management systems for partnerships;
- Strong management information systems and
- Clarity regarding incentives and penalties.

But partnerships with the private, for-profit sector face political and legal obstacles. Sometimes collaboration with the private sector is misconstrued as attempts at privatization. In many societies, fears about the private commercial sector emerge from a widely shared image that the private sector is exploitative. There are also differences in work culture and performance standards between the public and private sectors. The bureaucracy may be more willing to partner with the for-profit sector for administrative efficiency, whereas political and popular sentiments prevent overt attempts at collaboration. Although the not-for-profit sector may be easier to engage as partners, there are concerns raised about the difficulties faced by NGOs which work with the government (Mukhopadhyay 2000). Ahmed (2000) questions whether NGOs are truly partners in development or only interested in bidding for government grants like any other commercial contractors. In India concerns have been raised about the dubious nature of some NGOs which are established by political figures to garner funds from the state.

THE STUDY

While there are many experiments with public–private partnerships underway, both in India and in other developing countries, there is little data to indicate the relative merits of one partnership type over another. Evidence is scarce about aspects of partnerships such as the scope and coverage of services; institutional capacities of government agencies to design, implement and monitor partnerships; methods to select private-sector partners; monitoring performance and quality of services; resource implications including incentives; operational constraints and stakeholder perspectives. Because partnering with the private sector requires significant changes in how government departments function, evidence-based ways are needed to develop the capacity of government institutions and systems for this task.

The services covered in our case studies in rural areas and urban slums include clinical care, non-clinical support, stationary establishments and mobile clinics. These span diagnostic services, general curative care, maternal and child health, community-health financing, health promotion and information communication technology (ICT)-based health services. To assess different types of public–private partnerships, we compiled 16 cases in nine of India's 28 states. Cases were selected after a careful review of various partnership models in different states. Contract documents, government orders and other documents were reviewed, while stakeholders, including patients, public officials and private agencies, were interviewed. We also examined operational issues related to the management and functioning of the programs.

Appendix 7.A1 lists the 16 case studies. Partnerships ranged from the provision of tertiary care (Rajiv Gandhi Hospital, Raichur; SMS Hospital, Jaipur) to primary care (Karuna Trust, Karnataka) and maternal and child care in slum communities (Arpana Swasthya Kendra, Delhi; Urban Slum Health, Adilabad, Andhra Pradesh). Two community health insurance initiatives were documented (the Arogya Raksha scheme in Andhra Pradesh and the Yeshasvini scheme in Karnataka). Three different mobile health services were also documented (emergency ambulance service in Tamil Nadu; health camps for diagnostics and general consultation in Uttaranchal; boat-based health services in West Bengal). Other partnership initiatives studied include an integrated telemedicine and tele-health project (Chamarajnagar, Karnataka) and contracts for cleaning, catering and laundry (Baghajatin Hospital, Kolkata). Rogi Kalyan Samiti, a hospital autonomy initiative under local self-government control in the city of Bhopal (Madhya Pradesh) was examined to understand whether the concept fits the public–private partnership framework.

Analyses of the case studies are grouped under two categories: operational issues in managing partnerships and policy perspectives on public–private partnerships. The operational perspective examines the following: types of partnerships and the scope of services, target beneficiaries and partnership objectives, enabling conditions for partnerships, dynamics in selecting private partners and mutual obligations, quality of services and performance monitoring, functional autonomy for the private partner, technical and managerial capacity of the partners and stakeholder perspectives. From the policy perspective, issues related to the benefits and risks of partnership as well as equity and accessibility are reviewed along with resource implications, including user-fee options and payment mechanisms as well as sustainability and scalability of partnerships. The summary highlights policy implications.

OPERATIONAL ISSUES

Types of Partnership and Scope of Services

Although contracting is the predominant model of partnership, our study documented other forms of partnership, such as performance management agreements, technology demonstration pilot projects, voucher schemes, community-based health insurance and hospital autonomy. State governments are experimenting with different models, thereby providing insights for the contextual relevance of one model of partnership over another. Table 7.2 sketches the types of partnership and the scope of services in the 16 case studies.

The private-sector partners ranged from individual entrepreneurs or physicians through commercial contractors and large corporate hospitals to not-for-profit NGOs. Of the 16 cases and 19 partnership agreements, eight private partners were NGOs. Partnerships ranged from simple contract agreements involving individual contractors (catering, cleaning, retail pharmacies) to more complex agreements involving many stakeholders. For example, the

Table 7.2   Partnership Types and Scope of Services

Partnership type	Partnership project (case study)	Scope of services
Contracting in	SMS Hospital, Jaipur	Radiological diagnostics (CT Scan/ MRI)
	Life Line Fluid Store (SMS Hospital)	Drugs and medical supplies store
	Bhaga Jatin Hospital, Kolkata	Catering and kitchen services; cleaning and scavenging services; laundry services
Performance management contracts	Arpana Swasthya Kendra, Delhi	Management of a maternity health centre
	Karuna Trust, Karnataka	Management of Primary Health Centers
	Shamlaji Hospital, Sabarkantha District, Gujarat	Management of Community Health Center
	Rajiv Gandhi hospital, Raichur, Karnataka	Super-specialty clinical care services
Contracting out	Urban Slum Health Care Project, Adilabad, Andhra Pradesh	Maternity and child care and reproductive health services
	Chiranjeevi Yojana, Sabarkantha district, Gujarat	Private obstetricians and gynaecologists to conduct deliveries in their own clinics
	Emergency Ambulance Services, Theni district, Tamil Nadu	Transport for emergency obstetric cases
	Mobile Health Services The Sunderbans, West Bengal	Mobile (boat based) health services
Technology demonstration (collaborative partnership)	Uttaranchal Mobile Hospital and Research Center, Bhimtal	Mobile health vans delivering diagnostic and health care services
	Karnataka Integrated Telemedicine and Telehealth project, Karnataka	Tele consultation and in patient services for cardiac and other specialist care
Community health insurance	Yeshasvini Health Insurance Scheme, Karnataka	Health insurance to the members of farmers co-operatives
Voucher scheme	Arogya Raksha Scheme, Andhra Pradesh	Hospitalization services to those who had undergone sterilization after two children
Hospital autonomy	Rogi Kalyan Samiti, JP Hospital Bhopal	Decentralized management of hospital and improve the quality of care
Public–private mix	RNTCP, Mahavir Trust Hospital, Hyderabad	Surveillance and treatment of Tuberculosis patients, under disease control program

Yeshasvini scheme in Karnataka, a community-based self-financed health insurance scheme, not only involves the public sector and members of farmers cooperatives as beneficiaries, it also includes several private hospitals, a corporate funds manager and a large hospital which provides guidance and supervision. In most partnerships, the principal public partner is the provincial (state) government's department of health and family welfare, that signed the agreement either directly or through local health facility committees.

In terms of the monetary value, the lowest value contract is to provide catering at a rate of 27 rupees ($0.67) per meal for about 30 meals daily (Bhagajatin Hospital, Kolkata). The most expensive is engaging a corporate hospital chain (Apollo Hospitals, Ltd.) to operate the government-built super-specialty Rajiv Gandhi Hospital in Raichur, Karnataka (over 600 million rupees or $15 million). While the Chiranjeevi scheme in the state of Gujarat (engaging private doctors to conduct institutional deliveries) has operated only since December 2005, the adoption and management of primary health centers by the Karuna Trust in Karnataka, as well as the outsourcing of hospital laundry, catering and cleaning services in Bhagajatin Hospital, Kolkata, are more than a decade old. All private partners in the partnership projects, except Uttaranchal's Birla Institute of Scientific Research, had prior experience in the health sector. In scope of services, a dozen partnerships engage in providing community care and support services, three partnerships provided tertiary care and the remaining partnerships were non-clinical support services. Two-thirds of the partnership projects studied are in rural and tribal areas, including hilly regions and islands in a delta. Most projects concentrate services in a specific geographical region, although some are intended to benefit an entire state.

Target Populations and Objectives

While analyzing the background of these projects it became apparent that the objectives of each partnership had been carefully planned with well-defined beneficiary groups. Almost all partnership projects (except laundry and cleaning) focus on service benefits earmarked for women, children and the poor. Each partnership sought to alleviate the economic impact of costs associated with acute illness. This objective is reflected in the types of services: facilitating access to high-cost radiological services (SMS Hospital) and tertiary services (Rajiv Gandhi Hospital); better access to institutional deliveries and health protection to pregnant women in remote locations (Chiranjeevi scheme, emergency ambulance scheme, urban health scheme); facilitating access to services within the geographical vicinity of the patients (mobile health schemes in Uttaranchal and in West Bengal) or through telecommunication technology (Karnataka Integrated Telemedicine and Telehealth); ensuring 24-hour access (management of health centers by Karuna Trust, Shamlaji Hospital, Arpana Swasthya Kendra); subsidizing the cost of care with community-based health insurance (Yeshasvini scheme, Arogya Raksha scheme); and facilitating free access to medications and other services for patients afflicted with tuberculosis (Mahavir Trust Hospital). The free services are specifically earmarked for people below the poverty line and, in some cases, special privileges or concessions. However, the primary concern in partnership projects which provide super-specialty care is verification of the actual beneficiaries versus those excluded from a subsidy. No uniform procedures have been adopted to verify the status of beneficiaries.

Enabling Conditions

In most of the partnerships analyzed here, either the government or the private partner chose to consult each other, formally or informally, before venturing into partnership agreements. Successful partnerships require prior (informal) consultations, visionary personalities and relationships based on trust. Compelling circumstances or partners seeking mutual benefits are strong triggers for partnership initiatives. The following examples illustrate how crucial these prerequisites are for partnerships.

In the case of Arpana Swasthya Kendra, the Municipal Corporation of Delhi (MCD) built a maternity health center under the final installment of funds from the World Bank's India Population Project-VIII. However, staff shortages, due to the municipal government's failure to recruit personnel, the building was not operational. An NGO working in the same slum community approached the IPP-VIII project director and asked if the NGO could manage the health center. In order to obtain approval for the proposal to transfer the health center to the NGO under a formal agreement, the project director lobbied hard to convince the political leaders and administrative heads of the municipal corporation.

In the Yeshasvini health insurance program in Karnataka, Dr. Devi Shetty – the founder and director of Narayana Hrudayalaya and a widely acclaimed personality in India for his charitable pioneering work on low-cost cardiac surgeries – had been invited to endorse a milk product at a function organized by the Karnataka Milk Federation (KMF), a farmers' cooperative society with more than two million members. During the event Dr. Shetty offered to provide specialty medical services to all KMF members if each paid a monthly fee of five rupees ($0.12) per person. The government subsequently approved a formal proposal made by Dr. Shetty to the chief minister of the state and to the secretary of the cooperatives department, and it contributed half of the premium for each member of the scheme. Before an independent trust was given the responsibility for managing the program, Dr. Shetty and his staff designed, planned, implemented and supervised a trial period. Dr. Shetty used his personal contacts and persuasive skills to attract private hospitals throughout the state to be part of this scheme, so its members could use their medical benefits almost anywhere.

Beyond charismatic personalities in both the public and the private sectors, prior consultations and trust were important in facilitating these partnership. A critical factor is a combination of compelling circumstances, opportune timing and mutually beneficial outcomes, as illustrated in the case of the Rajiv Gandhi Hospital in Raichur. Built at a cost of 600 million rupees with a soft loan from OPEC, this super-specialty hospital is located in a drought-prone and economically underdeveloped region of northern Karnataka, where many people live below the poverty line. Before the hospital brought modern health facilities in the area, people had to travel long distances to Hyderabad or Bangalore for specialist medical care. But having built the hospital, the state government was then unable to retain specialists in such an impoverished and backward region. Consequently, the hospital went basically unused. At the same time a corporate hospital chain – Apollo Hospitals, Ltd. of Hyderabad – wanted to establish its own hospital in the region but hesitated, given the investment required. The government of Karnataka and Apollo Hospitals therefore established a partnership to run the Rajiv Gandhi super-specialty hospital. The arrangement offered mutual benefits: the government ensured free services for the poor, while Apollo Hospitals established business operations without having to invest in physical infrastructure. And because the corporate chain pays its staff well, it could retain the required specialists in Raichur.

Selecting Private Partners

Only a few projects selected the private partners through an open-tender bidding process. In most partnerships, either the government or the private partner initiated proposals after prior consultation. We found no uniform guidelines for eligibility other than registration of the organization and prior experience in the region. To avoid administrative scrutiny, eligibility conditions were tailored to the private partner's experience. Some states formalized partnerships after initial pilot projects. The governments of Gujarat, Karnataka and West Bengal, for example, based their policies for public–private partnerships on lessons learned from pilot projects.

The evidence suggests that a competitive process for selecting private-sector partners is less effective than partnerships based on prior consultations. The private partners chosen on the basis of competitive tendering (mainly for-profit, commercial contractors) are either dissatisfied or unable to perform according to the partnership agreements. One plausible explanation is that, while competing to win a contract, the primary concern of a private bidder is to showcase their low-cost solution, knowing that government procedures invariably choose the lowest bid. Contractors tend to misjudge the volume of 'business' or to presume lax supervision by a government establishment. They expect to recover costs by 'cutting corners' or, in some cases, to negotiate upward tariff revisions. In the absence of such adjustments, the contractor is unlikely to deliver services at the same level of quality or effectiveness as specified in the contract.

Although open tendering has merits – transparency, competitiveness, objectivity – it is more appropriate in large infrastructural development projects where tenders have two parts: technical and financial. When delivering health services to the poor in a community, however, conventional tendering has problems. There is a need to evolve methods of selecting the private partners which will simultaneously be objective and legal as well as in the best interests of the community. The successful partnership projects documented here indicate the importance of prior negotiations with potential partners. However, civil servants fear that any procedural lapse will cost them dearly. Public sector managers are often more concerned about satisfying procedural requirements than about the needs of beneficiaries. To overcome complexities in selecting private partners, prior consultation through a committee structure (for example, discussions among the private partners, the community, government and eminent persons) followed by formal negotiations offer better outcomes.

Partner Obligations and Commitments

In any partnership each partner must abide by its obligations and commitments. Failing to fulfill mutual responsibilities leads to a lack of trust, conflicts and disaffection among all the stakeholders. In all of the partnerships analyzed here, the public sector is committed to providing premises, electricity, water and other appropriate physical infrastructure. In some cases the government also provides equipment, drugs, supplies, fuel or their equivalent in budgetary allocation or reimbursement of actual expenditures. Otherwise, the government provides financial resources through grants-in-aid.

Most projects clearly state the responsibilities of the private partners. One common mandate is to provide uninterrupted services to the target beneficiaries, i.e., patients below the poverty line. Other obligations include employment of qualified staff, upkeep of physical infrastructure, payment of rents and taxes and submission of periodic accounts and reports. Some partnership projects prescribe additional responsibilities under certain contingencies: emergency medical services for road accidents and trauma cases (Shamlaji Hospital, Gujarat), emergency services during natural disasters (Rajiv Gandhi

Hospital, Raichur) and health status baseline surveys (mobile health clinics, the Sundarbans, West Bengal). All hospital-based partnerships are expected provide services under national disease control, birth control and immunization programs.

Yet evidence reveals the absence of a monitoring authority to ensure that the partner obligations are fulfilled both in letter and in spirit. While it may be easier for the public sector to find deficiencies in services provided by the private partner, there is no neutral authority to monitor the obligations of the government. If the release of payments to the private partner is delayed, how can a private partner resolve this issue? One possible solution would be an ombudsman.

Service Quality and Performance Monitoring

One justification for partnership with the private sector is to deliver the health services more efficiently and at better quality. But while all the partnership agreements have clear operational guidelines for the private partners, specific performance indicators are conspicuously absent in all but three partnership projects. Similarly, except for CT/MRI images at SMS Hospital in Jaipur, no specific indicators for quality of services have been mentioned. Only in the urban slum project of Andhra Pradesh are performance parameters made explicit in the contract, that uses a weighted score of 200 points.

There are several explanations for this lapse. Since the public sector itself is unable to provide quality services efficiently, it lacks an understanding about performance indicators. Since the public sector has rigid procedural formalities in its selection process, the 'high caliber' of a chosen agency is presumed to provide better services. Government contracts tend to pay more attention to input factors (minimum eligibility conditions, competitive bidding, cost) rather than to outcome indicators. Finally, since most partnerships engage in the delivery of primary care, quality issues have not been specified.

Functional Autonomy

True partnership is characterized by relative autonomy for all partners to conduct their day-to-day operations as well as in overall management of the partnership. From the private partners' perspective, autonomy is non-intrusiveness and liberty to take operational decisions without requiring cumbersome bureaucratic approval. Although partnership agreements provide the public sector with enormous scope for an active and interventionist role, the private partner's functional autonomy in most cases had not been restricted by the public sector. Indeed, the private partners in almost all partnership projects were free to offer additional services, to generate additional resources (except through user-fees) to appoint staff and to specify their service conditions. Only in the cases of 'contracting out' ancillary services (SMS Hospital; Bhagajatin Hospital) did the private partners complain about constant interference from hospital administrators.

How well the public sector exercised its oversight role is a debatable issue. Government agencies may lack either the technical skills or the willingness to take an active oversight role. Even if government officials play more active roles in monitoring the partnership projects, a corollary question asks what prevents them from taking a similar interest in monitoring their own functionaries. The general perception that the private sector is vulnerable to losing its autonomy if it works with the public sector is misplaced. Evidence indicates that the private sector played a subtle role in influencing the state's policy on private-sector partnerships (Arpana Swasthya Kendra, Karuna Trust, Narayana Hrudayalaya, Mahavir Trust Hospital, Southern Health Improvement Samity). In some partnerships, the public sector played a more dominant role (Yeshasvini, Chiranjeevi, urban slum health, Karnataka integrated telemedicine project).

Technical and Managerial Capacity

For partnerships to function effectively, all partners need to have common organizational systems and institutional structures in place. While the public sector has a complex set of administrative systems, the private sector lacks a commensurate system. The private not-for-profit sector tends to operate on a small scale in an informal and flexible manner. It lacks elaborate structures and systems. The for-profit sector has more elaborate systems in place but tends to be more flexible in its interpretation. Private agencies may be unable to understand the rigidities and the formalities associated with a bureaucratic system. Bureaucracy requires a great deal of documentation and procedural details usually unfamiliar to the private sector, especially non-profit NGOs. Many NGOs are unable to calculate the unit cost of their services or to follow the detailed accounting systems required by government agencies. Such differences between public- and private-sector practices often cause misunderstandings and conflicts.

The bureaucratic system is unlikely to accept private-sector practices, so it compels the private sector to function like a bureaucracy. However, the private sector requires skills to undertake partnership projects, skills which are more complex than managing conventional 'grant-in-aid' welfare-support schemes. As far as the public sector is concerned, some states have learned to understand the intricacies of public–private partnerships through their pilot projects; others continue to experiment or are still organizing themselves to engage the private sector. The public sector requires capacity-building in pricing services, identifying performance parameters, monitoring outcome indicators, etc. Functionaries in both government and private agencies are competent in managerial and technical skills, so government officials must be trained to exercise oversight functions without being intrusive.

Stakeholder Perspectives

Beneficiaries at all the partnership project sites reported satisfaction with the services they received, although in many places they were not aware that a partnership existed. They indicated that current services are better than in the past and that patients are not turned away due to the lack of physicians or medicines. Deciphering this feedback suggests that a public–private partnership is better than government service delivery. Despite positive feedback, however, respondents in almost all partnerships raised specific concerns such as insufficient clinical hours in Uttaranchal's mobile health scheme, the cost of travel by emergency ambulance in Theni, etc. A common concern has been the inadequate supply of drugs, forcing patients to buy them at full price from the market. While Transparency International rated public-sector health services as being among the most corrupt civic services in India, no bribery or corruption was reported in any project – although conjectures have been made about the utilization of funds under the Arogya Raksha scheme in Andhra Pradesh.

Although the not-for-profit private sector is able to attract motivated staff at low wages, staff turnover remains a major concern. While expressing satisfaction with the purpose of their jobs, staff working for the private partners expressed dissatisfaction about workload, long hours, low pay, job insecurity, political interference and turnover among colleagues. The public sector health employees were critical of partnerships, although they expressed a willingness to work with them.

Managers of the private agencies were circumspect in their comments about partnerships with the public sector. Among their concerns are tardy release of funds, lack of a sufficient volume of business, interference by local community leaders, overbearing attitudes of public-sector managers, pressure to provide free services to ineligible beneficiaries, lack of clarity about who is exempt from user-fees, insufficient infrastructure support or frequent disruption in such support and lack of grievance mechanisms. However, the managers expect these problems will be addressed through better coordination and joint control.

POLICY PERSPECTIVES

Government regulations require public–private partnerships to deliver services to everyone – particularly those intended to benefit from the policy – on the basis of equity, efficiency, accessibility and quality. Public–private partnerships are expected to deliver efficient, cost-effective services, ameliorate economic distress among the poor, facilitate wider reach and easy access by beneficiaries and ultimately produce a sustainable policy. Based on the analysis of the case studies, each goal is evaluated below.

Equity and Access for the Poor

Each of the profiled partnership projects provides special benefits to the poor. In some partnerships, the benefits were exclusively for the poor (Yeshasvini, urban slum health, Arogya Raksha, Chiranjeevi), while in others a certain proportion of services was earmarked for the poor with upper limits or restrictions to avoid misuse of the services. For example, patients in the Yeshasvini scheme are not allowed inpatient medical treatment unrelated to surgery, and only two unmarried children plus the spouse of the cooperative society member are allowed membership in the scheme. In the now-defunct Arogya Raksha scheme in Andhra Pradesh, the beneficiary was eligible for free hospital treatment (for minor surgery or other ailments needing hospitalization) only if his or her sterilization had been carried out in a government hospital. While the policy of targeting the poor has been successful in providing maternal and child health as well as primary and community care, targeting the poor in tertiary-care services poses greater challenges. In Jaipur's SMS Hospital and in Raichur's Rajiv Gandhi Hospital, there are no uniform procedures to verify whether beneficiaries are eligible. One hospital staff member in Raichur sums up the difficulty in verifying the antecedents of the poor patients: 'People drive into the hospital by a *Honda City* [a popular luxury car in India] car and claim that they are below-poverty-line patients'. Identity papers are easy to obtain, yet there is no mechanism to verify whether they are authentic or if the patients actually belong in the poverty category. In refusing to treat such patients, hospital staff could face physical altercations while management is subjected to political pressure.

Since poor patients are more likely to exhaust their resources for tertiary-care services, perhaps public–private partnerships would be more appropriate for these highly complex procedures. Similarly, the cost of reimbursement by the government for tertiary-care services is higher. When powerful members of the local community lay claim to services designated for the poor, the poor patients lose. If there is no fixed quota for the poor, and if the government works on a reimbursement mode, the hospital administration has no motivation to prevent ineligible patients from using the services. Any tertiary-care services partnership should address this issue with appropriate checks and control systems. Currently contracts and agreement documents do not spell out verification mechanisms, an authority for verification or penalties for violations.

Resource Implications and Cost Effectiveness

Cost effectiveness is a primary objective of public–private partnerships. In practice, however, there are no guidelines to assess the cost-effectiveness of services delivered under a partnership agreement. We need evidence about how partnerships affect public-sector health budgets. There is also a need to evolve uniform guidelines on resource allocation to private partners, depending on the nature and scope of services. Evidence suggests that the government is very circumspect about granting full budgetary allocation to non-profit agencies, while for-profit organizations have obtained excessive concessions. Such inconsistency often exists under the same state government. In Karnataka the government supports both the Rajiv Gandhi Hospital in Raichur and the Karuna Trust state-wide to run primary-health centers. However, the Karuna Trust is given only 90 per cent of the salary costs of staff plus minimal material support, while the service contract with Apollo Hospitals to manage the Rajiv Gandhi Hospital reimburses all expenses plus a service fee (3 per cent of total expenses) on top of the enormous initial capital investment. The agreement also provides the private partner with a share of the profits up to 30 per cent. It is not clear whether such discrepancy is due to better negotiating skills by the private sector, a perception that it is unacceptable for not-for-profit agencies to negotiate cost margins, or because the government is more than eager to engage for-profit agencies. Compounding this muddle is a lack of incentives for better performing partnerships, while poorly performing projects have no disincentives other than non-renewal of the contract.

Another issue is the timely release of grants or reimbursements to private partners, especially to non-profit agencies whose existence often depends entirely on government grants or reimbursements. Research found instances of delayed disbursement payments and, in one case, a state government did not release the grant to an NGO for nearly 13 months. Being relatively large, that particular NGO was able to cope with the delay, but for most agencies such delay would have terminated the project. Neither current state policies for public–private partnerships nor contractual agreements mention timely release of payment or, in the event of non-release, the consequences thereof.

Allocations of resources to public–private partnerships are made either fully through government grants or through a mixture of government grants and user fees or insurance premiums. There is no pattern of whether partnerships fully supported by government grants can charge user fees. For example, user fees are not allowed in the Andhra urban health project, Karuna Trust and Chiranjeevi scheme, whereas the mobile health scheme in the Sundarbans in West Bengal, Shamlaji Hospital in Gujarat and Karnataka's Integrated Telemedicine Project do charge user fees. Most non-competitive partnerships (that is, private partners selected only after prior consultation rather than open tendering) allow user fees in both primary- and tertiary-care services. But in no public–private partnership are poor patients charged for any services. The relevance and the utility of user fee charges are debatable. Revenues from such user fees, especially in primary-care services, are meager and benefit neither the health facility nor the private partner. In Uttaranchal's mobile health scheme, revenue from user fees over a three-year period was less than one-tenth of the expenditure incurred. Accounts of user fees were not found in any partnership project except Bhopal's Rogi Kalyan Samiti.

Analysis of the case studies indicates that the government grants under public–private partnerships are invariably directed toward primary-care services. This finding repudiates the claim in some quarters that partnerships with the private sector divert government resources toward specialist care. Even in primary care, the argument that public–private partnerships lead to privatization is untrue. Without government grants, the private sector cannot sustain operations at these locations, so government responsibilities have become more indispensable than ever.

Benefits and Risks

The success of public–private partnerships hinges on another critical factor, namely, the assessment by all partners of risks and benefits from the partnership. For not-for-profit partners, apart from community service ideals, the benefits are financial sustenance. For private for-profit commercial contractors, benefits include increased business and profit margins. Other than several commercial contractors, no private partner claimed not to have benefited from a partnership project. The benefit for the public sector in terms of services delivery to poor patients was already mentioned.

Risk assessment depends on two factors: rule-bound behavior by the partners, with strict disincentives for any deviance, and the degree of trust among partners. Different levels of health functionaries perceive risks differently, while perceptions also vary according to the scope of services under a partnership.

At the policy level, the risks are likely to political in nature. Pressure from the media, political parties, health-action groups or employee unions may inhibit the government from making overtures to the private sector, especially its for-profit component. In the context of economic liberalization, where public-sector activities are slowly being removed from government control, there is a strong suspicion that the government may resort to similar steps in the health sector. This suspicion is strengthened by the fact that the government has not been effective in regulating the asymmetrical growth of the private sector in health care and its misdeeds. The private sector, in turn, has not been able to demonstrate its interest in public health activities like primary care. Rather, the private sector shows great enthusiasm about 'collaborating' with the government in tertiary-care services and in medical education – setting up medical schools. This pattern reinforces the view that the private sector collaborates with the government only if there are monetary benefits without risks.

Not-for-profit organizations, on the other hand, are popularly perceived to be 'givers', an image advantageous for them. Recently, however, bogus organizations masquerading as NGOs have raised doubts about the integrity of the NGO sector. Governments face fewer hurdles when partnering with NGOs, but the latter have severe limitations: limited scope of services (mostly primary care), limited geographical operations, dependence on grants-in-aid, short-term focus, limited sustainability and a lack of technical and managerial capacity.

Risk assessment for all partners follows other dimensions as well. Financial risks are higher among non-profit agencies. Any procedural lapses (e.g., in accounting) may cause a wide range of risks: administrative strictures, temporary stoppage of funds and audit inspections or, worse, a ban on bidding by the agency on future projects. Apart from denting the image of the agency, any of these actions would cripple service delivery to the beneficiaries. Another concern is accountability for service delivery. Under a partnership, the government is ultimately responsible for the delivery of services. If deficiencies occur in service provision under a partnership, the onus falls on the government to fill the vacuum. A third concern is the relationship among key stakeholders and their personalities. Differences in personalities and their respective styles sometimes lead to conflicts and jeopardize the functioning of a partnership.

From a policy perspective, there is the question of whether partnerships run higher risks if partners are chosen through an objective, competitive process of tenders than through selectively negotiated agreements. A competitive process cannot guarantee the performance of an agency which wins a bid although, given lack of 'prior intimacy', it may be easier to monitor its activities. On the other hand, selecting partners on the basis of their prior track record may ensure more judicious choices. Evidence suggests that public–private partnerships based on prior consultation experience fewer difficulties than competitively chosen partners. But further research is needed on whether private non-profit agencies prefer relationship-based partnerships, whether the private for-profit sector prefers the competitive selection process and whether the state bureaucracy prefers for-profit or non-profit partners selected competitively or through prior consultation.

Sustainability and Scalability

Although collaboration between the public and private sectors is not new, the concept of a public–private partnership is a novel strategy. Some states where health-sector reform projects were initiated with World Bank funding – West Bengal, Karnataka, Andhra Pradesh and Gujarat – have established separate health-sector reform cells whose officials are trained in public–private partnership concepts and systems. They are able to design policy guidelines, tenders, eligibility conditions, financial details, including costing of the services, and performance indicators. But without commensurate modifications in the legal, administrative and procedural systems of the state bureaucracy, new initiatives with the private sector are not be easy.

Also, due to transfers of top officials, there is a lack of continuity in strategizing about public–private partnerships. Officers who have been trained in health sector reforms or who initiated the partnerships are often subsequently posted out of the health department. New officials are rarely able to understand or appreciate the systems developed by their predecessors. Sometimes the strategies and systems are modified or completely abandoned, depending on the likes and dislikes of the new incumbents. On the other hand, having not been consulted about policy decision, lower functionaries in the health department are either untrained or inadequately briefed about the objectives of the initiatives or do not share the enthusiasm of the senior officials. Subordinate health officials lack the necessary skills to understand a partnership proposal, evaluate its benefits, identify performance outcomes or monitor the functioning of a partnership.

As a formal policy instrument, the public–private partnership is at a nascent stage. Many state governments are still organizing themselves to engage the private sector. Some have evolved a detailed policy framework based on pilot experiments, but others continue to experiment. In the 1990s, for example, Tamil Nadu introduced public–private partnerships by inviting the corporate sector to manage primary health centers. After initial interest, however, this initiative was not sustained. Other than a government notification, however, no formal policy document has been developed.

Most partnerships originate in specific contextual circumstances. Contextual factors include trust between leaders in the public and private sectors, the scope of services to be delivered, the availability of a willing private provider, geographical terrain, community support, technical and managerial capacity as well as political and administrative support. Replicating or scaling-up partnership projects depend on such contextual factors.

CONCLUSION

This chapter reflects the experiences of public–private partnerships in the delivery of health services to the poor in India. The experiences of 16 partnership projects across nine Indian states provide insights into the operational management of the projects as well as critical policy perspectives. No pattern emerged whether the public–private partnership model was guided by donor agencies, the product of resource constraints or due to the initiatives of pro-reform bureaucrats – or a combination of these. However, health-sector reform initiatives backed by financial support from international institutions stimulated the policy of public–private partnerships. Successful partnerships have also been prompted by visionary individuals in the bureaucracy and in civil society.

Our analysis suggests that states which experiment with partnership ideas before formalizing a policy are more successful than those that promulgate a policy without prior experience. Policy pronouncements by the government alone are not sufficient for public–private partnerships to succeed. Visionary leadership, social entrepreneurship and relationships based on trust among stakeholders are equally important for success. While there is no uniform pattern to suggest which type of services are best provided through partnerships or what services should be 'off limits' to the private sector, our analysis suggests that the most successful partnerships are with private non-profit organizations.

Partnership failures were often caused by insufficient consultations with facility managers. Pre-negotiated partnerships are more effective than competitive bidding. And partnerships initiated by the bureaucracy tend to be less successful than those initiated by the private partners.

The primary objective of reaching the poor and making health services accessible has been achieved through public–private partnership. But the relative economic benefit for the poor through accessing services under the partnerships is yet to be empirically verified. The capacity of both private partners and public officials to manage partnerships is yet to be fully developed. Public-sector managers perceive the new initiative as a burdensome task which requires them not only to placate their own subordinates, but also to seek better performance from their private partners. Known for their informal and flexible systems and organizational processes, private partners are uncomfortable with the rigid organizational and managerial procedures which characterize the public sector. Bureaucracy has yet to become conversant with the principles of new public management.

Partnership with the private sector is not a substitute for provision of health services by the public sector. And public–private partnership initiatives cannot be uniform across all regions or suitable under all kinds of political and administrative dispensations. While private partnerships are an administrative decision, an obvious but important point is that they must enjoy political and community support. In states where the private sector is prevalent, partnership initiatives could be an alternative not necessarily because of competitive efficiency but to prevent further pauperization of the poor and deprived sections of society. Any policy initiatives to strengthen the flagging public sector health services in India would be welcome. But a government unable to deliver quality social services due to a lack of basic administrative capacity would not be able to contract either clinical or non-clinical services. The first step must be to improve basic administrative systems. To obtain a clear rationale for partnering with the private sector, it is important to understand not only what services are to be provided under public–private partnerships but also to understand the basis on which such decisions are made.

NOTE

The research study was funded by the Indo-Dutch Programme on Alternatives in Development (IDPAD).

BIBLIOGRAPHY

ADBI (2000), 'Public Private Partnerships in Health', Tokyo, Asian Development Bank Institute, Executive Summary Series No. S34/01, Executive Summary of Proceedings (30 October–3 November), Ayutthaya, Thailand.
—— (2001), 'Partnership Issues in the Social Sector', Tokyo, Asian Development Bank Institute, Executive Summary Series No. S51/01.
Ahmed, Manzoor (2000), 'Promoting Public-Private Partnership in Health and Education: The Case of Bangladesh', in Yidan Wang (ed.), *Public–Private Partnerships in the Social Sector: Issues and Country Experiences in Asia and the Pacific*, Tokyo: Asian Development Bank Institute, pp. 219–91.
Axelsson Henrik, Flavia Bustreo and April Harding (2003), 'Private Sector Participation in Child Health: A Review of World Bank Projects, 1993–2002', Washington, DC, World Bank Health, Nutrition and Population Discussion Paper.

Baru, Rama (1998), *Private Health Care in India: Social Characteristics and Trends*, New Delhi: Sage Publications.

Bazzoli Gloria et al. (1997), 'Public-Private Collaboration in Health and Human Service Delivery: Evidence from Community Partnerships', *Milbank Quarterly*, **75** (4), 533–61.

Bennett Sara (1991), 'The Mystique of Markets: Public and Private Health Care in Developing Countries', London, London School of Hygiene and Tropical Medicine PHP Departmental Publication No. 4.

Bennett Sara et al. (1994), 'Carrot and Stick: State Mechanisms to influence Private Provider Behavior', *Health Policy and Planning*, **9** (1),1–13.

Blagescu, Monica and John Young (2005), 'Partnerships and Accountability: Current Thinking and Approaches among Agencies Supporting Civil Society Organizations', London, Overseas Development Institute Working Paper No. 255.

Bloom David E., Patricia Craig and Marc Mitchell (2000), 'Public and Private Roles in Providing and Financing Social Services: Health and Education', in Yidan Wang (ed.), *Public–Private Partnerships in the Social Sector: Issues and Country Experiences in Asia and the Pacific*, Tokyo: Asian Development Bank Institute, pp. 17–29.

Brinkerhoff Jennifer M. (2002), 'Government-Non-profit Partnership: A Defining Framework', *Public Administration and Development*, **22** (1), 19–30.

CII–McKinsey (2004), *Healthcare in India: The Road Ahead*, New Delhi: Indian Health Care Federation.

India, Government of (2001), *Tenth Five Year Plan, 2002–2007*, New Delhi: Planning Commission.

—— (2002), *National Health Policy, 2001*, New Delhi: Ministry of Health and Family Welfare.

—— (2005a), *Concept Note on Public Private Partnerships*, New Delhi: Department of Family Welfare, Ministry of Health and Family Welfare.

—— (2005b), 'Report of the National Commission on Macroeconomics in Health', New Delhi: Ministry of Health and Family Welfare.

Kulkarni, Suresh (2003), 'India Sector Paper: Health – Overview and Prospects', New Delhi, Centre for Media Studies, Report submitted to Asian Development Bank.

Mahal, Ajay, et al. (2002), 'Who Benefits from Public Sector Health Spending in India?', New Delhi: National Council for Applied Economic Research.

Mitchell-Weaver, Clyde and Brenda Manning (1992), 'Public-Private Partnerships in Third World Development: A Conceptual Overview', *Studies in Comparative International Development*, **26** (4), 45–67.

Mukhopadhyay, Alok (2000), 'Public-Private Partnership in the Health Sector in India', in Yidan Wang (ed.), *Public–Private Partnerships in the Social Sector: Issues and Country Experiences in Asia and the Pacific*, Tokyo: Asian Development Bank Institute, pp. 343–56.

Paoletto, Glen (2000), 'Public Private Sector Partnerships: An Overview of Cause and Effect', in Yidan Wang (ed.), *Public–Private Partnerships in the Social Sector: Issues and Country Experiences in Asia and the Pacific*, Tokyo: Asian Development Bank Institute, pp. 35–54.

Roemer, M.I. (1984), 'Private Medical Practice: Obstacle to Health for All', *World Health Forum*, **5** (3), 195–210.

Rosenthal Gerald (2000), 'State of the Practice: Public-NGO Partnerships for Quality Assurance', Boston, LAC-HSR Health Sector Reform Initiative, Family Planning

Management Development Project, Management Sciences for Health.

Selvaraju, V. and V.B. Annigeri (2001), 'Trends in Public Spending on Health in India', New Delhi: National Institute of Public Finance and Policy, Commission on Macroeconomics and Health.

Wang, Yidan (ed.) (2000), *Public-Private Partnerships in the Social Sector: Issues and Country Experiences in Asia and the Pacific*, Tokyo: Asian Development Bank Institute.

World Bank (2001), 'India: Raising the Sights: Better Health Systems for India's Poor', Washington, DC, World Bank Health, Nutrition and Population Sector Report No. 22304.

—— (2004), 'India: Private Health Services for the Poor', Draft Policy Note, available at http://www.sasnet.lu.se/EASASpapers/11IsmailRadwan.pdf.

World Economic Forum (2005), 'Building on the Monterrey Consensus: The Growing Role of Public-Private Partnerships in Mobilising Resources for Development', Geneva: United Nations High-Level Plenary Meeting on Financing for Development.

World Health Organization (1999), *WHO Guidelines on Collaborations and Partnership with Commercial Enterprise*, Geneva: World Health Organization.

—— (2001), 'Making a Public-Private Partnership Work: An Insider's View', *Bulletin of the World Health Organization*, **79** (8), 795–96.

Appendix 7.A1 Case Studies

Type of partnership	Case/State	Type of services	Private partner(s)	Objectives	Benefits to the poor
Contracting in	SMS Hospital Jaipur, Rajasthan	Radiological diagnostics (CT/MRI)	Private Company	Operate CT /MRI facility; Provide high tech diagnostic services at low cost.	Free for all BPL patients, above 70 years age, freedom fighters.
	Bhagajatin hospital, Kolkata West Bengal	Drugs and medical supplies store	Individual Entrepreneur	Quality medicines and supplies at lowest possible rate compared to market prices.	Provision of 20% services to the poor patients is not clear.
		Dietary and kitchen services	Individual Entrepreneur	Improve the quality of diet to the indoor patients; Improve the cleanliness and better hygiene; Establishing mechanized laundry.	BPL (free bed) patients are supplied diet free of charge; all others pay 50% of the charges.
		Cleaning and scavenging services; Laundry services	Individual Entrepreneur Private Company		
	Arpana Swasthya Kendra, Delhi NCT of Delhi	Management of a maternity health center	Non Profit NGO	Provide medical and diagnostic services, build referral system, provide RCH and child care services.	Lab tests, ANCs, select surgeries are free to the poor patients.
Performance Management contracts	Karuna Trust, Bangalore Karnataka	Management of Primary Health centers (PHC)	Non-Profit NGO	Provide round the clock health services, maintain and manage the primary health centre and its official sub-centres.	All patients are provided health services free of cost for diagnosis, treatment, drugs or for any other purpose.
	Shamlaji Hospital, Sabarkantha District, Gujarat	Management of a Community Health center (CHC)	Non-Profit NGO	Provide quality health care to tribal population, through community health centre.	No user fee on immunization; sterilization; maternal and child health services, diagnosis and treatment of poor people.
	Rajiv Gandhi Super speciality hospital, Raichur, Karnataka	Super specialty clinical care services	Large Corporate Hospital	Provide super-specialty clinical care services and management of the hospital.	Free out patient services to BPL patients. 40% beds are for BPL in patients free of cost.

Appendix 7.A1 (continued)

Type of partnership	Case/State	Type of services	Private partner(s)	Objectives	Benefits to the poor
	Urban Slum Health Care Project, Adilabad, Andhra Pradesh	Providing maternity and child care and RCH services	Non-profit NGO	Provide health and family welfare services to slum dwellers; reduce morbidity and mortality among women and children. ensure safe deliveries and child survival;	Services are meant for only the people (Women and children) in urban slum community. All services are free.
Contracting out	Chiranjeevi Yojana, Sabarkantha District, Gujarat	Enrolment of the private obstetricians and gynecologists for deliveries	More than 45 individual private doctors	Increase the proportion of institutional deliveries, reduce the maternal mortality rate and infant mortality rate.	Free services for the BPL women beneficiaries. Scheme is primarily targeted to pregnant women of BPL families.
	Emergency ambulance services, Theni District, Tamil Nadu	Providing ambulance services to emergency cases	Non-profit NGOs (2)	Provide round-the-clock emergency transport to pregnant women for obstetric care, improve institutional deliveries.	10% of the cases provided ambulance services free of cost. Other pay Rs. 5 per Km.
	Mobile Health Services in Sunderbans, West Bengal	Providing mobile (boat based) health services	Non-profit NGO	Improve access to health services in remote and inaccessible areas through mobile boat clinics, regular health camps.	No explicit statement about any specific benefits to poor patients.

Appendix 7.A1 (continued)

Type of partnership	Case/State	Type of services	Private partner(s)	Objectives	Benefits to the Poor
Technology Demonstration Project (Collaborative partnership)	Uttaranchal Mobile Hospital and Research Centre, Bhimtal, Uttaranchal	Mobile health vans delivering diagnostic and health care services	Non-Profit Research Institute Autonomous GOI Agency	Provide clinical and diagnostic services in the hilly region in the form of health camps.	Free services for patients with BPL card, including OPD consultation, radiological diagnostics and pathological tests.
	Karnataka Integrated Telemedicine & Telehealth project, Karnataka	Teleconsultation and in-patient services for cardiac and other specialist care	A large private hospital Autonomous GOI agency A large private hospital	To provide tele-diagnosis and consultation for coronary care.	Free diagnostics, medicines and treatment for BPL patients and Yeshasvini card holders. Medicines are free.
Community based co-operative health insurance	Yeshasvini Health Insurance Scheme, Karnataka	Health insurance to the members of farmers co-operatives	A corporate TPA More than 160 private hospitals in the state	Provide access to clinical care to farmers, who are members of farmer co-operative societies through health insurance.	Scheme is principally targeted towards the poor farmers.
Voucher Scheme	Arogya Raksha Scheme, Andhra Pradesh	Hospitalization services to those who undergo sterilization after two children	Public sector company One private clinic per block	Low-cost insurance to provide hospitalization benefits and personal accident benefits to patients below poverty line.	Beneficiaries are restricted to only those below poverty line with only one or two children.
Hospital Autonomy	Rogi Kalyan Samiti (RKS), JP Hospital Bhopal, Madhya Pradesh	Decentralized management of hospital and improve the quality of care	State run district hospital	Improve the patient facilities through augmenting alternate sources of financing.	All services free for BPL patients, ex-defence personnel and physically handicapped patients.

Type of Partnership	Case/State	Type of Services	Private partner(s)	Objectives	Benefits to the poor
	Yeshasvini Health Insurance Scheme, Karnataka	Health insurance to the members of farmers co-operatives	A large private hospital A corporate TPA More than160 private hospitals in the state	Provide access to clinical care to farmers, who are members of farmer co-operative societies through health insurance.	Scheme is principally targeted towards the poor farmers.
	Arogya Raksha Scheme, Andhra Pradesh	Hospitalization services to those who undergo sterilization after two children	Public sector company One private clinic per block	Low-cost insurance to provide hospitalization benefits and personal accident benefits to patients below poverty line.	Beneficiaries are restricted to only those below poverty line with only one or two children.
	Rogi Kalyan Samiti (RKS), JP Hospital Bhopal, Madhya Pradesh	Decentralized management of hospital and improve the quality of care	State-run district hospital	Improve the patient facilities through augmenting alternate sources of financing..	All services free for BPL patients, ex-defense personnel and physically handicapped patients.
Public-Private Mix	RNTCP, Mahavir Trust Hospital, Hyderabad	Surveillance and treatment of Tuberculosis patients, under disease-control program	A large private hospital Number of private doctors and nursing homes	Create network of private doctors for surveillance, diagnosis and drugs delivery.	The entire program is covered under the national (RNTCP) program, and no charges are asked from any of the patients.

8. Labor Market Informalization and Implications for Sustainable Growth

Du Yang, Cai Fang and Wang Meiyan

In the late 1990s China's labor market entered a steep decline characterized by increasing unemployment and reduced labor-force participation. The severe unemployment crisis has three causes. First, state-owned enterprises (SOEs) lost their comparative advantage, leaving them unable to fully utilize their production capacity, and they began operating at a loss. Second, the radical reform of the SOE guaranteed-employment system, known as the 'iron rice bowl', further exacerbated unemployment. Third, massive numbers of rural laborers have migrated to cities to seek urban jobs, creating competition for urban labor markets. As a result, several million workers have been laid off from SOEs, who either remain unemployed or exit the labor force altogether.

At the same time, researchers have expressed doubts about official statistics on employment and unemployment, uncertainties which create misunderstandings about the real status of labor-market developments and give the impression that unemployment in China is not manageable. Meanwhile, this uncertainty prevents policymakers from identifying priorities for coping with the situation. To properly understand China's labor market, observers must bear in mind that the Chinese economy is rapidly growing and drastically changing. With the fastest growth rate in the world, China will inevitably witness an increase in total employment, although the accompanying industrial-structural change and institutional transition have two effects on current workers. First, industrial-structural adjustments required by World Trade Organization (WTO) membership commitments will spur the economy to follow its comparative advantage – labor-intensive industries – and therefore should create more jobs. Meanwhile, the same structural adjustment generates structural unemployment as new sectors with comparative advantages emerge and those without comparative advantages decline. Second, the market-oriented institutional transition has fostered a labor market and made labor-force allocation much more efficient than before. On the other hand, marketization inevitably involves breaking the iron rice bowl, causing redundant workers and staff to be laid-off from their workplaces.

The serious unemployment situation had the following two effects. First, it pushed local governments toward policies which protect local jobs. Local governments are responsible for social stability in their jurisdictions and thus often implement short-term policies which obstruct the expansion of labor markets (See Cai, Du and Wang 2001). More often than not, local governments intervene during labor adjustments in enterprises and sometimes ask enterprises not to fire workers with local *hukou* (household registration). In order to reduce the employment competition between outside and local laborers, the government asks enterprises not to hire outside laborers and encourages them to increase the costs of labor migration. Second, local governments depend on the labor market to solve the problems of employment and reemployment, and they adopt more deregulated policies to encourage development of the labor market, small- and medium-sized enterprises and diversified employment. These two effects have both led to the informalization of employment in China. More workers are working without contracts, temporary jobs or outside formal sectors.

DATA AND PROJECT DESIGN

We utilize data from various sources to depict labor market developments in different regions of China. Specifically, we use aggregated data at the macro-level and data at the micro-level. Each dataset has its advantages and drawbacks, but taken together they provide a fairly complete picture.

The macro-level data, mostly at the provincial or national level, allows us to identify the faster growing regions. The advantage of macro data is the comprehensiveness. But the drawbacks are obvious. First, the high aggregation of macro-level data can potentially bias labor market information. Second, too few indicators are available at the macro level to reflect concrete cases. When analyzing and comparing the labor markets among regions, we have to use data from sample surveys at the individual and household levels. The tradeoff is necessary, since we have to sacrifice some variations among regions because only a few regions are selected in those sample surveys. Another disadvantage of using micro survey data is that regions usually are not randomly selected and the samples are not nationally representative, so we should be careful about drawing conclusions for whole country from those datasets but focus on comparisons between fast-growing regions and other regions identified by macro data.

China's market-oriented economic reform resembles conventional marketization policy. Still at an early stage and characterized by deregulation, labor market development in China has been accompanied by the informalization of employment. More and more people are employed in informal sectors or employed as informal workers in formal sectors. In this section, we start with the definition of informal employment, examine a series of key components and take advantage of survey data on firms and households to understanding informal employment. We analyze the informalization of employment by comparing relevant characteristics in fast-growing regions and other regions in order to understand the relevant policy implications.

Defining Informal Employment

With more and more gaps developing between the total employment number and the number of employees in formal work units, as well as between the total employment number and the number of individuals employed in private enterprises or self-employed, labor statistics cannot compile the actual total employment figure in a timely manner. The gaps also reflect the increased pressure for employment, the serious unemployment situation, the growing labor market and the expansion of employment outside work-unit accounting. (In China, the Ministry of Labor and Social Security prefers using the phrase 'flexible employment', to 'informal employment'.) Overall employment has increased in recent years, and an increasing number of workers are employed in new ways, including through the emerging labor market.

'Informal employment' generally refers to employment in informal sectors, small production units such as self-employed individuals, family enterprises and micro-enterprises. They do not have integrated, independent accounting and cannot be clearly differentiated from family and other activities. The informal-sector work units do not have clear organization structures. Labor and capital are seldom separated from each other, and the production line is very narrow. The laborers' relationship with their employer is based on temporary employment, kinship or personal and social relationships; it is not based on formal contract arrangement which have a formal guarantee (International Labor Organization 2001).

Informal employment in China's cities and towns is similar to employment in informal sectors as defined by the International Labor Organization, but it is not identical. In general, employment by enterprises which do not register their business or production, do not participate in social security and have informal labor relations, can be regarded as informal employment. Employment which is not registered according to the state 'Labor Comprehensive Reporting System' and the Industrial and Business Administration can be considered informal employment. One unique Chinese variety concerns employment in formal sectors, but under informal practices.

Informal employment is characterized by low costs, market dependency and flexible ways of hiring and firing, etc, all of which are very suitable to create jobs in a dual economy undergoing the process of transformation. Data indicate that employment in informal sectors has been universally growing in the developing countries of Asia, Africa, and Latin America. From 1990 to 1994, 80 per cent of the new jobs in Latin America and 93 per cent of those in Africa were created by informal sectors. Statistics indicate that informal sectors constitute 57.2 per cent of total employment in Africa, 36.2 per cent in Latin America and 32.8 per cent in the Asia–Pacific region (Xue 2000).

Even developed countries which practice market economics have to use flexible modes of informal employment to cope with the intensified competition from globalization and the increased uncertainty of enterprises. This trend affects patterns of employment by reducing full-time jobs and permanent positions and encouraging temporary work, contract jobs, freelancing and part-time work. This trend is related to the transformation of industries, and it is especially evident in regions with concentrations of new industries, such as California's Silicon Valley. Some 27–40 per cent of employment in Santa Clara County, California, is contract work. New positions there are almost 100 per cent contract jobs (Benner 1996). In recent years, other governments in other countries have noticed the trend toward temporary employment, also known as the 'new flexible economy', along with related policies used to address the phenomenon.

The number of employees in work units in China's cities and towns has been gradually decreasing since 1990, while the number of persons employed outside official work units has been increasing alongside the growing economy. While in 1996 the number of employees in the informal sector was only 25 per cent of the level in official work units, by 2001 the informal sector had almost half of the work-unit level. Therefore, general statistical data can underestimate the actual growth of employment. In reality, the overall employment level in China has indeed increased, only the conventional, formal employment in cities and towns has reduced.

It can be difficult to identify informal employees even by combining the internationally accepted definition and one adapted with Chinese characteristics. Therefore in this study we use whether or not workers sign contracts with their employer as the criterion for distinguishing informal and formal employment. According to the Labor Act issued in 1994, the employment contract is the most important employment document, as it defines labor relations and specifies the rights and obligations of both sides. Although a contract is not a sufficient condition to guarantee employee rights, it still plays a vital role.

Since the widespread layoffs and unemployment at SOEs which emerged in 1998 was accompanied by radical restructuring, we define the following categories of people as informal workers: a blue-collar worker who began a job in or after 1998 without a contract; an individual working in the private sector without a contract and the self-employed. Next we estimate the size of informal employment in China's urban labor market.

Missing Workers and Informal Labor Markets

Both the surveyed and estimated unemployment rates documented by Cai (2004) are lower than what most researchers and observers expected, because people who had experienced unemployment and later quit the labor market, as well as people who took new jobs which are informal and not secure, are not counted as unemployed. Based on 2000 census data, we calculate both unemployment rates and labor-force participation rates for the population aged 16 and above by province and plot them on the maps in Figure 8.1. The contrast between the two maps is obvious. Provinces which have high unemployment rates have low labor-force participation rates, and provinces with low unemployment rates have high levels of labor-force participation. Statistically, the correlation coefficient between the two rates is −0.64, indicating a discouraged-worker effect.

Because a cursory look at China's labor market reveals an increase in the unemployment rate and a decrease in labor participation, many observers mistakenly conclude that there has been no increase in employment in China since the 1990s or even that there has been an absolute decrease in employment. For example, Rawski (2001) takes 'zero employment increase' as a basis for questioning China's GDP growth performance since the late 1990s. If we just look at the state and urban collective sectors, traditionally the only absorbers of urban employment, then employment has indeed declined year-by-year since the latter part of the 1990s, as shown in Table 8.1. However, because the components of China's economy became diversified, the national employment structure experienced huge changes. Consequently, focusing only on changes in work unit employment levels no longer fully reflects changes in total employment.

In practice, urban employment has grown steadily since the reform era started, reaching 256.4 million in 2003 – 8.6 million more than the previous year. During the entire period from 1978 to 2003, the average annual growth rate was 4.1 per cent – that is, 6.45 million extra jobs were created each year on average. In the same period, the share of state-owned units in total urban employment declined from 78.3 per cent to 26.8 per cent; the share of collective work units declined from 21.5 per cent to 3.9 per cent, while employment created

Figure 8.1   Comparison of Labor Market Situation by Province

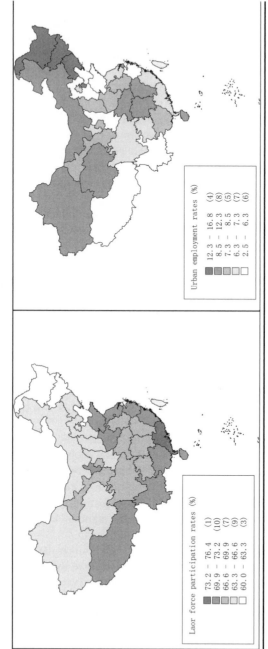

Laor force participation rates (%)

73.2 – 76.4   (1)
69.9 – 73.2   (10)
66.6 – 69.9   (7)
63.3 – 66.6   (9)
60.0 – 63.3   (3)

Urban employment rates (%)

12.3 – 16.8   (4)
8.5 – 12.3   (8)
7.3 – 8.5   (5)
6.3 – 7.3   (7)
2.5 – 6.3   (6)

Source: Authors' calculation from 1 per cent sampling of 2000 census, long form.

by newly emerging units such as limited-liability corporations, share-holding corporations, private enterprises, enterprises with funds from Hong Kong, Macao and Taiwan, foreign-funded enterprises and self-employed businesses increased from zero to two-thirds of the total, making a quite diversified employment pool. However, the substantial increase of unit employment in such newly emerged sectors does not sufficiently offset the decline in state and collective employment, causing a gap between classified and total employments. This 'leftover' employment represents 96.4 million urban employees in 2002, more than the sum of state and collective employment, and accounts for 39 per cent of total urban employment. Explaining why this residual employment emerges statistically and practically will help us better understand the attributes of the employment growth and the changes in employment structure under a more liberalized labor market.

Statistically, the residual between total and unit employments appeared in 1990. Previous urban employment figures were collected through all production units with independent accounts and individually registered enterprises. Currently, official statistics on employment come from three sources.

One source is the Comprehensive Labor Statistics Reporting System (CLSRS), that provides employment information covering all independent accounting units. Under the CLSRS, the information about employed people in enterprises (units) comes from mandatory statements about the labor situation of all units, whether state-owned, collective-owned units, share-holding corporations, etc. A second source, the State Administration for Industry and Commerce (SAIC), reports numbers for self-employment and private enterprises. Together, these two figures should match the total urban employment figure calculated by CLSRS.

However, there are at least three factors which might cause the CLSRS to underestimate employment statistics. First, some units were never included in the numerical statement system, creating the problem of 'missing units', as a result of enormous changes in the boundaries of enterprises due to SOE restructuring. Second, units had a motivation to deliberately underreport the numbers of employees – or even not report at all – because some obligations, such as paying premiums to the social security program, are based on unit employment numbers. Third, the employment levels for private enterprises and self-employed businesses obtained from the registration of enterprises and family business at SAIC are usually the level at registration; they may not include subsequent increases as the enterprise develops. At present, the boundary between self-employed business households and private enterprises is not very clear. According to state regulations, a self-employed business is one which employs seven people or less. When a business's employment exceeds this cap, it should be re-registered as a private enterprise. However,

Table 8.1   Changes in Employment Structure since the Reform

	SOU	COU	SHC	JOU	LLC	SHCL	PE	HMT	FIU	IND	RDL	Total
1990	103.5	35.5	0.0	1.0	0.0	0.0	0.6	0.0	0.6	6.1	23.1	170.4
1991	106.6	36.3	0.0	0.5	0.0	0.0	0.7	0.7	1.0	6.9	22.0	174.7
1992	108.9	36.2	0.0	0.6	0.0	0.0	1.0	0.8	1.4	7.4	22.4	178.6
1993	109.2	33.9	0.0	0.7	0.0	1.6	1.9	1.6	1.3	9.3	23.2	182.6
1994	112.1	32.9	0.0	0.5	0.0	2.9	3.3	2.1	2.0	12.3	18.5	186.5
1995	112.6	31.5	0.0	0.5	0.0	3.2	4.9	2.7	2.4	15.6	17.0	190.4
1996	112.4	30.2	0.0	0.5	0.0	3.6	6.2	2.7	2.8	17.1	23.8	199.2
1997	110.4	28.8	0.0	0.4	0.0	4.7	7.5	2.8	3.0	19.2	30.9	207.8
1998	90.6	19.6	1.4	0.5	4.8	4.1	9.7	2.9	2.9	22.6	57.0	216.2
1999	85.7	17.1	1.4	0.5	6.0	4.2	10.5	3.1	3.1	24.1	68.4	224.1
2000	81.0	15.0	1.6	0.4	6.9	4.6	12.7	3.1	3.3	21.4	81.6	231.5
2001	76.4	12.9	1.5	0.4	8.4	4.8	15.3	3.3	3.5	21.3	91.6	239.4
2002	71.6	11.2	1.6	0.5	10.8	5.4	20.0	3.7	3.9	22.7	96.4	247.8
2003	68.8	10.0	1.7	0.4	12.6	5.9	25.5	4.1	4.5	23.8	99.1	256.4
2004	67.1	9.0	1.9	0.4	14.4	6.3	29.9	4.7	5.6	25.2	100.2	264.8

Notes:
SOU: State-owned units   COU: Collective-owned Units   SHC: Share-holding cooperative units   JOU: Joint ownership units
LLC: Limited liability corporations   SHCL: Shareholding corporations, Ltd.   PE: Private enterprises
HMT: Units with Funds from Hong Kong, Macao and Taiwan   RDL.: Residual   FIU: Foreign-investment units
IND: Self-employed individuals   RDL.: Residual
Source: National Bureau of Statistics (2005).

many enterprises with many more than seven employees stay registered as self-employed business and report a smaller employment number. This leads SAIC to inadvertently underestimate the employment numbers in private enterprises and self-employed business.

Another data source is based on China's Sample Survey of the Population Changes (SSPC), that covers 1 per cent of the total population. Initiated in 1996, SSPC takes urban samples based on residence, but not *hukou*. With a multi-stage systematic PPS cluster-sampling scheme, about 400,000 individuals are randomly chosen. Because this survey follows common statistical methods and the ILO-recommended definitions of employment and unemployment, the resultant data are relatively accurate and comparable. The difference between the larger numbers of urban employment collected from SSPC and the smaller number of employment from CLSRS results in an employment deficit (Cai and Wang 2004). Many researchers incorrectly claim a zero increase in employment and minor elasticity of employment to economic growth because their research is based on employment data from CLSRS, the only available source for disaggregating the employment by sector and province.

The expansion of the employment gap not only proves that traditional labor statistics are unable to reflect the actual labor market situation in diversified, complicated economic structures, but it also indicates the progress of marketization and the tendency toward the informal allocation of labor, a result of increasingly severe unemployment and rising labor mobility. This informal channel has overwhelmingly employed rural-to-urban migrants and re-employed the urban laid-off and unemployed, contributing to the growth of gross employment in recent years.

Size and Components of Informal Employment

The informalization of the labor market is reflected by the increasing size of informal employment. As discussed in the last two sections, only relying on published labor statistics will not uncover exact numbers of informal employment; the only way to estimate its size is via other indicators. In fact, the discrepancy between total employment and aggregated unit employment is regarded as the approximate size of informal employment. Based on household survey data, we may estimate the size of informal employment in a more explicit way.

Table 8.2 displays the size of informal employment estimated from two rounds of CULS data. As we sample migration labor and local residents separately, we report the estimated size of informal employment for migrants and local residents. Official urban labor statistics rarely take into account migrant informal labor.

Table 8.2   Size and Components of Informal Employment (per cent)

	Fast-growing regions		Other		All	
	local	migr	local	migr	local	migr
CULS1						
Size of informal employment	14.5	72.1	21.4	72.8	18.5	72.5
% of self-employment	67	73	64	63	65	73
% of unregistered work	33	27	36	37	35	27
CULS2						
Size of informal employment	25.7	73.9	38.2	92.1	32.6	84.3
% of self-employment	39	62	35	73	37	69
% of unregistered work	61	38	65	27	63	31

Source: Authors' calculation from CULS2.

The results from household survey data show a consistent trend of increasing informal employment. Under our definition, 18.5 per cent of local residents worked in the informal sector in 2001, and the number went up to 32.6 per cent in 2005. The same trend is found in the sample of migration labor. Compared with other studies, we think our estimation based on the urban household survey is reasonable.

It is not surprising that most migrants are employed in the informal sector. Although this is the conventional wisdom, there are few studies which give a detailed estimation of informal employment among migrant workers. Our estimation of the size of informal employment of migration labor contributes to efforts to determine the actual proportion of informal work in total employment. As discussed elsewhere, migrants are seldom included statistics for work-unit employment. While the National Bureau of Statistics (NBS) labor-force survey used to report total employment claims to adequately include migrant labor, it is still insufficient. Thus the estimated number based on the discrepancy between total employment and its decomposition also risks underestimating the size of informal employment.

As far as the components of informal employment, in 2001 self-employment dominated unregistered work for both migrants and local residents. But things changed in 2005, when the self-employed share decreased dramatically from 65 per cent to 37 per cent. Urban residents apparently are increasingly accepting unregistered work.

Table 8.3   Characteristics of Informal and Formal Work: CULS1

	Fast-growing regions		Other		All	
	local	migr	local	migr	local	migr
Informal work						
Working days per week	6.3	6.8	6.5	6.9	6.4	6.8
Working hours per day	9.2	10.8	9.4	10.9	9.3	10.8
Monthly earning (yuan)	1455	1246	730	833	968	991
Formal work						
Working days per week	5.1	6.2	5.2	6.5	5.3	6.4
Working hours per day	8.2	9.2	8.1	9.7	8.3	9.5
Monthly earning (yuan)	1222	899	826	696	1001	776

CHARACTERISTICS OF INFORMAL WORK

In addition to quantity, we need to identify the characteristics of informal work. First, we want to know if the characteristics in fast-growing regions differ from those in other regions. Second, how does the informal sector differ from the formal sector? Third, how similar are the experiences of migrants and local residents? Finally, since we have two rounds of household survey data collected in different years, we can do temporal comparisons. Table 8.3 and Table 8.4 present data on work intensity and earnings in both the formal and informal work sectors, broken down by residence and by region. Below we discuss some of the issues raised during the calculations.

Earnings

Since workers in informal and formal sectors, with or without local *hukou* identity, have different work intensities, we calculated hourly earnings as a comparable variable between groups. Figures 8.2 and 8.3 display the hourly earnings of local residents and migrants in both fast-growing and other regions using data from CULS1 and CULS2, respectively.

According to the data, all workers in formal sectors make higher hourly wages except for the migration group in CULS1. In each figure, the histograms in the left panel are higher than their right-handed counterparts. Although the human capital endowment of informal workers is lower than those in the formal sector – which could be an important explanatory variable – we can still hold that the relatively low earnings and the vulnerability of work for informal

Table 8.4   *Characteristics of Informal and Formal Work (CULS2):*
                Proportion of Workers with Social Security Benefits (per cent)

	Fast-growing regions		Other		All	
	local	migr	local	migr	local	migr
Informal work						
Pension	56.8	3.1	53.8	1.52	54.8	2.1
Unemployment insurance	13.6	0.9	12.1	0.16	12.6	0.4
Accident insurance	8.6	2.5	4.6	0.4	6.0	1.2
Health insurance	43.5	2.4	26.8	0.7	32.6	1.3
Working days/week	5.9	6.7	6.2	6.9	6.0	6.8
Working hours/day	8.8	10.7	9.0	10.6	8.9	10.6
Monthly earning (yuan)	1197	1300	702	790	1094	976
Formal work						
Pension	84.4	38.2	79.9	10.0	82.1	29.0
Unemployment insurance	36.1	24.1	43.1	4.6	39.7	17.8
Accident insurance	35.6	42.4	22.8	9.6	29.1	31.7
Health insurance	72.2	40.2	70.6	7.9	71.4	29.7
Working days/week	5.1	5.9	5.5	6.2	5.3	6.0
Working hours/day	8.2	8.7	8.2	8.8	8.2	8.7
Monthly earning (yuan)	1763	1422	1020	883	1387	1247

Notes:
1. The codes for industries are:
   3 = manufacturing; 7 = transportation, shipping and warehousing; 9 = wholesale, retail trade and catering service; 12 = social service; 16 = education.
2. For migration labor, only rural to urban migrants are included.

workers are significant features of the informalization phenomenon. In 2001 there was no major difference in hourly earnings between migrant workers engaged in the formal and informal sectors; however, the situation changed in 2005, partly because new government policies favoring migrants could only reach those employed in formal sectors. Most observers assume that labor market discrimination against migrants exists in urban areas, meaning that even migrants working in the formal sector could not earn a higher income than their counterparts in informal sectors in 2001. But things changed in 2005, a change which implies an improved environment for all migrants, but it is true only for formally employed migrants.

    Second, no matter which sectors they work in and what *hukou* positions they hold, workers in faster-growing regions earned higher hourly rates than their

Figure 8.2   Hourly Earnings of Local Residents and Migrants (CULS1)

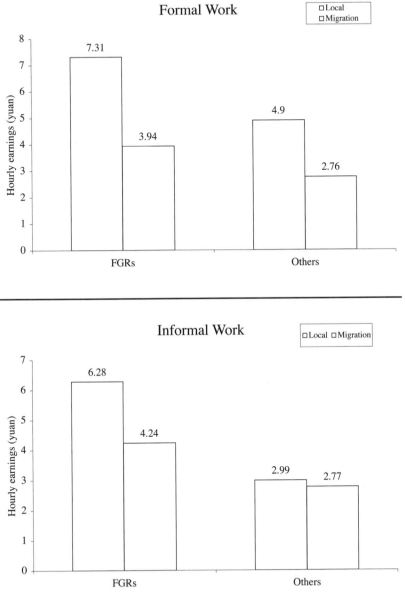

Figure 8.3   Hourly Earnings of Local Residents and Migrants (CULS2)

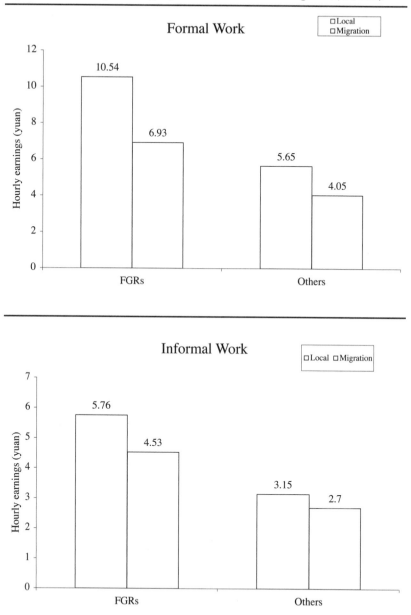

counterparts in other regions. This is not surprising and mirrors the common regional disparities in incomes. If our samples are somewhat representative at the city level, they should reflect the trend of increased regional disparities which is well documented elsewhere.

For comparisons between local residents and migrant laborers, we look at the earning ratio of these two groups and take migrant groups as one. In 2001 for faster-growing regions and other regions the ratios were 1.86 and 1.78 in formal sector, while they were 1.48 and 1.08 in informal sector, respectively. The same calculation for 2005 produced 1.52 and 1.40 in formal sector, versus 1.27 and 1.17 in informal sector, respectively. This suggests that there is less discrimination against migrant workers in the informal sector.

Finally, there are some long-term changes in terms of earnings disparities: (1) disparities between local residents and migrants are getting smaller, (2) disparities between the formal and informal sectors increased and (3) disparities between faster-growing regions and other regions increased. Next we explain why these changes happened and how they are related to the evolving causes and nature of informal employment over time.

Blinder–Oaxaca Decomposition

Given the fact that migrant workers are a major component of the informal labor force in urban sectors, it is important to know how they become informalized while entering the urban labor market. Based on the descriptive statistics above, we know that wage differentials exist between migrants and local residents. Since the factors contributing to wage differentials are multifaceted, we have to control for other effects in order to get the net effects of discrimination from overall wage differentials. To look further into the causes of wage differentials between migrant and local workers, we apply a traditional Blinder–Oaxaca decomposition to CULS2 data. To eliminate the potential selection bias, we use household composition variables as selection variables, because we believe that those household variables affect individual decisions about labor-market participation and employment but not wages. Our main interest here is to observe how much of the wage differentials come from the discrimination against migrants and the relative sizes of the discrimination in faster-growing and other regions. As is shown in Table 8.5, after controlling for the wage determinants, discrimination accounts for 9.6 per cent of wage differentials between migrants and local residents in faster-growing regions and 44.8 per cent in other regions. It is obvious that faster-growing regions have less discrimination against migrants and suggests that labor markets in faster-growing regions are more competitive than those in other regions.

Work Intensity

Working longer hours is another prominent feature of informal work. Following the procedure for wage differentials, we next compare work intensity between the formal and informal sectors with extension to regional and residential dimensions. Both rounds of the survey ask questions about working hours. Our findings suggests that: (1) informal workers tend to work more hours compared with workers in formal sectors, (2) migrant workers work more hours than local workers and (3) workers in faster-growing regions work much less than their counterparts in other regions.

Over time, workers tend to work fewer hours, as indicated by the differences between the working hours for CULS1 and CULS2. However, formal workers in other regions slightly increased their work hours during the interval between the two surveys. This could indicate that labor market behavior tends to be more rational, although the size of informal employment increased over time.

Social Protection

Our data raise two issues related to social protection. Workers with formal employment contracts are much better protected than workers with informal employment arrangements. According to CULS2, 82.1 per cent of local workers and 29 per cent of migrant laborers joined pension programs, whereas the numbers are 54.8 per cent and 2.1 per cent, respectively, for informal workers. Similarly, local workers are better protected than migrant laborers. For example, even among local workers who work in informal sectors, more than one-half have pension plans and near one-third have health insurance. Those two figures are much higher than their migrant counterparts. This suggests that while the employment shocks resulting from SOE restructuring deprived many SOE employees of formal jobs, they still could, more or less, benefit from social security programs and other government protections. However, even within the informal sector, there is a huge gap between local workers and migrant laborers.

CHARACTERISTICS OF INFORMAL WORKERS

As mentioned above, we are also interested in the characteristics of workers employed informally. In Tables 8.6 and 8.7, demographic characteristics, human capital and working history are presented by residence and by region for both rounds of the survey.

Table 8.5 Blinder-Oaxaca Wage Decomposition with Heckman Selection (CULS2)

	Fast–growing regions		Other	
	Local	Migrants	Local	Migrants
Wage Equation:				
dependent variable = log of hourly earnings				
Years of schooling	0.095	0.062	0.077	0.05
	(15.60)	(6.51)	(13.92)	(7.89)
Age	−0.0048	−0.0014	−0.0049	−0.001
	(2.85)	(0.43)	(2.87)	(0.48)
Sex (1= male)	0.039	0.12	0.12	0.096
	(0.87)	(1.54)	(2.93)	(2.07)
Log of years on the job	0.14	0.08	0.11	0.039
	(10.78)	(3.29)	(9.81)	(2.46)
Log of height	2.78	1.07	1.07	1.45
	(5.84)	(1.21)	(2.30)	(2.56)
Party membership (1=yes)	−0.049	−0.11	0.11	−0.15
	(1.19)	(0.53)	(2.71)	(1.09)
Self-employment (1=yes)	−0.19	0.14	−0.16	−0.16
	(3.11)	(2.19)	(3.30)	(3.55)
Self-reported health status	−0.068	0.02	−0.47	−0.079
	(3.57)	(0.53)	(2.77)	(3.62)
Negative impacts of deformity or				
chronic diseases on work	−0.057	0.25	−0.031	−0.01
	(0.91)	(1.93)	(0.53)	(0.15)
Work in public sector (1=yes)	0.25	−0.036	0.25	0.065
	(2.72)	(0.38)	(6.05)	(0.94)
Work in private sector (1=yes)	0.23	0.28	0.23	0.29
	(4.13)	(3.15)	(4.97)	(4.41)
Heckman selection				
Household size	−0.027	−0.23	−0.01	−0.20
	(1.04)	(5.97)	(0.69)	(7.26)
Fraction of member > 60	−1.81	−0.035	−1.66	−0.36
	(14.35)	(0.06)	(17.43)	(1.43)
Fraction of member < 16	−0.78	−2.22	−0.22	−1.20
	(4.61)	(11.42)	(1.60)	(8.50)
ρ	−0.37	0.033	−0.078	0.81
	[0.13]	[0.15]	[0.14]	[0.030]
δ	0.57	0.90	0.58	0.85
	[0.02]	[0.018]	[0.011]	[0.021]
λ	−0.21	0.030	−0.045	0.69
	[0.078]	[0.13]	[0.08]	[0.039]
Summary of Decomposition Results (as %)				
Due to endowments (E)		58.9	34.8	
Due to coefficients (C)		830.5	−148.1	
Shift coefficient (U)		−824.2	176.4	
Endowments as % total: E/(E+C+U)		90.4	55.2	
Discrimination as % total: (C+U)/ (E+C+U)		9.6	44.8	

Note: Absolute value of t value in parenthesis, standard errors in bracket.

Table 8.6   Characteristics of Workers Employed Informally (CULS1)

	Fast-growing regions		Other		All	
	local	migr	local	migr	local	migr
Informal workers						
Age	40.1	31.3	40.6	30.1	40.4	30.6
Sex (% male)	60.5	61.7	55.2	59.9	56.9	60.6
Health status	6.42	6.10	6.42	6.01	6.42	6.04
Years of schooling	9.3	7.76	9.9	8.10	9.7	7.97
Party membership (%)	4.4	1.79	7.7	1.85	6.6	1.83
Experience being laid-off, registered unemployment, or involuntary retirement (%)	20.2		40.7		33.9	
Formal workers						
Age	41.2	30.5	40.7	28.5	40.9	29.3
Sex (% male)	57.1	62.8	58.2	72.2	57.7	68.5
Health status	6.40	6.19	6.60	6.11	6.51	6.14
Years of schooling	11.3	8.33	11.8	8.69	11.6	8.55
% Party membership	21.5	2.16	25.5	2.53	23.7	2.4
Experience being laid-off, registered unemployment, or involuntary retirement (%)	15.2		11.2		13.0	

Basic Individual Characteristics

Both surveys found migrant laborers to be younger than local workers, but there is no significant difference between the informal and formal sectors or between faster-growing regions and other regions. For most indicators, male workers have advantages over females, because males have higher labor-market participation rates and migration probability. Laborers with fewer years of schooling tend to work more in the informal sector, and local workers generally have higher educational attainment. There is no significant difference in health status, which we take as a selective process – only healthy workers stay in the labor market.

Experience with Shocks

We asked workers from urban areas about their past experience with labor-market shocks. (This question is not relevant for rural-to-urban migrants.)

Table 8.7   *Characteristics of Workers Employed Informally (CULS2)*

	Fast-growing regions		Other		All	
	local	migr	local	migr	local	migr
Informal workers						
Age	41.7	33.8	40.0	34.4	40.6	34.2
Sex (% male)	52.8	56.0	52.3	56.3	52.5	56.2
Health status	6.18	6.48	5.86	6.41	5.97	6.44
% Party membership	8.8	1.80	7.49	1.20	7.95	1.42
Years of schooling	10.9	8.45	11.1	8.27	11.0	8.34
Training (%)	2.8	3.61	6.21	4.33	5.02	4.07
Experience being laid-off, registered unemployment, or involuntary retirement (%)	45. 9		55.6		52.2	
Formal workers						
Age	41.7	31.6	39.9	32.0	40.8	31.7
Sex (% male)	56.2	56.6	60.9	63.3	58. 6	58.8
Health status	6.26	6.58	6.16	6.41	6.21	6.52
Party membership	18.7	2.61	23.6	1.25	21.2	2.17
Years of schooling	12.30	9.67	12.43	9.75	12.37	9.70
Training (%)	5.54	7.23	6.97	10.83	6.26	8.40
Experience being laid-off, registered unemployment, or involuntary retirement (%)	15.4		19.3		17.4	

Note: For migration labor, only rural-to-urban migrants are included.

Informal workers are more likely to experience involuntary job separation in various forms. On average, about one-third of informal workers in 2001 and more than one-half of informal workers in 2005 had experienced employment shocks, whereas a much lower proportion of workers in the formal sector have suffered employment shocks. The proportion of workers with shock experience in faster-growing regions is generally lower than in other regions, suggesting that the fast-growing regions have more stable labor markets due to the greater number of job opportunities thanks to their economic boom. Labor market employment shocks are the main contributor to the formation of informal employment.

LINKS BETWEEN INFORMAL AND FORMAL SECTORS

Why Stay in the Informal Sector?

We regressed a linear probability model to see what influences a worker to enter the informal sector. As shown in Table 8.8, more young people tend to work informally, but the relationship is not linear. Male laborers are more likely to work in formal sectors, but this does not hold in faster-growing regions For both types of regions, workers with past experience with involuntary unemployment have more than 30 per cent probability to work in informal sectors if other things are equal. Better political status helps workers enter the formal sector, but statistically it has only marginal significance in faster-growing regions, where the labor market is more competitive.

Less-educated people are more likely to work informally, and one additional year of schooling will reduce the probability of entering the informal sector by about 3 per cent in faster-growing regions and 2 per cent in other regions. Training programs also help individuals find work in the formal sector. In faster-growing regions, a person involved in a training program has about 15 per cent greater probability to enter the formal sector. In the other regions, the number is 6 per cent, but it is not very significant statistically. The coefficients of human capital variables in both regions not only reflect the fact that labor markets in fast-growing regions are more developed, but they also imply that improving education and skills are effective ways to help workers enter the formal sector. On the contrary, if policymakers try to formalize the labor market by interfering with employers' decisions, labor markets can actually become more rigid.

Moving between Informal and Formal Sectors

As discussed above, employment in urban labor markets has become increasingly informalized in recent years. Our survey data show that informal employment accounted for 18.5 per cent total employment in 2001; the number increased to 32.6 per cent in 2005. Retrospective data in CULS2 also confirmed this trend: 26 per cent of workers were employed in the informal sector in 2002. Figure 8.4 shows the links and mobility between formal and informal sectors by job turnover.

According to Figure 8.4, workers in the informal sector are more mobile than those in formal sectors. According to CULS2 data, in 2002 3,180 sampled individuals worked in both sectors, and the informal sector accounted for 26 per cent of the total workforce. From 2002 to 2005 one-third of informal workers experienced job turnovers, while the ratio of job turnover is about 16

Table 8.8   *Linear Probability of Determination of Entrance to Informal Sector*

1 = informal employment, 0 = formal	All	FGRs	Other
Age	−0.04	−0.03	−0.06
	7.60	3.80	7.30
Age square	0.00	0.00	0.00
	6.91	3.27	6.86
Sex (1=male)	−0.04	−0.02	−0.05
	2.69	1.01	2.62
Experience with involuntary unemployment	0.34	0.32	0.37
	19.97	12.18	16.04
Party membership (1=yes)	−0.09	−0.05	−0.12
	4.37	1.75	4.27
Years of Schooling	−0.03	−0.03	−0.02
	9.83	7.39	6.36
Self-reported health status	−0.02	−0.02	−0.02
	2.38	1.53	1.78
Household size in 2002	−0.01	−0.01	−0.01
	0.92	0.98	0.46
Share of kids below 16 in household	0.10	0.17	0.07
	1.62	1.80	0.77
Share of labor in household	−0.02	0.00	−0.05
	0.39	0.04	0.54
Getting dibao transfer since 2002	0.20	0.05	0.23
(1=yes)	6.83	0.69	6.94
Private transfer (1=yes)	0.05	0.06	0.03
	2.92	2.76	1.11
Trained (1=yes)	−0.10	−0.15	−0.06
	3.10	3.04	1.56
FGRs (1=yes)	−0.08		
	5.14		
Adj R-squared	0.22	0.15	0.24
Obs	3355	1502	1853

Source: Authors' calculation from CULS2.

per cent in the formal sector. Based on our dataset, high mobility appears to be a common feature of informal work, although more workers move from formal sectors into informal sectors than vice versa.

Figure 8.4   Links and Mobility between Formal and Informal Sector

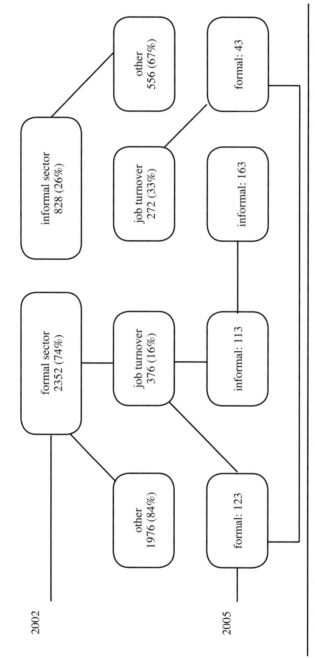

Note: In Figure 8.4, the box 'other' includes those who did not experience job turnovers and retirement over the three-year periods and those whose information was missing in the questionnaires. The definition of job turnovers is kept the same as used above.
Source: Authors' calculations from CULS2.

194

IMPLICATIONS OF LABOR MARKET INFORMALIZATION

The general trend toward informalization has significant impacts on China's labor market. We mainly explore the effects of informal employment on China's competitiveness, a key factor for sustainable development.

The prevalence of informal employment reduces the workforces' social security coverage to a great extent. For example, from 1990 to 2002 the proportion of retirees who joined the basic state pension program increased from 40.6 per cent to 84.1 per cent, but the proportion of urban employees who joined the program only increased from 30.5 per cent to 44.9 per cent. Popular coverage did not increase, because the rising number of informal workers lack access to the social security system. Although the flexibility of informal employment encourages jobs which provide more effective security than the social security system does, the lack of access to social security of the informal laborers has to be solved in the future, otherwise the social burdens will greatly increase.

Furthermore, although migrant laborers might earn higher incomes compared with the opportunities available in their home towns, employment stability, working conditions and social protection for them are severely inadequate. This is especially true since migrant workers' jobs are usually dangerous, dirty and physically demanding. This disparity has harmed many workers and contributed to many labor disputes. Migrant laborers also lack the residency registration which provides access to many services. Existing laws and regulations about labor protection have not been effectively implemented for the informal sector. For example, according to data from the fifth population census, compared with local urban workers, the proportion of migrant laborers who work six days a week in urban labor markets is two times higher, and the proportion of migrant laborers who work seven days a week is 58 per cent higher.

While causing problems in terms of job security, social protection and wage rates, this emerging form of employment does help utilize the immature labor market to relocate labor and solve the problems of urban unemployment and rural underemployment during the transition period. Thus, the employment trend should be understood in a broader perspective. The development of the labor market involves a whole set of institutional arrangements. The levels of the labor market function differently at different stages of labor-market development. The current informal modes of employment in China come with the advantages of market competition and actually have become the main path of labor-market development. Letting the market work, therefore, is the first and the most important step, that will allow the rest of the market to develop accordingly. China still enjoys the advantages of its abundant labor force, and market-determined wage rates should still be lower than those set by central planning.

POLICY RECOMMENDATIONS

This study has used empirical analysis of firm-level and household-level data to focus on two important emerging issues. First, we compared labor-market developments between fast-growing regions and other regions. Second, we discussed the new trend of informalization in China's labor market. Some policy recommendations can be drawn from the empirical analysis.

Compared with other regions, faster-growing regions have performed well in creating employment opportunities, whether measured at household level or at firm level. To a great extent, this advantage comes from better developed labor markets in these higher performing regions. The implication is that, for regions with less developed labor markets, promoting an effective labor market should increase job opportunities. Based on the studies in this chapter, Beijing should implement policies facilitating long-term job creation and human resource utilization, such as increasing labor market flexibility, creating a favorable environment for the development of small enterprises, granting more autonomy to SOEs regarding hiring and firing and delivering incentives for investment in education and training.

Recently the informalization of employment has become a significant phenomenon in China's labor-market development. In this chapter, we clarified the definitions and statistics of informal employment and described in detail the characteristics of the informal sector, links between the informal and formal sectors and the impacts of informalization.

Marketization and informalization are simultaneous and interactive at the early stages of labor-market development and during economic transition. Bearing that in mind, policymakers must realize the positive side of informal employment in an appropriate way. Even in an informal way, wage formation and employment determination in the informal sector follow basic market principles. In practice, the experience of dealing with the informal sector can help introduce market forces into the current employment mechanism. Therefore, while regulating the labor market, the government must take into account the positive effects on job creation and poverty reduction generated by the informal sector. If the focus is only on creating a well-regulated and formalized job market, China will miss chances to increase employment and make full use of its rich human resources. When comparing faster-growing regions with other regions, we may find that labor markets in faster-growing regions are more formal and more developed, implying that labor markets in other regions could be formalized in a marketized way. In other words, informalization can serve as a process of transition and facilitate the development of labor markets.

Since migrant labors mostly work informally in urban areas, they actually constitute the major part of the group missing in labor statistics. Consequently, the actual size of informal employment is underestimated even when the discrepancy between total employment and its disaggregated components is considered. The underestimated size of informal employment is not a good basis for policymaking and policy implementation. Policymakers and the public have only recently started monitoring the welfare, protection and social issues relating to informal employment. In fact, if we realize the heterogeneity between the two groups in informal sectors – urban workers and rural-to-urban migrants, we may conclude that the former, who experienced employment shocks, is protected fairly well, although they work in a informal way. To the contrary, a more urgent and essential task for policymaking is to provide better protection to migrant laborers, since they are excluded from the social security system and even from current labor statistics. Job informality and lack of residence registration should not be an excuse for ignoring their demand for public services and social protection.

As China's labor market develops, the role of informal employment has been modified over time. From the aspect of income generation, informal employment had positive effects on enhancing incomes when the labor-market shocks were serious, but the effects are not significant anymore. Given the inherent shortcoming of informal employment in job security, pay and supervision, the expansion of labor market informalization challenges labor-market regulation efforts. Apart from direct regulations aiming to formalize employment, some policies aimed at the labor-supply side might be helpful to created a regulated but efficient labor market. Those policies include enhancing education and providing training to people who are potentially informal workers.

NOTE

Comments from Ana Revenga and Xiaoqing Yu are appreciated. The authors take all responsibility for possible errors in the chapter.

BIBLIOGRAPHY

Benner, Chris (1996), 'Shock Absorbers in the Flexible Economy: The Rise of Contingent Employment in Silicon Valley', at http://www.wpusa.org/pubs/.
Blinder, Alan S. (1973), 'Wage Discrimination: Reduced Form and Structural Estimates',

Journal of Human Resources, **18** (4), 436–55.

Cai, Fang (2004), 'The Consistency of China's Statistics on Employment: Stylized Facts and Implications for Public Policies', *Chinese Economy*, **37** (5), 74–89.

Cai, Fang, Yang Du and Meiyan Wang (2003), *The Political Economy of Labor Migration* (Laodongli Liudong de Zhengzhi Jingjixue), Shanghai: Shanghai Sanlian Press.

—— (2005), 'How Far is China to a Labor Market?' (Zhongguo laodongli shichang zhuanxing yu fayu), Beijing: China Commerce Press.

Cai, Fang and Meiyan Wang (2004), 'Irregular Employment and the Growth of the Labor Market: An Explanation of Employment Growth in China's Cities and Towns', *Chinese Economy*, **37** (2), 16–28.

Giles, John, Albert Park and Fang Cai (2006), 'How has Economic Restructuring Affected China's Urban Workers?', *China Quarterly* (185), 61–95.

International Labor Organization (2001), *Main Labor Force Indicators*, Beijing: China Labor and Social Security Publishing House.

National Bureau of Statistics of China (NBS) (2005), 'A Statistical Analysis on China's Flexible Employment', at http://www.molss.gov.cn/news/2005/0107a.htm.

Oaxaca, Ronald (1973), 'Male-Female Wage Differentials in Urban Labor Markets', *International Economic Review*, **14** (3), 693–709.

Rawski, G. Thomas (2001), 'What's Happening to China's GDP Statistics?' *China Economic Review*, **12** (4), 298–302.

Solinger, Dorothy J. (2001), 'Why We Cannot Count the Unemployed', *China Quarterly* (167), 671–88.

—— (2002), 'Economic Informalization by Fiat: China's New Growth Strategy as Solution or Crisis?', in Luigi Tomba (ed.) *On the Roots of Growth and Crisis: Capitalism, State and Society in East Asia*, Rome: Annali Della Fondazione Giangiacomo Feltrinelli (36), 373–417.

United Nations Development Programme (UNDP) (1999), *China Human Development Report – 1999: Transition and the State*.

Wu, Yaowu and Fang Cai (2006), 'Informal Employment in Urban China: Size and Characteristics', Beijing, Chinese Academy of Sciences, Institute of Population and Labor Economics, unpublished paper.

Xue, Zhao (2000), 'Developing Informal Sector and Increasing Informal Employment', *China Economic Times*, (6 December).

Zhang, Junsen, Yaohui Zhao, Albert Park and Xiaoqing Song (2005), 'Economic Returns to Schooling in Urban China, 1988 to 2001', *Journal of Comparative Economics*, **33** (4), 73–52.

Zhu, Ling and Yu Yao (2006), 'Report on China's Flexible Employment', Report for World Bank.

9. Financing China's Entrepreneurs: The Role of Legislative Membership

Wubiao Zhou

China's rapid economic growth in the past two decades is widely considered to be one of the major economic miracles since World War II. However, state-owned enterprises (SOEs) have been stagnant during most of this period (Lin, Cai and Li 1996; World Bank 2002). Township- and village-owned enterprises (TVEs) prospered from the mid-1980s until the mid-1990s (Nee 1992; Oi 1992; Walder 1995), but declined drastically in the late 1990s. The only domestic sector which has experienced steady growth paralleling the rapid national economic development is the domestic private sector, referred to here as the 'private sector'. The size of the private sector and its significance in the national economy snowballed even before the central government began to privatize SOEs and TVEs in 1998. By 1997 the private sector contributed one-third of the total national industrial output and one-fifth of the total national non-farm employment (Gregory 2000). By the early 2000s, this sector reportedly contributed slightly more than 50 per cent of the national GDP (*China Industry News* 26 April 2005).[1]

Nevertheless, the private sector has developed under a harsh regulatory environment (ADB 2003; Byrd and Lin 1990; Gregory 2000; Nee 1992; Peng 2004; Tsai 2002; Zhang and Ming 1999, 2000). Among the unfriendly state policies, the loan practices of the state banking system affect this sector most, because Chinese private entrepreneurs, like entrepreneurs everywhere, are often wealth constrained and need to obtain external financing to pursue their opportunities (Casson 1982). Most banks – even the newly established shareholding ones – are not entirely independent from the government, and they have discriminated against lending to private firms (ADB 2003; Tsai 2002). Nevertheless, the private sector flourished.[2]

Not surprisingly, Chinese private entrepreneurs have depended overwhelmingly on internal sources, particularly retained earnings and principal-owner financing (ADB 2003; Nee 1992). However, both regional and national surveys suggest that bank financing was the second-most important

Table 9.1   *Sources of Finance (Post-Start-Up Investments) for Chinese Private Firms, 1993–98 (per cent)*

	1995[a]	1998[a]	1993[b]	1997[b]
Retained earnings and principal owner	52.1	62	70.7	58.7
Loans from banks, including formal credit unions	22.6	18.0	18.2	32.6
Informal finance	12.6	9.0	7.8	5.45
Outside equity	1.0	1.3	0	2.8
Corporate bonds	1.0	0.3	0	0.27
Other	10.7	9.4	1.4	0.82

Notes:
a. The data are based on the four-city survey on private enterprises conducted by the International Finance Corporation in 1999.
b. The sources of the data are the 1993 and 1997 National Surveys of Chinese Private Enterprises conducted by the All China Federation of Industry and Commerce.

source of funding for private firms (Zhang and Ming 1999, 55). According to these surveys informal finance,[3] observers identified as the primary source for the economic miracle of the private sector (e.g., Tsai 2002), contributed only modestly to finance the private sector (see Table 9.1).

Given the difficulties in obtaining bank loans, how could bank financing play a significant role in China's private sector growth? From the supply (bank) side, it seems that firm size matters. According to this argument, although private firms in general are discriminated against by banks, as there are high financial risks associated with lending to them, large private firms could still secure bank loans easily because they are more transparent and have a greater ability to provide collateral and guarantee. While this view makes sense economically, it sees private firms as rather passive actors.

Based on the insights from resource-dependence theory (Pfeffer and Salancik 1978; Pfeffer 1982), I offer a demand-side view by arguing that firm strategies also matter. This study analyzes one strategy used by private entrepreneurs; namely, obtaining membership in various levels of the Chinese legislative (or semi-legislative) system, such as the People's Congress (PC) and the People's Political Consultative Conference (PPCC). Specifically, the research questions are: Why and how does membership in the PC or PPCC help private enterprises obtain bank financing? How do such memberships affect the probability of obtaining bank loans for firms of different sizes?

A SUPPLY-SIDE VIEW: CAUTION PREVAILS

Many economic and policy researchers adopt a supply-side view on bank financing in China's private sector (e.g., ADB 2003; Gregory 2000). According to this view, there are high financial risks associated with lending to private firms in China, primarily because of the unfavorable regulatory environment faced by such firms. As such, banks and other financial institutions will impose a number of stringent contracting methods, such as collateral requirements and relationship lending, in order to induce entrepreneurs to self-select in ways which offset the financial risks, or they will use signals to choose less-risky borrowers (Berger and Udell 1998). But what is the source of the unfavorable regulatory policies? How do these policies affect the financial risks faced by banks?

Beijing allowed the private sector to reemerge for very pragmatic reasons. After 30 years (1949–78) under a socialist planned economy, by the late 1970s China had encountered severe shortages in consumer goods and services, low morale in factories and collective farms and high real unemployment rates in the cities (Lin, Cai and Li 1996). In many regions, peasants called for collective farms to be dismantled. The central reformers finally supported the Household Responsibility System (HRS) that had been initiated by peasants in a remote village in Anhui province. Over the next five years (1979–84), HRS was adopted throughout the country (Naughton 1995). The tremendous success of the HRS in increasing agricultural production greatly alleviated the long-standing food shortages and inspired the central reformers to allow peasants, as well as unemployed urban residents, to establish small businesses to produce consumer goods and services. Many families and individuals subsequently created private firms.

The development of private firms, however, was severely restricted in the early 1980s, because of harsh critiques from ideologically conservative forces. Although the pragmatic reformers defended their policy on liberalizing private businesses in terms of economic needs, they did not want to openly challenge the socialist ideology for fear of losing their political legitimacy. As a result, there were many restrictions on private businesses initially. For example, a private firm could not employ more than seven employees; it could enter only a short list of industrial sectors (mainly consumer goods and services); it could not get factor resources directly from state-owned institutions; it encountered higher real tax rates, etc. (ADB 2003; Byrd and Lin 1990; Gregory 2000). With these restrictions, the state intended to use the private sector to play only a marginal, stop-gap role in the economy.

Some of these regulatory restrictions were lifted, such as the limit on firm size, and others were loosened in 1988. After 1988, and especially after Deng

Xiaoping's Southern Tour in 1992, Beijing adopted a more pragmatic approach to the private sector (Naughton 1995). Nevertheless, two problems remained almost unchanged in the 1990s. First, the central government did not provide substantive legal protection and enforcement of private property rights. Second, it still arbitrarily kept the private sector in a subordinate, near pariah status. These problems were not resolved even after 2004, when a constitutional change was introduced to protect private property rights and level playing field for all firms, because 'there is a long way to go from official proclamations to real results on the ground' (Gregory 2000, 53). Such a regulatory environment greatly increased the financial risks banks faced when lending to private firms.

First, although it affects all financial markets, the information asymmetry problem is especially severe for Chinese private firms because of the weak protection of private property rights. Many private firms have deliberately made themselves more opaque and are especially cautious about revealing information to outsiders – including banks. For example, in order to avoid high local levies and other potential liabilities resulting from unprotected private property rights, private firms usually avoid formal accounting systems or keep several sets of books, thus making auditing difficult – if not impossible (Gregory 2000, 52). As a result, banks – not only state-owned banks, but also other banks less controlled by the state – are reluctant to accept financial statements from private firms and remain conservative in extending loans to private firms (ADB 2003; Tsai 2002).

Second, as a result of the unequal playing field between the SOEs and private firms, state policies are somewhat biased against lending to private firms. For example, the state will step in if a state-owned enterprise fails to amortize a loan, so that the bank does not have to absorb the entire loss on its own balance sheet (Lardy 1998). However, if a private enterprise fails, banks will have to absorb the loss from their own provisions and profits. Under such policies, banks would naturally favor state-owned enterprises, but they must be careful about lending to private firms.

Since Chinese banks face high financial risks, they typically impose a number of stringent contracting methods when lending to private firms. For example, researchers have found that Chinese banks often have more stringent requirements on collateral and guarantees, charge higher interest rates and use more relationship lending when they extend loans to private firms. Banks, however, may also use simple indicators to evaluate the potential financial risks of a private firm.

One commonly used indicator is firm size. Previous studies consistently show that financial risks are negatively associated with firm size (e.g., Beck, Demirguc-Kunt and Maksimovic 2005; Schiffer and Weder 2001). There are two reasons for this theory. First, larger firms have a stronger capacity to provide adequate collateral and/or proper guarantees. Second, larger firms usually are more transparent with their financial information because they have more formal organizational structures. In China, because information asymmetry is very common, banks have very stringent requirements on collateral. Real estate assets appear to be the most common collateral accepted by Chinese banks. Since larger private firms generally have more real estate assets, they are favored much more than smaller ones by banks when applying for a loan. According to Hypothesis 9.1, from a supply-side view, it appears that the larger the size of the private firm, the fewer the financial risks faced by banks, and therefore, the less the bank financing obstacle faced by the firm. Thus large private firms would be the major beneficiaries of bank financing among all private firms.

A DEMAND-SIDE VIEW: POLITICAL STATUS REMOVES BARRIERS

While the supply-side view makes sense economically, it looks at the bank-financing problem faced by private entrepreneurs primarily from the bank side. It seems to treat firms as passive actors and does not ask whether or how private firms could break down the financial constraints. This could result in prediction errors. One problem, for example, is that it could not answer why the same bank may often treat same-sized firms very differently. Thus, a balanced view should consider the problem not only from the supply side but also from the demand – i.e., firm – side.

Resource-dependence theory has long argued that when facing external constraints, organizations would respond more to the demands of those organizations or groups in the environment which control critical resources. In particular, organizational entrepreneurs would develop strategies to manage their external dependencies in order to ensure the survival of their organization and to acquire more autonomy and freedom from external constraint (Pfeffer 1982, 193). Based on resource-dependence theory, this study offers a demand-side view which focuses on the active political strategies which private entrepreneurs use to secure high political status which, in turn, can exert influence over the allocation or source of a critical resource (Oliver 1991; Pfeffer and Salancik 1978, 113–42). With these strategies and the resulting high political status, private entrepreneurs obtain legitimacy and institutionalized social capital, both of which facilitate resource mobilization; as a result, they could enjoy uninterrupted growth (Oliver 1991; Pfeffer 1982).

Joining the Legislative System

Previous research has shown that Chinese private entrepreneurs have been very keen to manipulate their environment through strategies which could improve their political status. Many entrepreneurs have obtained membership in the Chinese Communist Party (CCP) to pursue both individual and collective goods (Dickson 2003). Recent reports, however, have suggested that many entrepreneurs have also participated in Chinese politics more directly through getting a seat in China's legislative or semi-legislative systems, namely, the national and local People's Congress (PC) and People's Political Consultative Conference (PPCC) (Jiang 1999, 103–17).[4]

Since 1954 China's formal legislative system consists only of People's Congresses. People's Political Consultative Conferences once served as China's legislative system (1949–54), but changed into the organ of the United Front, which has been used to control members of the non-socialist classes since 1955. However, these two political organizations have their annual meetings at the same time; both have little real political power and simply convene and endorse the decisions of the national or local CCP committees (Dreyer 1999, 88). In addition, a significant proportion of the positions in both the PC and the PPCC are reserved for semi-retired party or government officials. As the PC and PPCC have quite similar functions in Chinese politics, the PPCC could be considered as a semi-legislative organization.

Citizens can participate in multiple levels of either the PC or the PPCC, but they cannot hold membership in both. For a private entrepreneur, like all citizens, there are two official ways to join one of the bodies. He can acquire a position either through being co-opted by the Party branch at the same level as the PC or PPCC or through self-nomination (Jiang 1999, 109). In practice, however, it is very difficult to join either organization through the self-nomination process. Thus co-optation by the Party is the predominant route.

Why does the CCP co-opt private entrepreneurs into these two political organizations? One important reason is related to the overall objective of the CCP – to maintain political control. The CCP has always faced challenges from opposition forces outside the one-party political system which threaten its monopoly on power, although the Party has always been very harsh toward such groups (Dickson 2003; Tong 1994).[5] Given their wealth, private entrepreneurs are considered a potential direct or indirect challenge to the Party Leadership because they could support opposition forces. One way for the Party to resolve such a problem is to co-opt selected people from outside the political system, installing private entrepreneurs into these two political organizations (Dickson 2003, 100; Jiang 1999).

Private entrepreneurs have also been very responsive to the political co-optation strategy. Many entrepreneurs have attempted to get a PC or PPCC seat through the Party-nomination process using various formal or informal ways. Some entrepreneurs even try self-nomination, although their chance of being elected this way would be very small (Jiang 1999). By the late 1990s, a substantial proportion – about 10 per cent – of private entrepreneurs with firms larger than seven employees were already members of either the PC or the PPCC (Zhang and Ming 1999, 163–64).

Why are entrepreneurs so interested in getting a seat in the PC or PPCC? The answer is the substantial benefits which such a membership could bring to them. Such membership signals the high political status of the entrepreneur to society and can greatly enhance the organizational legitimacy and institutionalized social capital of the private firm, thus facilitating the acquisition of critical resources including bank loans controlled or regulated by the state.

Organizational Legitimacy

Organizational legitimacy is 'a generalized perception or assumption that the actions of an entity are desirable, proper or appropriate within some socially constructed system of norms, values, beliefs and definitions' (Suchman 1995). In this study, organizational legitimacy refers more narrowly to a perception of the desirability of the organizational activity within the larger economic and political system. As mentioned above, throughout the 1980s and early 1990s the state regarded the Chinese private sector as inferior to the state-owned sector because it is not 'socialist' in nature. Its status was improved first during the 1992–94 regulatory reforms and then in the late 1990s when the state began to protect private ownership and level the playing field between public and private firms. The secure private property rights and the level playing field, however, have not materialized, primarily because of problems in policy implementation. As a result, private firms lacked full organizational legitimacy throughout the reform period.

The lack of organizational legitimacy has severe consequences for private firms. First, because they are less legitimate, private firms have difficulty in obtaining many critical resources which are controlled by government officials who distribute the resources more on the basis of political considerations – meaning favoring politically legitimate firms such as state-owned enterprises – than economic ones (Nee 1992). This is clearly demonstrated in the financial constraints faced by private entrepreneurs, as discussed above. Even in Zhejiang, the province famous for government policies relatively supportive of the private sector, until the late 1990s local officials still limited the quantities available to businesses of many economic resources, such as land, water, electricity, raw materials and bank loans (He 1999, 194–205). Second, because of the lack of organizational legitimacy, local state-controlled media and even public opinions in many regions have often been prejudiced against private entrepreneurs.

Achieving high political status could bring political legitimacy, thus helping solve the demand-side problems. As argued above, the CCP co-opts private entrepreneurs into the political system in order to transform potential system challengers into system supporters, thus stabilizing the one-party political regime. Since those entrepreneurs who are offered a seat in the PC or PPCC are considered system supporters, they and their firms can enjoy beneficial treatment in resource acquisition and positive media coverage. Many private entrepreneurs in Fuyang, Zhejiang province, for example, reported that they enjoyed 'the freedom of doing business', such as easy access to loans, protection from unfair competition and positive media coverage, only after being co-opted into the PC or PPCC (He 1999, 202).

Institutionalized Social Capital

No only can membership in the PC or PPCC bestow organizational legitimacy, it can also bring institutionalized social capital to the private firm and entrepreneur. According to Bourdieu (1986), social capital consists of all actual or potential resources linked to possession of a durable network of more or less institutionalized relationships of mutual acquaintance or recognition. It is a personal asset which provides tangible advantages to those individuals, families or groups which are better connected.[6]

Sociologists have argued that social capital can be viewed as based on social similarity (Burt 1992). Thus, people with a high sociopolitical status have a greater probability of having other high-status people in their personal networks (Suchman 1995). In this study, high sociopolitical status attached to membership in the PC or PPCC could increase the probability of an entrepreneur having other high-status people, such as politicians, bureaucrats and bankers,[7] in their personal networks. These high-status contacts are very useful when the entrepreneurs need financing.

First, high-status contacts could facilitate relationship lending and ease the information asymmetry problem, that is especially severe because of weakly protected private property rights. Banks often use relationship lending to solve information asymmetry problems (Berger and Udell 1998; Gregory 2000). However, Chinese banks usually do not have incentives to establish relationships with private entrepreneurs, given the unfavorable regulatory environment for the private sector (Gregory 2000; Tsai 2002). But an entrepreneur who is a member of the PC or PPCC can use their high-status contacts to help him or her establish relationships with bank officials. Because direct and indirect ties between the entrepreneur and bank officials may create social obligations between the two parties, causing them to behave generously toward each other, the high-status contacts may facilitate relationship lending (Gulati 1995; Shane and Cable 2002).

Second, high-status contacts can sometimes directly intervene on behalf of an entrepreneur regarding bank credit decisions. As discussed above, Chinese banks often discriminate against lending to private firms, compared with state-owned enterprises, because of state policies which are biased against private firms. However, bank officials could hardly make independent credit decisions in China. Local governments and officials had strong control over state-owned banks during the reform period until very recently (Naughton 1995). During the late 1990s, the central government reorganized the provincial network of the People's Bank and eliminated the credit quota system in order to break the links between local governments and state-owned banks. Nevertheless, local governments are finding new ways to preserve some role in the allocation of financial resources through the banking system. Under such an institutional environment, an entrepreneur who is a member of the PC or PPCC can easily use their high-status contacts to intervene on his behalf in the bank credit decisions (Gregory 2000, 55).

Hypotheses from the Demand-Side View

Given the above discussion, it seems likely that membership in the PC or PPCC (hereafter 'legislative membership') can help the private entrepreneur get access to bank financing. Furthermore, not only does legislative membership matter, but the level of the membership is also important, with members of higher-level PCs or PPCCs enjoying more advantages. For example, a provincial-level PC or PPCC member may enjoy more benefits than a member of a county-level one. A member of a higher level PC or PPCC can secure support from a higher-level – and thus more resourceful – government and may enjoy social ties with higher-level political elites. Thus Hypothesis 9.2, from a demand-side view, states that legislative membership can help a private entrepreneur get access to bank financing; and the higher the level of the legislative membership, the lower the financing obstacles faced by the entrepreneur.

Combining the supply-side view and the demand-side view into Hypothesis 9.3, it appears that legislative membership may be more beneficial for smaller private firms, because smaller firms have been more constrained by the regulatory environment throughout the reform period. Therefore, smaller private firms may benefit more when an entrepreneur gains legislative membership. In sum, the smaller the firm, the more benefits it can obtain from the legislative membership of the entrepreneur.

METHOD AND DATA

The data used to test the hypotheses were created from the 2000 National Survey of Chinese Private Enterprises. This survey was designed and administered by a joint research team on private enterprises from the All-China Federation of Industry and Commerce (ACFIC) and the Chinese Academy of Social Sciences (Zhang and Ming 2000). Following the definition of private enterprise specified in the Tentative Stipulations on Private Enterprises promulgated in 1988 by the central government, the 2000 survey included only domestic private businesses which had at least eight employees and were owned by private entrepreneurs. A total of 3,073 private firms from all 31 provinces (including provincial districts and province-level municipal cities) were selected in early spring 2000, and a total of 39 questions were asked to collect information about both the firms and their owners (the entrepreneurs) in 1999.

Dependent Variables

Table 9.2 reports all study variables with their means and standard deviations and the number of non-missing observations. I use four variables to indicate bank financing obstacles. (1) Degree of Difficulty in Obtaining Bank Loans is an ordinal variable ranging from 1, meaning 'very difficult', to 5, meaning 'very easy'. (2) Working capital Primarily Relying on Bank Loans and (3) Investment Capital Primarily Relying on Bank Loans, two binary variables, are coded 1 if the firm relies on bank loans as the most important source for working capital or investment capital, but 0 if it relies on its own savings, informal financing or other sources. If a firm relies on bank loans for working capital or investment capital, then it should have lower financing obstacles. (4) The Interest Rate Paid for the Most Recent Borrowing from Banks is a continuous variable. Higher interest rates are commonly considered an indicator for higher bank financing obstacles.

Independent Variables

Consistent with the economic literature (Beck, Demirguc-Kunt and Maksimovic 2005; Gregory 2000; Schiffer and Weder 2001), I create three dummy variables to indicate firm size. A firm is defined as Small Size if it has less than 50 employees; Medium Size if its employee size is no less than 50 but

Table 9.2   Means and Standard Deviations of Variables (before imputation)

Variables	Mean	S.D.	N
Bank loan variables			
Difficulty in obtaining bank loans (1 = very difficult, 5 = very easy)*	2.228	1.093	2857
Working capital primarily relying on bank loans	.114	.318	2960
Investment capital primarily relying on bank loans	.310	.463	2771
Whether borrowed money from banks before	.649	.477	3000
Interest rate paid for the most recent borrowing from banks (%)*	5.836	3.364	1315
Loan term for the most recent borrowing from banks (month)*	9.481	5.533	1322
Characteristics of the firm owner			
Level of legislative membership (0 = none, 1 = town, 5 = national)*	1.502	1.290	2516
Female	.111	.314	3070
Human capital[a]			
High school graduate	.391	.488	3066
College graduate or above	.384	.486	3066
Natural logarithm of work experience*	3.131	.433	2951
Political capital			
Communist cadre before establishing the firm	.235	.424	2717
Current Party member	.198	.399	3073
Characteristics of the firm			
Natural logarithm of firm age*	2.231	.673	3022
Firm Size [b]			
Small (< 50 employees)	.462	.499	2861
Medium (50 ≤ number of employees < 499)	.473	.499	2861
Firm scope = number of industrial sectors the firm entered*	1.415	.717	3073
Main Industrial sector the firm was in			
Agriculture	.043	.203	3073
Mining	.011	.105	3073
Manufacturing	.363	.481	3073
Utility	.010	.100	3073
Construction	.058	.234	3073
Geological	.001	.018	3073
Transportation	.021	.143	3073
Restaurant	.187	.390	3073
Financial	.002	.040	3073
Real estate	.029	.167	3073
Social service	.056	.231	3073
Health care	.010	.102	3073
Educational	.009	.095	3073
Technical research and service	.023	.151	3073
Others	.087	.282	3073
Industrial data missing	.089	.285	3073
Location of the firm[c]			
Villages	.144	.351	2869
Towns	.584	.493	2869
Registration status			
Firm previously registered as a state or collective firm	.212	.409	3004

Notes: All variables from 1999. All variables are binary, except when marked with '*'.
a. The omitted category of educational level of the owner is lower than high school degree.
b. The omitted category of firm size is large firm (number of employees ≥ 500).
c. The omitted category of location of the firm is firm located in cities.

smaller than 500 and Large Size if it has 500 or more employees. Large Size is designated as the reference category and thus is not shown in Table 9.2.

Level of Legislative Membership is an ordinal variable ranging from 0 to 5. It is coded as 0 if the owner was not a member of a PC or PPCC, 1 for a member of the town-level legislature; 2 for a member of the county-level body; 3 for a member of the prefecture-level legislature; 4 for a member of a province-level body and 5 for a member of the national-level PC or PPCC.[8]

Control Variables

One set of control variables describes the characteristics of the owner of the firm (the entrepreneur). Gender and human capital are often used as control variables in entrepreneurship studies (e.g., Evans and Leighton 1989; Amit, Glosten and Muller 1990; Hamilton 2000). Female is a binary variable with 1 meaning the owner is a female and 0 otherwise. The survey asked the owners their level of education. I created three dummies to indicate their educational level: (1) Lower than Senior High School Diploma, (2) Senior High School Graduate and (3) College Graduate or Above. There is no indicator variable for entrepreneurs with lower than senior high school education in Table 9.2 because it is designated as the reference category for the educational level. Work experience is defined as 2000 minus the first year the owner began to work. As the distribution of this variable spreads widely, its natural logarithmic form is used.

In addition, the market transition literature suggests that other types of entrepreneurial political capital also play an important role for resource acquisition in transitional economies (Róna-Tas 1994). Thus, two other commonly used political capital variables for the owners are also included in all regressions. One is whether the owner was a communist cadre before establishing the firm.[9] 'Cadre Position' here refers to any government position. The other is whether the owner was a member of the Communist Party at the time of the survey.

Another set of the control variables analyzes the characteristics of the firm. Variables about Firm Age, Firm Scope, and dummies for Main Industrial Sector the firm entered are all self-explanatory and are commonly used variables in organizational or economic studies on firms (e.g., Acs and Audretsch 1988; Hannan and Freeman 1989). Firm Age is taken in its natural logarithm to adjust for its skewness.

The location of the main establishment of the firm, i.e., villages, towns or cities, is controlled to capture possible environmental differences among these three areas. Firm Located in Cities is designated as the reference category for this variable. I also control for whether the firm was once registered as a state-owned or collective firm. Being registered as a state-owned or collective firm might help the firm get access to bank loans more easily (Nee 1992). No firm was currently registered as a state-owned/collective firm in the data. Whether Borrowed Money from Banks before is a binary variable, coded as 1 if the firm once borrowed money from banks but 0 otherwise. Loan Term for the Most Recent Borrowing from Banks is a continuous variable. These two variables are used for estimating the Heckit model.

Models

The firm data analyzed here are a multi-stage stratified sample of private enterprises nested within provinces, that were heterogeneous in their stages of market reforms and thus had very different policies toward the private sector (Gregory 2000; Naughton 1995). Therefore, I estimate fixed-effects models with each province dummy added as a group-specific constant term in the regression models to control for environmental heterogeneity across regions (Greene 2000, 560).

Concretely, among the four dependent variables, Working Capital Primarily Relying on Bank Loans and Investment Capital Primarily Relying on Bank Loans are binary variables. Therefore, I use fixed-effects logit models (Greene 2000, 839). Degree of Difficulty to Obtain Bank Loans is an ordinal variable, and thus I use a fixed-effects ordered logit model (Long 1997, 138).

For Interest Rate Paid for the Most Recent Borrowing from Banks, since it is observed only if the private firm has borrowed money from banks before, there is a sample selection problem. To solve this problem, I use Heckman's two-step estimation procedure (Greene 2000, 930; Heckman 1979). Detailed model specification for the two-step estimation procedure will be discussed in the next section.

In estimating all of the models above, the missing values of all enterprise-level independent variables are imputed with best-subset regression imputation models which use a reliable procedure for handling missing data. With this imputation procedure, missing values for the independent variables of a regression model are imputed as a function of whatever non-missing data are available on the other independent variables in the model. All observations with at least some non-missing data are therefore included in the model (Morgan 2001). This procedure is easily defendable, because a set of values are imputed for each missing value, and the variances of these imputed sets are explicitly incorporated into the standard errors of the resulting parameter estimates (Little and Rubin 1987; Morgan 2001).

RESULTS

Degree of Difficulty to Obtain Bank Loans

Table 9.3 reports coefficients from fixed effects ordered logit models predicting Degree of Difficulty to Obtain Bank Loans. Model 1 is a baseline model which includes all variables in Table 9.2 about the characteristics of the entrepreneur and the firm, except for the Level of Legislative Membership and the interactions between membership and firm size. Large Size is the comparison group and thus is not shown in the model. From the negative signs and the high significance level of the coefficients for the two firm size dummies, Model 1 suggests that larger firms are much easier to obtain bank loans. Thus, Hypothesis 9.1 is strongly supported.

Model 2 adds the Level of Legislative Membership into the baseline model. Although it makes little sense to interpret the coefficient associated with this variable, since it is an ordinal scale, the coefficient is positive and statistically significant, indicating legislative membership, together with the level of the membership, facilitates access to bank loans. Overall, the results in Model 2 provide support to Hypothesis 9.2.

Model 3 adds the interactions between the Level of Legislative Membership and all three firm size dummies into the baseline model. The results in Model 3 suggest that legislative membership may benefit medium firms more than small and large ones in terms of access to bank loans. For large firms, legislative membership did not bring many benefits, perhaps because they already had easy access to bank loans. Small firms, on the other hand, might not need much capital and had seldom asked for bank loans, although they were severely constrained by bank loan policies. Thus, legislative membership also may not benefit them much in access to bank loans. Medium firms, however, were both constrained by bank loan policies and hungry for capital and can thus benefit from legislative membership. Therefore, Hypothesis 9.3 is only partly supported.

Models 1–3 also suggest that the effects of the Party Membership of the Entrepreneur are positive but not statistically significant. This may be because, unlike membership in the PC or PPCC, that authorizes the entrepreneurs to play an active role in Chinese politics, Party membership does not guarantee entrepreneurs a role in local politics. Many entrepreneurs were actually brought into the Party reluctantly by local party branches and seldom went to Party meetings.[10]

Table 9.3   *Coefficients from Fixed Effects Ordered Logit Model Predicting the Degree of Difficulty to Obtain Bank Loans*

Independent Variables	Model 1	Model 2	Model 3
Small firm	−.926***	−.829***	−.868***
	(.159)	(.162)	(.267)
Medium firm	−.561***	−.515***	−.675*
	(.150)	(.150)	(.270)
Level of legislative membership		.100**	
		(.037)	
Level of legislative membership small firm			.042
			(.058)
Level of legislative membership medium firm			.155**
			(.051)
Level of legislative membership large firm			.059
			(.106)
Selected other variables[a]			
Communist cadre before establishing the firm	−.069	−.061	−.062
	(.097)	(.097)	(.097)
Party membership	.089	.091	.095
	(.088)	(.088)	(.088)
Natural logarithm of firm age	.099+	.073	.073
	(.055)	(.056)	(.056)
Firm once registered as a state or collective firm	−.027	−.014	−.019
	(.091)	(.091)	(.091)
Firm located in villages	.216+	.207+	.206+
	(.125)	(.125)	(.124)
Firm located in towns	.237**	.236**	.232**
	(.089)	(.088)	(.089)
Cut point 1[b]	−.490	−.529	−.632
Cut point 2	.970	.935	.834
Cut point 3	2.291	2.258	2.157
Cut point 4	4.231	4.200	4.100
Log likelihood	−3858.065	−3854.234	−3852.640
Number of Cases	2857	2857	2857

Notes:
a. All other variables on the characteristics of the firm and the owner of the firm as shown in Table 9.2 are controlled in the models. In parentheses are robust standard errors.
b. In ordered logistic regression, STATA sets the constant to zero and estimates the cut points for separating the various levels of the response variable.
+ $p < .10$; * $p < .05$; ** $p < .01$; *** $p < .001$ (two-tailed tests).

Table 9.4   *Coefficients from Fixed Effects Logit Model Predicting Working Capital Primarily Relying on Bank Loans*

Independent Variables	Model 4	Model 5	Model 6
Constant	−20.070***	−19.969***	−19.649***
	(1.182)	(1.211)	(1.396)
Small firm	−.444+	−.281	−.549
	(.266)	(.277)	(.406)
Medium firm	−.173	−.094	−.460
	(.242)	(.247)	(.398)
Level of legislative membership		.171**	
		(.060)	
Level of legislative membership small firm			.150
			(.103)
Level of legislative membership medium firm			.224**
			(.080)
Level of legislative membership large firm			.033
			(.148)
Selected Other Variables[a]			
Communist cadre before establishing the firm	.027	.025	.026
	(.165)	(.165)	(.165)
Party membership	.215	.234	.238
	(.150)	(.150)	(.150)
Natural logarithm of firm age	−.072	−.122	−.126
	(.098)	(.100)	(.100)
Firm once registered as a state or collective firm before	.161	.186	.182
	(.151)	(.151)	(.151)
Firm located in villages	.609***	.586**	.586**
	(.198)	(.198)	(.198)
Firm located in towns	.355*	.347*	.343*
	(.155)	(.155)	(.155)
Log likelihood	−972.549	−968.676	−967.744
Number of Cases	2960	2960	2960

Notes:
a. All other variables on the characteristics of the firm and the owner of the firm as shown in Table 9.2 are controlled in the models. In parentheses are robust standard errors.
+ $p < .10$; * $p < .05$; ** $p < .01$; *** $p < .001$ (two-tailed tests).

Working Capital Primarily Relying on Bank Loans

Table 9.4 reports coefficients from fixed-effects logit models predicting working capital primarily relying on bank loans. As with Model 1 in Table 9.3, Model 4 is a baseline model that includes all variables in Table 9.2 about the characteristics of the entrepreneur and the firm, except the level of legislative membership and the membership-firm size interactions. Large Size is still the comparison group and thus is not shown in the model. Note that larger firms are more likely to rely on bank loans as their primary source for working capital, since the coefficients of both small size and medium size are negative, although only the coefficient of small size is statistically significant. Holding all other variables constant, the odds of securing working-capital loans are expected to change by a factor of 0.64 ($e^{-0.444}$) from being a large firm to a small one, and, though not statistically significant, by a factor of 0.84 ($e^{-0.173}$) from being a large firm to a medium one. Thus, Hypothesis 9.1 from the supply-side view is largely supported.

Model 5 adds the Level of Legislative Membership into the baseline model. The coefficient associated with this variable is positive and statistically significant, indicating legislative membership, together with the level of the membership, helps firms secure bank loans as the primary source for working capital. Thus, the results in Model 5 provide support to Hypothesis 9.2.

Model 6 adds the interactions between the level of legislative membership and all three firm-size dummies into the baseline model. Similar to the pattern found in Model 3, the results in Model 6 suggest that legislative membership may benefit medium-size firms more than small and large ones. Thus, Model 6 only provides some support to Hypothesis 9.3. In addition, as with Models 1–3, Models 4–6 also suggest that the effects of the owner's party membership are positive but not statistically significant, indicating that benefits of party membership are not guaranteed.

Investment Capital Primarily Relying on Bank Loans

Models 7–9 in Table 9.5, that are structurally equivalent with Models 4–6, report coefficients from fixed-effects logit models predicting Investment Capital Primarily Relying on Bank Loans. Results in Models 7 and 8 are remarkably similar to those in Models 4 and 5, and thus will not be discussed in detail here. Results in Model 9, however, are different from those in Models 3 and 6. According to Model 9, legislative membership may benefit small firms more than large and medium ones in securing bank loans as the primary source for investment capital. This may be because even small firms needed to borrow from banks, since the amount of capital needed was often too large for retained profits to cover. And since small firms were the most constrained, legislative membership could thus provide greater support to them. This result largely supports Hypothesis 9.3.

In addition, Models 7–9 suggest that party membership of the owners has almost zero effect on securing bank loans as the primary source for investment capital, further indicating that benefits from party membership are not guaranteed.

Interest Rate

As mentioned in the previous section, predicting the last dependent variable – the Interest Rate Paid for the Most Recent Borrowing from Banks – involves a sample-selection problem. The sample-selection problem resides in the fact that those firms which have reported the Interest Rate Paid for the Most Recent Borrowing from Banks obviously must have borrowed money from some bank. Thus, those not having borrowed from banks previously are incidentally truncated, and the average interest rate in the data would be misleading as an indication of the average interest rate in the population. If I ran OLS regression of interest rates on its determinants using only data for the firms having reported their interest rates, it would produce inconsistent estimates for the coefficients. To solve this problem, Heckman (1979) suggested a two-step estimation procedure, known as the Heckit model (Greene 2000, 926–34).

Step one is a probit equation predicting Whether the Firm Has Borrowed Money from Banks before, using all variables on the characteristics of the firms and the owners of the firms in Table 9.2, the Degree of Difficulty in Obtaining Bank Loans, Working Capital Primarily Relying on Bank Loans, and Investment Capital Primarily Relying on Bank Loans as predictors. The more easily a firm obtains bank loans and the more a firm relies on bank loans for either working or investment capital, the more likely it is that the firm would have borrowed money from banks before. From the probit estimation, the propensity to have borrowed money from banks for each firm in the selected sample – λ – is calculated.

Second, I estimate the coefficients of the covariates by least-squares regression of Interest Rate on X_{ij} and λ - with fixed effects. Here X_{ij} includes not only variables on the characteristics of the firm and the entrepreneur in Table 9.2, but also the Loan Term for the Most Recent Borrowing from Banks.

Models 10–12 in Table 9.6 report coefficients from the fixed-effects Heckit models. Every model has two equations. The loan equations, that are the same across the three models, correspond to the first step, and the interest equations the second step. The loan equations suggest that Working Capital Primarily Relying on Bank Loans has a significantly positive effect on Whether the

Table 9.5   *Coefficients from Fixed Effects Logit Model Predicting*
Investment Capital Primarily Relying on Bank Loans

Independent Variables	Model 7	Model 8	Model 9
Constant	−981[+] (.519)	−948[+] (.519)	−983[+] (.571)
Small firm	−.253 (.193)	−.175 (.198)	−.196 (.324)
Medium firm	.004 (.182)	.041 (.183)	.159 (.320)
Level of legislative membership		.085* (.043)	
Level of legislative membership small firm			.169* (.071)
Level of legislative membership medium firm			.036 (.058)
Level of legislative membership large firm			.112 (.124)
Selected other variables[a]			
Communist cadre before establishing the firm	.114 (.113)	.117 (.113)	.120 (.113)
Party membership	−.001 (.110)	.005 (.110)	.004 (.110)
Natural logarithm of firm age	−.091 (.072)	−.115 (.073)	−.121[+] (.073)
Firm once registered as a state or Collective firm	.080 (.108)	.090 (.108)	.094 (.108)
Firm located in villages	.167 (.149)	.157 (.150)	.158 (.150)
Firm located in towns	.225* (.105)	.224* (.105)	.227* (.105)
Log likelihood	−1652.010	−1650.131	−1648.679
Number of Cases	2771	2771	2771

Notes:
a. All other variables on the characteristics of the firm and the owner of the firm as shown in
   Table 9.2 are controlled in the models. In parentheses are robust standard errors.
+ $p < .10$; * $p < .05$; ** $p < .01$; *** $p < .001$ (two-tailed tests).

Table 9.6 *Coefficients from Fixed Effects Heckit Model Predicting Interest Rate Paid for the Most Recent Borrowing from Banks*

Independent Variables[a]	Model 10		Model 11		Model 12	
	Interest equation	Loan equation	Interest equation	Loan equation	Interest equation	Loan equation
Constant	3.010 (3.230)	2.499*** (.649)	1.173 (3.246)	2.499*** (.649)	1.157 (3.315)	2.499*** (.649)
Small firm	.859* (.428)	−.223 (.264)	.727+ (.451)	−.223 (.264)	.814 (.738)	−.223 (.264)
Medium firm	.108 (.382)	−.053 (.246)	.026 (.401)	−.053 (.246)	−.402 (.723)	−.053 (.246)
Level of legislative membership		.065 (.055)	−.193+ (.105)	.065 (.055)		.065 (.055)
Level of legislative membership small firm		−		−	−.486** (.169)	−
Level of legislative membership medium firm		−		−	−.029 (.130)	−
Level of legislative membership large firm		−		−	−.281 (.270)	−
Loan term for the most recent borrowing from banks	−.012 (.018)	−	−.013 (.018)	−	−.012 (.018)	−
Degree of difficulty obtaining bank Loans	−	.018 (.054)	−	.018 (.054)	−	.018 (.054)
Investment capital primarily relying on bank loans	−	−.105 (.127)	−	−.105 (.127)	−	−.105 (.127)
Working capital primarily relying on bank loans	−	.345* (.179)	−	.345* (.179)	−	.345* (.179)
λ		−1.923 (1.395)		−2.775* (1.388)		−2.816* (1.382)
Number of Cases		1237		1237		1237

Notes:

a. All other variables on the characteristics of the firm and the owner of the firm as shown in Table 9.2 are controlled in all equations in this table. In parentheses are two-step efficient estimates of standard errors.

+ $p < .10$; * $p < .05$; ** $p < .01$;*** $p < .001$ (two-tailed tests).

Firm Has Borrowed Money from Banks Before. Larger firms and legislative membership also have positive effects on borrowing, although the effects are not statistically significant.

The primary interest here, of course, is in the interest equations. The interest equation in Model 10 excludes the level of legislative membership and membership-firm size interactions, and serves as the baseline model. Large Size is the comparison group and thus is not shown in the model. Note that smaller firms pay higher interest rates when borrowing from banks, since the coefficients for both small size and medium size are positive, although only the coefficient for small size is statistically significant. Holding all other variables constant, small firms pay 0.86 points more in interest rates than large firms; and, though not statistically significant, medium firms pay 0.11 points more than large firms. Thus, Hypothesis 9.1 from the supply-side view is largely supported.

The interest equation in Model 11 adds the level of legislative membership into the baseline model. The coefficient associated with this variable is negative and statistically significant (at the α level of 0.1), indicating legislative membership, together with the level of the membership, helps firms get cheaper bank loans. Thus, the results in Model 11 provide support to Hypothesis 9.2.

The interest equation in Model 12 adds the interactions between the level of legislative membership and all three firm size dummies into the baseline model. According to this model, legislative membership may benefit small firms more than both large and medium ones in access to cheaper bank loans. This may be because small firms were the most constrained by state interest policies (ADB 2003), and legislative membership could provide greater support to them. This result largely supports Hypothesis 9.3.

Discussion

For the reason of parsimony, I have used one ordinal variable: Level of Legislative Membership as the key independent variable to test the hypotheses. For robust check, I also used five dummy variables, that indicate township-level, county-level, prefecture-level, province-level and national-level legislative membership with no membership as the comparison group, to replace the ordinal variable. The results from using dummy variables support the hypotheses in general, but are not parsimonious.

Omitted variable bias is a fundamental and pernicious problem in regression analysis. In entrepreneurship research, omitted variable bias usually results from the unobserved ability of the entrepreneur. Could it be possible that both legislative membership and the lower bank financing obstacle are simply the results of the stronger ability of the entrepreneur? It is very possible that an unobserved ability of the entrepreneur may help him or her to both become a member in a PC or PPCC and reduce bank financing obstacles. For example, an entrepreneur with strong interpersonal skills may allow him to be co-opted by Party committees as a member of a PC or PPCC; he may also successfully persuade financial institutions to engage in relationship lending with him. However, legislative membership could also enhance the unobserved ability of the entrepreneur by providing both legitimacy and higher sociopolitical status to the entrepreneur. A capable entrepreneur with no legitimacy and low status may be more likely to succeed when the state is politically weak or when it is friendly to entrepreneurs. The Chinese government during the reform era, however, is politically very strong and unfriendly to entrepreneurs, and thus both legitimacy and higher sociopolitical status attached to the legislative membership are useful for the entrepreneur to succeed.

CONCLUSION

Entrepreneurs are often wealth constrained and need to obtain external financing, especially bank financing, to pursue their opportunities. Given the rapid expansion of private entrepreneurship and the discriminatory regulatory policies to the private sector, how has the Chinese private sector been financed? Previous studies have neglected the role played by bank financing for private firms because of the discriminative bank practices. This study, however, shows that bank financing has, in fact, played a significant role in private sector growth.

The goal of this study is to understand how private entrepreneurs obtain bank financing in China. The supply-side view argues that firm size matters. Larger firms, according to this explanation, have advantages when obtaining bank loans because they have more transparent structures and can provide adequate collateral. While the predictions of this view are largely supported by the firm-level data in this chapter, it views private entrepreneurs as passive actors subjected to the outside environment.

The key insight from the resource-dependence perspective is that entrepreneurs are actually very active in playing strategies to acquire critical resources from the environment. Given the significance of politics in businesses, many Chinese entrepreneurs are eager to obtain a political position, as is clearly shown in the multiple national surveys of Chinese private enterprises (Zhang and Ming 1999, 108). And memberships in PCs and PPCCs are among the most attractive positions for private entrepreneurs, because of the substantial legitimacy and social capital benefits that these positions could bring to the incumbents. This study suggests that memberships in PCs and PPCCs could indeed facilitate access to bank loans for private entrepreneurs; and they are especially helpful for small or medium private firms.

This research may be related to a broader debate on the role of corruption in economic development. As this study demonstrates, under the unfriendly regulatory environment, Chinese private entrepreneurs have resorted to premeditated political strategies and networks for resolving their financing problem. Such entrepreneurial political behavior may involve rent seeking and corruption. The competition among entrepreneurs for the legislative membership creates opportunities for local party officials to extract bribes from those competitors. Corruption may also emerge when the entrepreneur uses high-status contacts to establish relationship lending or to intervene on behalf of him in the credit decisions of banks.

Evidence in this chapter, however, seems to deviate from the findings of previous empirical research which suggests that corruption produces negative economic consequences (see, e.g., Mauro 1995; Tanzi and Davoodi 1997). This study suggests that corruption may have facilitated bank financing for Chinese private firms, especially small and medium ones, which are more constrained by the regulatory environment. In this sense, it provides some support to the view that corruption may serve as the grease for the wheels of commerce (Huntington 1968).

Nevertheless, the entrepreneurial political behavior discussed in this study could potentially damage the national economy in the long run. By bringing favored private entrepreneurs into the PC or PPCC and allowing them to enjoy economic privilege, the Communist Party may have transformed potential political enemies into allies. However, this will create an uneven playing field among private firms, thus discouraging many entrepreneurs or potential entrepreneurs from investment.

Since China was accepted into the World Trade Organization in 2001, the Chinese government has been taking measures to provide more protection to private property rights and to level the playing field for all firms. This is a blessing for private firms, especially small and medium ones. If such effort were to succeed, then the economic rationale for entrepreneurs to engage in political behavior would not exist any more – and the private sector as whole might grow even faster.

NOTES

I am grateful to Victor Nee, Paul Lee, Chris Yenkey, and the editors of this book for their helpful comments on earlier versions of the paper. However, the author is responsible for any remaining errors. A different version of the study has been accepted by *World Development*.

1. In this study, the private sector refers to the domestic private sector only. It does not include either private corporations established by foreigners or joint ventures between foreign direct investments and domestic firms. It only includes non-farming private enterprises (*siying qiye*) and non-farming individual enterprises (*getihu*). According to the Tentative Stipulations on Private Enterprises promulgated by the central government in 1988, the difference between private enterprises and individual enterprises is in the employee size: A private firm is called a private enterprise if its employee size is larger than seven, but called an individual enterprise if its employee size is fewer than eight. I do not differentiate the two types and call both 'private firms'.
2. To date, both public and private equity markets in China have served primarily to finance state-owned enterprises but not private firms.
3. Informal finance ranges from casual interpersonal borrowing and trade credit among wholesalers and retailers to more institutionalized mechanisms such as rotating credit associations, grassroots credit cooperatives and even full-service yet unsanctioned private banks (Tsai 2002, 3).
4. The People's Congress has five levels: town, county, prefecture, provincial and national. The People's Political Consultative Conference has four levels: county, prefecture, provincial and national.
5. During the 1989 Tiananmen Square student movement, for example, private entrepreneurs, most prominently Wan Runnan of Beijing Stone Corporation, supported students demonstrating for a democratic government, angering the Party leaders and resulting in the subsequent crackdown on private businesses from 1989 to 1992 (Dickson 2003, 99).
6. Nobility titles, for example, constitute an institutionalized form of social capital.
7. Remember, a significant proportion of the positions in both PC and PPCC have been preserved for semi-retired party or government officials, who may still have strong influences on politics. Being a member of a PC or PPCC, thus, increases the probability of establishing social ties to these officials.
8. I could also use five dummy variables indicating the level of legislative membership. Such coding strategy, however, does not change the overall results reported here. To keep it parsimonious, I use the ordinal variable.
9. According to government regulations, current communist cadres cannot also be private entrepreneurs.
10. As one private entrepreneur in Ningbo, Zhengjiang, told me in summer 2004, 'I am not interested in joining the party. How can it benefit me? But the party chief in my village asked me to join it for many times in order to fulfill his duty. [After 1997, the Party began to recruit private entrepreneurs into it and every village party branch is required to recruit a few entrepreneurs.] So I joined it several years ago. However, although I pay party membership fees every year, I never went to the meetings. That is a waste of my time'.

BIBLIOGRAPHY

Acs, Zoltan and David B. Audretsch (1988), 'Innovation in Large and Small Firms: An Empirical Analysis', *American Economic Review*, **78** (4), 678–90.

Amit, Raphael, Lawrence Glosten and Eitan Muller (1990), 'Entrepreneurial Ability, Venture Investments and Risk Sharing', *Management Science*, **36** (10), 1232–45.

Asian Development Bank (2003), *The Development of Private Enterprise in People's Republic of China*, Manila: Asian Development Bank.

Beck, Thorsten, Asli Demirguc-Kunt and Vojislav Maksimovic (2005), 'Financial and Legal Constraints to Growth: Does Firm Size Matter?', *Journal of Finance*, **60** (1), 137–77.

Berger, Allen and Gregory Udell (1998), 'The Economics of Small Business Finance', *Journal of Banking and Finance*, **22** (6–8), 613–73.

Bourdieu, Pierre (1986) 'The Forms of Capital', in John Richardson (ed.) *Handbook of Theory and Research for the Sociology of Education*, New York: Greenwood Press, pp. 241–58.

Burt, Ronald (1992), *Structural Holes*, Cambridge, MA: Harvard University Press.

Byrd, William and Qingsong Lin (1990), *China's Rural Industry*, New York: Oxford University Press.

Casson, Mark (1982), *Entrepreneur: An Economic Theory*, Totowa, NJ: Barnes and Noble Books.

Dickson, Bruce J. (2003), *Red Capitalists in China*, New York: Cambridge University Press.

Dreyer, June Teufel (1999), *China's Political System: Modernization and Tradition*, Boston: Allyn and Bacon.

Evans, David and Linda Leighton (1989), 'Some Empirical Aspects of Entrepreneurship', *American Economic Review*, **79** (3), 519–35.

Greene, William H. (2000), *Econometric Analysis*, 4th ed., Upper Saddle River, NJ: Prentice-Hall.

Gregory, Neil E. (2000), *China's Emerging Private Enterprises: Prospects for the New Century*, Washington, DC: International Finance Corporation.

Gulati, Ranjay (1995), 'Does Familiarity Breed Trust?', *Academy of Management Journal*, **38** (1), 85–112.

Hamilton, Barton H. (2000), 'Does Entrepreneurship Pay?', *Journal of Political Economy*, **108** (3), 604–31.

Hannan, Michael T. and John Freeman (1989), *Organizational Ecology*, Cambridge, MA: Harvard University Press.

Huntington, Samuel (1968), *Political Order in Changing Societies*, New Haven: Yale University Press.

He, Xiaan (1999), 'The Past, Current, and Future of Fuyang', [Fuyang de Guoqu Xianzai he Jianglai] in Houyi Zhang and Lizhi Ming (eds), *Zhongguo Siying Qiye Fazhan Baogao, 1978–1998* [The Development Report of Chinese Private Enterprises from 1978 to 1998], Beijing: China Social Science Literature Press, pp. 194–205.

Heckman, James (1979), 'Sample Selection Bias as Specification Error', *Econometrica*, **47** (1), 153–61.

Jiang, Nanyang (1999), 'On Entrepreneurial Political Participation', [Qiyejia de Zhengzhi Canyu] in Houyi Zhang and Lizhi Ming (eds), *Zhongguo Siying Qiye Fazhan Baogao, 1978–1998* [The Development Report of Chinese Private Enterprises from 1978 to 1998], Beijing: China Social Science Literature Press, pp. 103–17.

Lardy, Nicholas (1998), *China's Unfinished Economic Revolution*, Washington, DC: Brookings Institution Press.

Lin, Justin Y., Fang Cai and Zhou Li (1996), *The China Miracle: Development Strategy and Economic Reform*, Hong Kong: Chinese University Press.

Little, Roderick and Donald B. Rubin (1987), *Statistical Analysis with Missing Data*, Hoboken, NJ: John Wiley & Sons.

Long, J. Scott (1997), *Regression Models for Categorical and Limited Dependent Variables*, Thousand Oaks, CA: Sage Publications.

Mauro, Paolo (1995), 'Corruption and Growth', *Quarterly Journal of Economics*, **110** (3), 681–712.

Morgan, Stephen (2001), 'Counterfactual, Causal Effect Heterogeneity and the Catholic School Effect on Learning', *Sociology of Education*, **74** (4), 341–74.

Naughton, Barry (1995), *Growing out of the Plan: Chinese Economic Reform, 1978–1993*, New York: Cambridge University Press.

Nee, Victor (1992), 'Organizational Dynamics of Market Transition: Hybrid Forms, Property Rights, and Mixed Economy in China', *Administrative Science Quarterly*, **37** (1), 1–27.

Oi, Jean C. (1992), 'Fiscal Reform and the Economic Foundations of Local State Corporatism in China', *World Politics*, **45** (1), 99–126.

Oliver, Christine (1991), 'Strategic Responses to Institutional Processes', *Academy of Management Review*, **16** (1), 145–79.

Peng, Yusheng (2004), 'Kinship Networks and Entrepreneurs in China's Transitional Economy', *American Journal of Sociology*, **109** (55), 1045–74.

Pfeffer, Jeffrey (1982), *Organizations and Organization Theory*, Boston: Pitman.

Pfeffer, Jeffrey and Ferald R. Salancik (1978), *The External Control of Organizations: A Resource Dependence Perspective*, New York: Harper & Row.

Róna-Tas, Ákos (1994), 'The First Shall Be the Last? Entrepreneurship and Communist Cadres in the Transition from Socialism', *American Journal of Sociology*, **100** (1), 40–69.

Schiffer, Mirjam and Beatrice Weder (2001), 'Firm Size and the Business Environment: Worldwide Survey Results', Washington, DC, International Finance Corporation Discussion Paper No. 43.

Shane, Scott and Daniel Cable (2002), 'Network Ties, Reputation, and the Financing of New Ventures', *Management Science*, **48** (3), 364–81.

Suchman, Mark C. (1995), 'Managing Legitimacy: Strategic and Institutional Approaches', *Academy of Management Journal*, **20** (3), 571–610.

Tanzi, Vito and Hamid Davoodi (1997), 'Corruption, Public Investment, and Growth', Washington, DC, IMF Working Paper No. 97/139.

Tong, Yanqi (1994), 'State, Society and Political Change in China and Hungary', *Comparative Politics*, **26** (3), 333–53.

Tsai, Kellee S. (2002), *Back-Alley Banking*, Ithaca: Cornell University Press.

Walder, Andrew G. (1995), 'Local Governments as Industrial Corporations: An Organizational Analysis of China's Transitional Economy', *American Journal of Sociology*, **101** (2), 263–301.

World Bank (2002), *Transition: The First Ten Years: Analysis and Lesson for Eastern Europe and the Former Soviet Union*, Washington, DC: World Bank.

Zhang, Houyi and Lizhi Ming (eds) (1999), *Zhongguo Siying Qiye Fazhan Baogao, 1978–1998* [The Development Report of Chinese Private Enterprises, 1978–1998], Beijing: China Social Science Literature Press.

Zhang, Houyi and Lizhi Ming (eds) (2000), *Zhongguo Siying Qiye Fazhan Baogao, 1999* [The Development Report of Chinese Private Enterprises, 1999], Beijing: China Social Science Literature Press.

10. Grassroots Democracy, Accountability and Income Distribution: Evidence from Rural China

Yan Shen and Yang Yao

After the commune system was dissolved in the early 1980s, the state introduced village elections in rural China to enhance village governance. In 1987 the National People's Congress (NPC) passed a preliminary version of the Organic Law of Village Committee (OLVC), launching a ten-year experiment with village elections. In 1998 the NPC formally passed the final version of the law, and elections quickly spread to the whole country. However, since the first elections began in the mid-1980s, there has been controversy about their impact on daily life in Chinese villages.

The elections hardly take place in a friendly institutional environment. Within the village, the authority of the elected village committee is seriously constrained, if not superseded, by the Communist Party committee; outside the village, the township and county governments still maintain a heavy hand in village affairs. As a result, even if the elected village committee is willing to advance the interests of the villagers, it may not be able to do so. On the other hand, the decentralized nature of the elections may make it easier for local elites to capture local politics; in practice, democracy does not necessarily lead to a fairer provision of public goods (Bardhan and Mookherjee 2005). There is evidence that business elites have begun to dominate the local elections in some villages (Liu, Wang and Yao 2001). In addition, lineage influences political alignments in many village elections, and people worry that bias could distort the effects of the election.

However, there have been few empirical studies devoted to exploring the actual performance of village elections. Using survey data from 48 villages for the period 1987–2002, this study provides systematic evidence about how elections affect accountability and income distribution in the village.

The existing literature suggests that local elections generally increase a local government's responsiveness to its constituency. For example, Foster and Rosenzweig (2001) found that village elections in India led to more investment in road building instead of irrigation facilities. They interpreted this finding as evidence for a pro-poor policy, because road building provides jobs to the landless whereas investment in irrigation facilities augments the capacity of the landlords. Using data from a quasi-experiment in India in which a group of randomly selected villages were required to elect a woman to lead the village, Chattopadhyay and Duflo (2004) found that the villages headed by women tended to provide more female-friendly public services. Using a sample from China's Jiangsu province, Zhang, Fan, Zhang and Huang (2004) found that village elections had increased the share of public investment and has no effect on the amount of taxes handed over to the township. Gan, Xu and Yao (2005, 2006) further found that village elections helped to reduce the negative impacts of health shocks on farmers' income by an annual average of 11.6 per cent and to strengthen farmers' consumption-smoothing capabilities. Lastly, drawing on a sample from Shaanxi province which compared elections with government-appointed candidates, Kennedy, Rozelle and Shi (2004) found that more competitive elections, in which candidates were nominated by villagers, produced village leaders who were more accountable to villagers in decisions regarding land reallocation.

There are two ways that village elections can have positive effects on income inequality. First, democracy could lead the government to cater to the interests of the median voter, who generally prefers income redistribution because his income is usually less than the group mean (Alesina and Rodrik 1994; Benabou 1996). Second, democracy could press the government to spend more to increase the income of the poorer portion of the population, because poverty exerts negative externalities on the richer (Gan, Xu and Yao 2005). Existing studies using country-level data have not provided conclusive results, however (Milanovic and Ying 2001).

Our data covers a critical period of time which has witnessed a rapid increase in income inequality in rural China. Nationwide, the rural Gini coefficient increased from 0.29 in 1987 to 0.35 in 2000 (Riskin, Zhao and Li 2002). At the same time, government investment in the countryside decreased. Using the two-way fixed-effect panel method, we found four important outcomes. First, on average, introducing the village election has increased the share of public expenditures in the village government's total expenditures by 4.2 percentage points, equivalent to 22.8 per cent of the average share in the sample. Second, it has also reduced the share of administrative expenditures by 4 percentage points, equivalent to 18.2 per cent of the sample average. To the extent that public expenditures are used to advance the interests of the villagers and administrative expenditures are mostly spent to satisfy the needs of the village leaders, these two results suggest that elections have enhanced the accountability of the village committee. Third, village elections have not led to more income redistribution; on the contrary, they have reduced the progressiveness of income redistribution. This means that the increased share of public expenditures has been devoted to productive investments, since income transfer and investment are the only two components of public expenditures. Lastly, the introduction of elections, on average, reduces the Gini coefficient in a village by 0.016, equal to 5.7 per cent of the sample average. Because income redistribution has not increased, this improvement has to be the result of village pro-poor actions, such as increasing productive investments. These results show that the village election mechanism has worked, despite the many constraints imposed on it.

Below, we first review the performance of the village election experiment over the last 20 years and discuss the issues involved in the process. After describing the data and presenting descriptive evidence for the election, village expenditures, income redistribution and Gini coefficients, we turn to econometric analysis and conclusions.

VILLAGE ELECTIONS IN RURAL CHINA

The Chinese commune system was dissolved in the early 1980s. Administratively, townships replaced communes, while village committees (VC) replaced commune production brigades. The 1982 Constitution defines the village committee as a self-governing body of villagers (Clause 111). However, committee members were appointed rather than elected in all but a few localities. In 1987, under the leadership of Vice Chairman Peng Zhen, the NPC passed a tentative version of the OLVC which required elections for all village committees. This law triggered elections in Chinese villages, and by 1994 half had begun elections. By 1997, 25 of the 31 mainland provinces had adopted a local version of the law, and 80 per cent of the villages had begun elections (Ministry of Civil Affairs 1998). The NPC passed the formal version of the OLVC in 1998 and elections quickly spread to almost all the villages.

The VC is comprised of three to seven members, depending on the size of the village. The core members are the chairman, vice chairman and treasurer. Before 1998, candidates for the chairmanship were usually appointed by the township government although popular nomination, a mixture of government appointment and popular nomination, and nomination by village representatives also existed. The formal version of the OLVC requires candidates to be nominated by at least ten villagers. A primary election reduces the field of candidates to two, and the formal contest is run between these two candidates. This election scheme is popularly called *hai-xuan*. The term of the committee is three years, but there is no term limit.

Village elections in China operate in a weak institutional environment. In a typical village, the elected VC faces two major challenges which may hinder its ability to serve villager interests. First, although the Party committee is not popularly elected, the OLVC stipulates that the VC works under the leadership of the party committee, reflecting the nature of China's one-party political system. Since he is appointed by a higher authority, the party secretary often pursues an agenda different from the VC's. Backed by popular votes, however, the chairman of the VC often defies the direction of the party secretary, but the outcome is not always in his favor (Oi and Rozelle 2000; Guo and Bernstein 2004). To reconcile the conflicts between the VC and the party secretary, the central government has begun to encourage the party leader to seek election as the VC chairman. While this may ease the tension inside the village (Guo and Bernstein 2004), the VC still faces a second challenge.

Since village elections operate in an authoritarian institutional environment, where the upper-level governments – the township and county governments in particular – are not elected and often intrude on village elections and other village affairs, the VCs' ability to serve its constituents is in doubt. Evidence shows that informed local people tend not to trust elections. For example, in a survey conducted in Fujian province, Zhong and Chen (2002) found that villagers with low levels of internal efficacy and democratic values were more likely to participate in an election, and those with higher levels of internal efficacy and democratic orientation are more likely to stay away from elections because they are aware of the institutional constraints placed upon the VC.

Given these two challenges, will elections enhance the VC's accountability to the local population? This question is compounded by the possibility of elite capture inside the village. Studying India, Bardhan and Mookherjee (2005) found that decentralization could lead to elite capture at the local level if the financing of public goods provision was not properly designed. In the context of the Chinese village, rising business elites frequently dominate the village election (Liu, Wang and Yao 2001). Although there are not *a priori* reasons to believe that business elites would necessarily steer the VC to adopt pro-rich policies, this belief lingers within Chinese academic and policy circles. In addition, lineages have regained strength and voters frequently chose candidates based on family ties rather than policy orientation (Liu, Wang and Yao 2001). Some observers worry that the revitalization of lineage will distort the results of village elections.

Figure 10.1   Introduction of Village Elections in Sample Villages

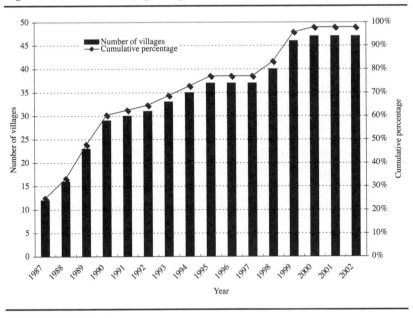

DATA AND RESEARCH DESIGN

Our data come from two sources: the Fixed-Point Survey (FPS), maintained by the Ministry of Agriculture's Research Center on the Rural Economy, and a retrospective survey we conducted in the spring of 2003. The FPS started in 1986 and has maintained a survey sample of about 340 villages and 30,000 households in all Chinese continental provinces. One advantage of the dataset is that it surveys a relative large number of households (50–100) in a village. This feature enables us to calculate the Gini coefficient in a village with a fair degree of accuracy. We obtained data on 48 villages in eight provinces for the period 1986–2002.[1] These eight provinces are Guangdong, Zhejiang, Hunan, Henan, Sichuan, Gansu, Shanxi and Jilin. They cover diverse geographic settings and income levels. The 2003 retrospective survey provides information on village elections in the 48 villages. Our household sample is smaller than the FPS sample. The FPS does not have a good record of the household codes, so we had to use household characteristics to match households in order to establish the panel structure. This led us to obtain a smaller sample of 1,118 households for household-level analysis. In addition, household data starts in 1987 instead of 1986.

Table 10.1   *First Election in Sample Villages and Adoption of the OLVC OLVC in Sample Provinces*

Province	Year OLVC adopted	Median year of first election	St. dev. of year of first election
Guangdong	1998	1999	0.5
Hunan	1989	1988	1.7
Zhejiang	1988	1989	3.9
Henan	1992	1991	4.6
Sichuan	1991	1989	1.7
Gansu	1989	1995	6.8
Shanxi	1991	1993	4.6
Jilin	1991	1989	2.7

Village Elections

As the first election is likely to have more dramatic impacts than subsequent elections, we focus on studying the effects of the first election. Figure 10.1 presents the number of villages holding elections and their cumulative percentage in each year. Village elections in China started in 1987, and 12 of our sample villages had their first election in that year. By 1990 more than 50 per cent of the sample villages had held at least one election; and by 2002 only one village – in a remote area of Gansu province – had not begun elections.

The introduction of elections had a clear regional pattern; villages in the same province tended to introduce elections around the same year that the province adopted the OLVC.[2] Table 10.1 shows the year when each sample province adopted the OLVC, as well as the median and standard deviation of the year of the introduction of elections in its villages. With the exception of Guangdong, all provinces adopted the OLVC between 1988 and 1992.[3] The median year of first election was close to the year when the province adopted the OLVC, and the standard deviation was small in all provinces except three: Henan, Gansu and Shanxi, that also had large standard deviations.[4] The median year and the adoption year were actually quite close in Henan and Shanxi, but far apart in Gansu, where the election was held long after the adoption of the OLVC. Overall, there were great regional and temporal variations in the introduction of the first election. One variation is especially pertinent to this study; namely, high-income and low-income villages were mixed in terms of the timing of the first election. The introduction of elections is an irreversible process, so if the timing of the first election were closely associated with the income level, it would be hard to distinguish between the true effects of elections and the effects of income. The mixed nature of our data removes this possibility.

Village Expenditures

Public goods provision in rural China is based on a joint effort among various levels of the government and the villages. For major projects which involve several villages, such as road construction, one or several levels of government usually provide part of the funding and the targeted villages provide the rest. For smaller projects within a village, the village budget is usually fully responsible, although governments may also provide some funds (Song 2004). Villages obtain their revenue from fees, collective firms profits and rents from village properties. Many fees are surcharges (*san-ti-wu-tong*), designated specifically for local public goods provision and intended to be shared with the township government to provide public goods within the township territory. Seven types of village spending are recorded in the National Fixed-point Survey: investment in village businesses, public expenditures, office maintenance, salaries of the VC members, revenue handed to the township government, other spending and surplus/deficit. To study VC accountability, we focus on public expenditures, office maintenance and VC salaries.[5] Public expenditures include transfers to households and spending on public projects such as local roads, schools, irrigation systems and healthcare facilities, so they are likely to benefit the majority of the villagers. In contrast, office maintenance costs are spent on the village government's daily operations and can easily be pocketed by VC members. Together with VC salaries, maintenance costs have exactly the opposite implication of public expenditures for the VC's accountability. Consequently, we will add them together and call them 'administrative costs'. In our econometric exercises, detailed below, we study the shares of public expenditures and administrative costs in total village spending.

Figure 10.2 presents the trends of the two shares over the period 1986–2002. The share of public expenditures in village spending was remarkably stable, at just below 20 per cent over the entire sample period. In contrast, the share of administrative costs increased dramatically after 1993. By 2002 43 per cent of total village spending was used to operate the village government, whereas the share was less than 20 per cent before 1993. These two time trends have an important implication for our tests of the role of elections. If we find that elections increase the share of public expenditures but reduce the shares of administrative costs, then we will obtain strong evidence to support the proposition that elections enhance VC accountability because the effects of elections run counter to the time trends.

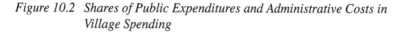

Figure 10.2   Shares of Public Expenditures and Administrative Costs in Village Spending

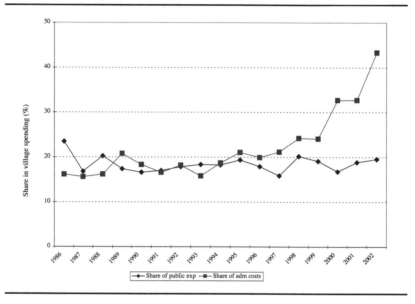

Income Redistribution

Before the central government announced plans to abolish the agricultural taxes and fees in 2005, households paid fees (*san-ti-wu-tong*) to the village to finance local projects.[6] In villages with income from village-sponsored businesses (such as factories and land rentals), households also get transfer income from the village. Figure 10.3 presents the trends of per capita fees, per capita transfer income, and per capita net transfer income based on 1,118 households in the sample villages in the period 1987–2002. The amount of fees increased in the early 1990s but stabilized after 1995. The amount of transfer income was high in the early years but declined substantially in subsequent years. This might be related to the privatization of collective enterprises in the 1990s. However, net transfer income was kept positive throughout.

Gini Coefficients

The Gini coefficient is calculated based on the per capita net income of the original FPS sample households (so that each village has 50–100 households). Household net income is defined as household income minus operational costs

Figure 10.3   Fees and Transfer Income

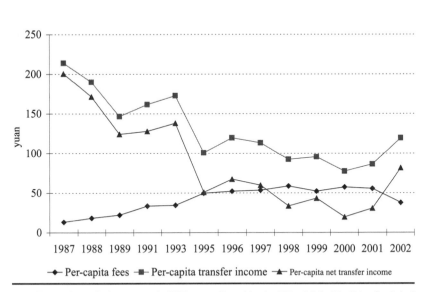

Note: Fees and transfer income are in 2002 yuan adjusted by the CPI published in China Statistical Yearbook. Data for 1990, 1992 and 1994 are missing.

and taxes but with transferred income from the government. We calculate the Gini coefficient for each village in each year. To minimize possible biases caused by household size, we weight the calculation by household size; that is, we record a household in the calculation by the number of its members. Figure 10.4 plots the average Gini coefficients of the 48 villages during 1987–2002. The data reveal increasing income inequality in the period, rising from 0.26 in 1987 to 0.28 in 1992, and then to 0.32 and 0.31 in 2001 and 2002. This trend matches the national trend. The Gini coefficient in rural China increased from 0.29 in 1987 to 0.35 in 2000 (Riskin, Zhao and Li 2002).[7]

Figure 10.5 shows the Lorenz curves for the within-village income distribution in the years 1987, 1999 and 2002. These curves are obtained by averages from the sample villages. The three curves do not cross each other, and the one for 1999 is below the one for 1987, while the one for 2002 is below the one for 1999. Therefore, income inequality increased unambiguously from 1987 to 2002.

To further understand the change of the within-village inequality, Figure 10.6 displays the histograms of the Gini coefficients in 1987, 1999 and 2002. They largely agree with the histograms provided by Benjamin, Brandt and

Figure 10.4   Gini Coefficients for Sample Villages, 1987–2002

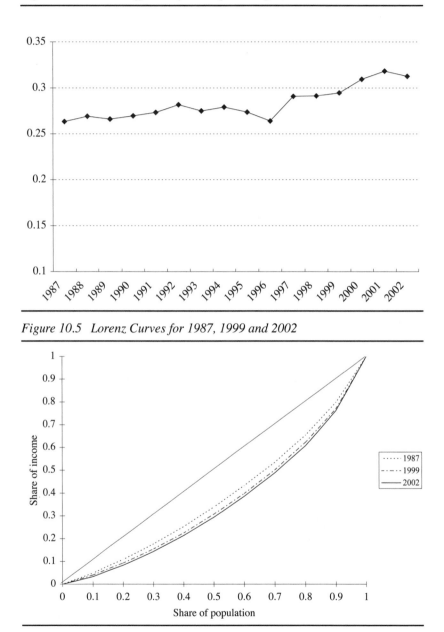

Figure 10.5   Lorenz Curves for 1987, 1999 and 2002

Figure 10.6   *Histograms of the Gini Coefficients in 1987, 1999 and 2002*

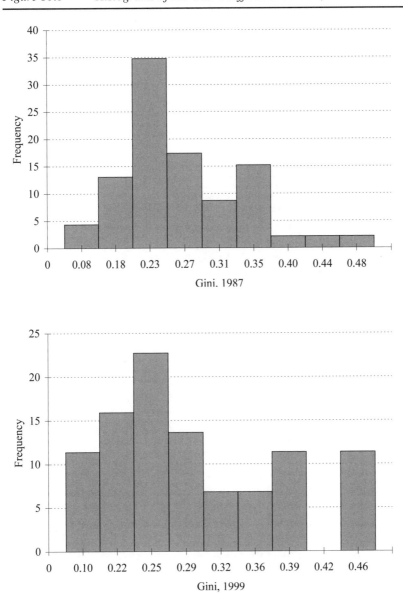

Figure 10.6   *(continued)*

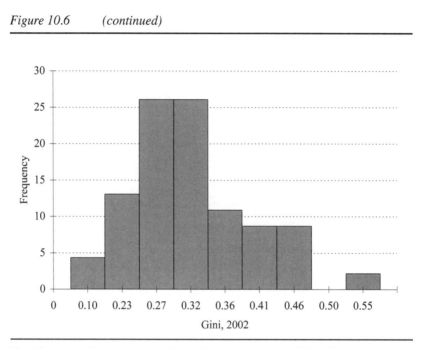

Note: The number for each bar in the figures is the average of the Gini coefficients represented by the bar.

Giles (2005), who used a sample which contained ours. Income distribution is clearly becoming more unequal, as both the mean and the distribution of the Gini coefficient shifted upward.

ECONOMETRIC RESULTS

We use the two-way fixed-effects panel model to do our estimations. This model allows us to control unobserved village or household characteristics and time events which may simultaneously determine the introduction of the election and the dependent variables. The main explanatory variable is a dummy variable indicating the introduction of the election. It is equal to 0 if a village had not begun elections by a certain year, and 1 if it had had at least one election. We will introduce the dependent and control variables when we study individual topics.

Elections and Accountability

As discussed above, we study the share of public expenditures and the share of administrative costs in a total village budget to determine the effect of elections on the accountability of the VC. Using a dataset for the years 1986 to 2002, the control variables include Village Population, Per Capita Net Income, Share of Collective Income in Total Village Income, Per Capita Land Territory, Unemployment Rate and Share of Migrant Workers Who Work outside the County. Village Population (entering the regressions in logarithm term) controls the village size. A larger population may make public decisions more difficult, so it would tend to have a negative effect on village governance. Per Capita Net Income (converted into 2002 Yuan and entering the regressions in logarithm term) controls the level of economic development of a village, and share of collective income in total village income controls the relative size of the collective economy. Studies frequently find that people in villages with higher income or a larger collective economy are more likely to participate in village elections, presumably because the stakes are higher in these villages. Per Capita Land Territory is introduced to represent the amount of resources which a village possesses. Land resources are particularly important in the coastal provinces, as the rapid growth of the local industry has significantly raised the demand for land. Recent literature suggests that natural resources can be a curse for a country, as they encourage elite capture (Hoff and Stiglitz 2004). It is thus interesting to see whether a larger territory reduces village government accountability.

Table 10.2 presents the results. Two regressions are run for each dependent variable, one without any control variables and one with them. The first regression provides the estimate for the total effect of elections, and the second provides the estimate for its marginal effect. For the share of public expenditures, both the total and marginal effects are statistically significant.[8] They are also economically meaningful, as they are equivalent to 22.8 per cent and 26.4 per cent of the average share of public expenditures in the sample. For the share of administrative costs, the total effect of the election remains statistically significant. The introduction of the election reduces administrative costs by about 4 percentage points, equivalent to 18.2 per cent of the sample mean. The marginal effect, however, turns out to be only weakly significant (the p-value is 0.12). This shows that the positive effect of the election on administrative costs comes through its impacts on the control variables.

The above results are very strong in terms of the two time trends shown in Figure 10.2. The share of public expenditures was stable, so our result that the election increases this share is not an artifact of the time trend. In the case of

Table 10.2   Election Effects on Public and Administrative Expenditures

Variables	Share of public exp.		Share of adm. costs	
	R1	R2	R3	R4
Constant	15.67***	−11.79	24.75***	−14.76
	(1.52)	(52.72)	(1.31)	(45.46)
Election dummy	4.21**	4.87**	−3.96**	−2.80
	(2.13)	(2.14)	(1.83)	(1.84)
Ln(population)		3.59		5.77
		(7.44)		(6.42)
Ln(per-capita income)		−1.65		2.14
(1000 yuan)		(1.62)		(1.40)
Share of collective income		−0.14***		−0.14***
in total income (%)		(0.05)		(0.04)
Per capita land		0.55***		−0.43***
territory (mu)		(0.15)		(0.13)
Unemployment rate (%)		−0.46		−0.38
		(0.98)		(0.85)
Share of migrant		0.03		−0.02
workers (%)		(0.05)		(0.05)
Adjusted R^2	0.26	0.28	0.44	0.45

Notes:
The regressions are based on data of 48 villages in the period of 1986–2002, and the total number of cases is 806. All the regressions use the panel model with village and year fixed effects. Standard errors are in parentheses. *significant at 10 per cent level; ** significant at 5 per cent level; *** significant at 1 per cent level.

the share of administrative costs, there was even a significant upward trend, so our finding that elections reduce the share runs counter to the time trend.

Income Redistribution

We use data from 1,118 households in the period 1987–2002 to study the net and total transfer income. In the regressions we have sets of control variables. One set is comprised of household variables including relative per capita earned income (RELINC), per capita land, per capita productive assets, average age, average education of family labor and male ratio. There are five dummies indicating whether a family has a member working in a government agency other than the village council, working in the village council, being a Communist Party member, working a regular wage job and serving in the army. Another dummy indicates whether a family has been designated *wubaohu*, i.e., a household receiving welfare from the village. Earned income is income earned by the household in agricultural production, businesses and labor hiring. We divide the per capita earned income by the village average income in each year to obtain the relative per capita earned income. This variable is included in the regressions to control for a household's relative position in the village. Its coefficient reflects the progressiveness (if it is negative) or regressiveness (if it is positive) of income redistribution. The other family attributes control for factors which may affect the amount of fees paid by a household and the amount of transfer income received by it. The other set is comprised of the village variables which we used in Table 10.2 to control for village characteristics.

The estimation results are presented in Table 10.3. Four regressions are performed. R1 and R2 study per capita net income transfer, and R3 and R4 study per capita total income transfer. R2 and R4 include the interaction term between RELINC and the election dummy, whereas R1 and R3 do not. The results are generally consistent with our expectations. Income redistribution is progressive. A household which is wealthier, has more land or assets or has at least one regular wage earner gets less net income transfer. In contrast, a *wubaohu* and a household with a member in the army gets more net income transfer. The progressiveness of the total income transfer is not as strong as the net income transfer, however. The somewhat surprising result is that households with a village cadre get significantly less net and total income transfers. This shows that on average the village cadres are not taking advantage of their positions in getting documented income from the village.[9]

R1 and R3 estimate the election dummy's average effects on the net and total income transfer. Neither is statistically significant, so village elections do not increase income redistribution. By adding the interaction term between RELINC and the election dummy, R2 and R4 tell us how village elections change the progressiveness of income redistribution. The coefficient of the interaction term is positive in both regressions, and, surprisingly, they are both significant. This means that elections have reduced the progressiveness of income redistribution. According to the estimate provided in R2, in a village without elections, a household gets 113.71 Yuan less of net transfer income for each of its members if its income is twice of the village average. Elections close this gap by 85.65 Yuan (75 per cent). The effect of elections is even stronger for the total income transfer in which case the gap is reduced by 107.19 yuan (94 per cent). The Chinese villages had decades of experience with the commune system, so their income redistribution had been quite progressive before any

Table 10.3 Elections and Income Transfers

Variable	R1 Estimate	R1 St. Err.	R2 Estimate	R2 St. Err.	R3 Estimate	R3 St. Err.	R4 Estimate	R4 St. Err.
Election dummy	−0.51	12.84	−56.34***	15.79	5.93	12.46	−63.94***	15.31
Household variables								
RELINC	−45.20***	6.86	−113.71***	14.13	−19.52***	6.66	−105.26***	12.81
RELINC×Election dummy			85.65***	13.21			107.19***	13.70
Per-capita landholding (mu)	−12.35***	3.60	−12.31***	3.59	−0.91	3.49	−0.87	3.48
Per-capita productive assets (yuan)	−0.84***	0.18	−0.81***	0.18	−0.87***	0.18	−0.83***	0.18
Ave. age	−0.46	2.10	−0.52	2.10	−0.26	2.04	−0.34	2.03
Ave. education	−3.60	5.21	−3.13	5.21	−5.55	5.06	−4.97	5.04
Ratio of male members	−20.44	21.55	−21.47	21.52	−15.88	20.91	−17.16	20.88
Have a member in government	−8.69	14.94	−4.57	14.93	−4.31	14.49	0.84	14.47
Have a member as village cadre	−111.23***	17.91	−109.83***	17.88	−121.75***	17.37	−120.00***	17.33
Have a member as CCP member	1.17	12.20	3.01	12.18	6.10	11.82	8.40	11.80
Have a regular wage earner	−7.86***	1.42	−7.94***	1.42	0.05	1.38	−0.06	1.37
Being a Wubaohu	84.83***	32.75	79.38***	32.72	69.40**	31.77	62.59**	31.71
Have a member in the army	46.52*	24.74	49.99*	24.71	40.48	24.00	44.82	23.95
Village variables								
Ln(village population)	5.89	49.13	13.03	49.07	−39.84	47.66	−30.91	47.56
Ln(village ave. income) (yuan)	41.41***	11.24	40.96***	11.23	41.31***	10.91	40.74***	10.89
Share of collective income (%)	6.39***	0.38	6.44***	0.38	6.32***	0.37	6.38***	0.37
Per-capita land territory (mu)	−1.32	1.14	−1.29	1.14	−1.49	1.10	−1.45	1.10
Unemployment rate (%)	−1.90	6.21	−2.64	6.20	−0.99	6.02	−1.91	6.01
Share of migrants (%)	1.21***	0.34	1.19***	0.34	1.12***	0.33	1.09***	0.33
Constant	−249.33	382.71	−261.79	382.15	116.41	371.27	100.81	370.36
Adjusted R²	0.38	0.38	0.38	0.38	0.38	0.38	0.38	0.38

Notes:

Regressions are based on 13,366 cases of 1,118 households in the period 1987–2002. R1 and R2 are for per capita net income transfer (in 2002 yuan), and R3 and R4 are for per capita total income transfer (in 2002 yuan). All the regressions use the panel model with household and year fixed effects. *significant at 10% level; ** significant at 5% level; *** significant at 1% level.

Table 10.4   Village Elections and Income Distribution

	R1	R2	R3	R4
Election dummy	−0.016***	−0.015**	−0.010	0.001
	(0.006)	(0.006)	(0.006)	(0.006)
Per-capita net income		0.197E−2***	0.150E−2**	0.167E−2***
(1,000 yuan)		(0.630E−3)	(0.631E−3)	(0.606E−3)
Per-capita net income squared		−0.307E−4***	−0.248E−4***	−0.288E−4***
		(0.679E−5)	(0.681E−5)	(0.657E−5)
Log village population		0.058***	0.057***	0.050***
		(0.021)	(0.021)	(0.020)
Share of collective income (%)			−0.794E−3***	−0.768E−3***
			(0.151E−3)	(0.145E−3)
Per-capita land territory (mu)			−0.385E−3	−0.115E−3
			(0.457E−3)	(0.446E−3)
Unemployment rate (%)			0.127E−4	−0.479E−3
			(0.269E−2)	(0.259E−2)
Share of migrants (%)			0.133E−4	−0.500E−4
			(0.168E−3)	(0.167E−3)
CV of household size				0.166***
				(0.032)
CV of average education				−0.006
of household adults				(0.035)
CV of per-capita				−0.007
household landholding				(0.005)
CV of household wage earners				0.013***
				(0.002)
Constant	0.266***	−0.124	−0.111	−0.153
	(0.007)	(0.151)	(0.149)	(0.144)
Adjusted R^2	0.662	0.677	0.689	0.715

Notes:
The regressions use data of 48 villages in the period of 1987–2002. The number of observations is 706. Both regressions use the panel model with village and year fixed effects. Standard errors are in parentheses. * significant at 10% level; ** significant at 5% level; *** significant at 1% level.

election happened. To the extent that it empowers not just the poor, but also the richer, the village election can lead to less progressive income redistribution.

Income Inequality

To study how elections affect income inequality, we run four regressions on the Gini coefficient which we obtained in the last section. In the first regression, whose results are presented in R1 of Table 10.4, we only include the election dummy and control the village and year fixed effects, so this regression provides us with an estimate for the election's total effect. The election reduces the Gini coefficient by 0.016, and this effect is significant at the 1 per cent level. It is equivalent to 5.7 per cent of the sample average of 0.28, but it is 32 per cent of the Gini coefficient's increase in the period 1987–2002. This is a large effect. In particular, it is obtained against the growth trend of the Gini coefficient.

In the other three regressions, we have included different sets of control variables to obtain different estimates for the marginal effect of the village election. R2 adds village per capita income, its square and the logarithm of village population. The two income variables are added to represent the Kuznets curve, that measures increasing inequality during periods of growth. The coefficient of the election dummy has remained essentially the same as in R1, and it is still significant at the 1 per cent level. The Kuznets curve is verified. In addition, a larger village tends to have a larger Gini coefficient.

R3 then adds the other village variables which we used before: the share of collective income in total village income, per capita land territory, unemployment rate and the share of migrants. Now the coefficient of the election dummy becomes barely significant (the p-value of the t-statistics is 0.12) and its magnitude becomes smaller. The three old control variables remain significant. Among the new control variables, only the share of collective income has a significant coefficient. An increase of one percentage point of the collective income would reduce the Gini coefficient by 0.008, that is a very strong effect. The average of the share of collective income is 6.8 per cent in the sample, and the standard deviation is 15.2 per cent, so there are wide variations in the data. If the share of collective income increases by one standard deviation, the Gini coefficient will decrease by 0.122.

R4 further adds four coefficients of variations to the regression; namely, household size, household average education of adult members, per capita household landholding and number of regular household wage earners. These four coefficients are meant to capture the variations which affect the Gini coefficient and which in the meantime are possibly correlated with the election. The previously significant control variables are still significant. Among the new control variables, the coefficients of household size and household wage earners are significant and increase the Gini coefficient – an understandable result. However, the election dummy has become highly insignificant.

The above results show that the village election can significantly reduce income inequality, and this effect is mainly channeled through increased village collective income, creating wage jobs, or changing the distribution of land. With more collective income, the elected VC can engage in more income redistribution and public investment. However, our early study of the net and total income transfer showed that the election has not increased income redistribution. Therefore, its positive effect on reducing income inequality must come from greater public investment. The creation of wage jobs often is also tied to the growth of collective income. In the past, village-run enterprises were the main source of village-generated jobs. In the last decade, most of the collective enterprises have been privatized and collective income is now mainly coming from renting land and buildings to outside investors who set up factories on village land. With more investors coming in, the number of jobs in the village increases. Finally, the VC can redistribute land to make it more equally held among the households. According to the Constitution land is collectively owned by the villagers, so each of them is entitled to the village land (Liu, Carter and Yao 1998). This provides the legal basis for the VC to undertake land redistribution.

CONCLUSION

The village election has been a significant milestone in China's progression toward a full democracy. Using a unique panel dataset, we found that elections have played a significantly positive role in enhancing the accountability of the village committee and has reduced the income inequality in the village. This second effect is not brought about by additional redistribution of income, but rather by more public investment. These results have significant implications for the current debate in China.

First, our results show that grassroots democracy can work even in a distorted institutional environment. It seems that village elections have only created numerous isolated democratic islands, because the village is still administratively controlled by the township and county governments, that are not directly elected. The upper-level governments still intervene in village affairs either through direct orders or through the village party secretary. In some cases, the upper-level governments directly intervene in the village election to make sure that the people they like get elected. These people then would care more about their reputation in the higher governments than about villagers' concerns. However, our results show that on average elections have made the elected village committee more accountable to the villagers. Indeed, the elected village committee often uses the mandate created by the election to defy the directives of the party secretary and sometimes of the higher authorities (Liu, Wang and Yao 2001).

Second, our results also show that villagers can quickly learn how to run a functioning democracy. At least at the beginning of the village election process, many people had doubts about whether farmers could run a successful democracy in China. Such doubts have diminished, but there are still many people who have doubts about whether the experience of the village election can be transplanted to the higher-level governments. At the other extreme, however, there are people who believe that only the direct election of government officials constitutes true democracy. A possible compromise might be direct election of the delegates to the local and national People's Congress. Such a move does not require extensive Constitutional changes, but still would enhance the accountability of the local governments.

Third, our finding that the village election has not led to more income redistribution but yet has improved income distribution defies the conventional wisdom that democracy leads to more distributive policies. This may be related to the small scale of the village election. Within the village context of lineage and other intimate ties, it may be easier for the villagers to reach more productive decisions than to fight for greater short-term redistribution. However, our findings are still relevant for larger-scale democracies.

NOTES

We thank Abhijit Banerjee, Samuel Bowles, Esther Duflo, Justin Lin, John Strauss, Xiaobo Zhang, and participants of the 2007 GDN conference for their valuable comments. We also thank Dwayne Benjamin, Loren Brandt and John Giles for their generosity to share with us part of their data. Mengtao Gao, Ang Sun, Shuna Wang, and Shenwei Zhang provided excellent research assistance. We are grateful for financial supports from the Chinese Medical Board and the National 211 Projects Fund and thank the excellent data collection efforts provided by the Research Center of Rural Economy, the Ministry of Agriculture, People's Republic of China.

1. The FPS did not conduct survey in 1990, 1992, and 1994. We computed the village-level data for these years by averaging the nearest two years, but we leave the household data intact.
2. When the NPC passes a law which involves government actions, each province enacts a local law which specifies the details of the implementation of the central law. Most provinces actually adopted the OLVC even when it was in the experimental stage.
3. Guangdong adopted the OLVC in 1999. Before that year, Guangdong did not treat the village as a self-governing administrative unit, but rather as a branch of the township government.
4. On Hunan, Henan, Sichuan and Jilin, the median year of election was earlier than the year of adopting the OLVC. It seems that these provinces waited after some experiments to provide the implementation details of the law.
5. The implication of investment in village businesses to accountability is unclear. In many cases, village businesses are either pet projects or pork barrels for village leaders. However,

they can also benefit the villagers if the VC is relatively honest.
6. Since local taxes and fees were abolished, villages must obtain approval from the villager conference to finance local public projects on a case-by-case basis.
7. It is understandable that the national Gini coefficients were larger than those in our sample villages, because the latter are calculated within a much smaller number of observations.
8. The fact that the marginal effect is larger than the total effect shows that there are correlations between the election and the control variables, and these correlations reduce the impact of the election on the dependent variable.
9. Our results do not tell us whether village cadres get under-the-table income from the village.

BIBLIOGRAPHY

Alesina, Alberto and Dani Rodrik (1994), 'Distributive Politics and Economic Growth', *Quarterly Journal of Economics*, **109** (2), 465–90.

Bardhan, Pranab and Dilip Mookherjee (2005), 'Decentralizing Antipoverty Program Delivery in Developing Countries', *Journal of Public Economics*, **89** (4), 675–704.

Benabou, Roland (1996), 'Inequality and Growth', Cambridge, MA, National Bureau of Economic Research (NBER) Working Paper No. 5658.

Benjamin, Dwayne and Loren Brandt and John Giles (2005), 'The Evolution of Income Inequality in Rural China,' *Economic Development and Cultural Change*, **53** (4), 769–824.

Chattopadhyay, Raghabendra and Esther Duflo (2004), 'Women as Policy Makers: Evidence from a Randomized Policy Experiment in India', *Econometrica*, **72** (5). 1409–43.

Foster, Andrew and Mark Rosenzweig (2001), 'Democratization, Decentralization and the Distribution of Local Public Goods in a Poor Rural Economy', Providence, RI, Brown University, Department of Economics, unpublished paper.

Gan, Li, Lixin Xu and Yang Yao (2005), 'Local Governance, Finance and Consumption Smoothing', World Bank Research Group, memo.

Gan, Li, Lixin Xu, and Yang Yao (2006), 'Health Shocks, Village Elections, and Long-term Income: Evidence from Rural China', CCER Working Paper No. E2006012; NBER Working Paper No. 12686. Hsiao, Cheng (2003), *Analysis of Panel Data*, New York: Cambridge University Press.

Guo, Zhenglin and Thomas Bernstein (2004), 'The Impact of Elections on the Village Structure of Power: The Relations between the Village Committees and the Party Branches', *Journal of Contemporary China*, **13** (39), 257–75.

Hoff, Karla and Joseph E. Stiglitz (2004), 'After the Big Bang? Obstacles to the Emergence of the Rule of Law in Post-communist Societies,' *American Economic Review*, **94** (3), 753–63.

Kennedy, John, Scott Rozelle and Yaojiang Shi (2004), 'Elected Leaders and Collective Land: Farmers' Evaluation of Village Leaders' Performance in Rural China', *Journal of Chinese Political Science*, **9** (1), 1–221.

Liu, Shouying, Michael Carter and Yang Yao (1998), 'Dimensions and Diversity of Property Rights in Rural China: Dilemmas on the Road to Further Reform', *World Development*, **26** (10), 1789–806.

Liu, Yigao, Wang, Xiaoyi and Yao, Yang (2001), *The Chinese Village: Inside and Out*, in Chinese, Shijiazhuang: Hebei Renmin Press.

Milanovic, Branko and Yvonne Ying (2001), 'Democracy and Income Inequality: An

Empirical Analysis', Washington, DC, World Bank Policy Research Working Paper No. 2561.

Ministry of Civil Affairs (1998), *Civil Affairs Statistical Report: 1997*, Beijing.

Oi, Jean and Scott Rozelle (2000), 'Elections and Power: The Locus of Decision-Making in Chinese Villages', *China Quarterly*, (162), 513–39.

Riskin, Carl, Renwei Zhao and Shi Li (eds) (2002), *China's Retreat from Equality: Income Distribution and Economic Transition*, Armonk, NY: M.E. Sharpe.

Song, Hongyuan (2004), *Public Finance in Chinese Villages*, in Chinese, Beijing: Finance and Economics Press.

Tan, Qingshan (2004), 'Building Institutional Rules and Procedures: Village Election in China', *Policy Sciences*, **37** (1), 1–22.

Yang, Zhong and Chen Jie (2002), 'To Vote or Not To Vote: An Analysis of Peasants' Participation in Chinese Village Elections', *Comparative Political Studies*, **35** (6), 686–712.

Zhang, Xiaobo and Shenggen Fan (2000), 'Public Investment and Regional Inequality in Rural China', Washington, DC, International Food Policy Research Institute, Environment and Production Technology Division Discussion Paper No. 71.

Zhang, Xiaobo, Shenggen Fan, Linxiu Zhang and Jikun Huang (2004), 'Local Governance and Public Goods Provision in Rural China', *Journal of Public Economics*, **88** (12): 2857–71.

Index

Abed-el-Rahman, Kamel 82
accountability 225–9, 231–2, 237–8,
    243–4
Acharya, Shankar xx, xxi, xxvi, xxvii,
    xxx
administrative expenditure 226–7, 231–2,
    237–8, 243–4
advertising intensity 125–6, 129–37
Africa 49, 50, 51, 176
Aghion, Philippe 121
agriculture
    China 9, 11, 63, 201, 226
    India xxx, 26, 28, 37–8
Ahmed, Manzoor 150
Airtel 31
Álvarez, Roberto xxii, 98, 104, 106, 113
Apollo Hospitals Limited 155, 161
Arogya Raksha Scheme, Andhra Pradesh
    152, 160, 171, 172
Arpana Swasthya Kendra, Delhi 152,
    154, 169
Asia
    Chinese exports, effect of 98, 109–10
    development barriers xxvii–xxxii
    development drivers xviii–xxvii
    economic growth 46–51, 54–8
    education 51–2
    exports 51
    global role xi–xiv, xvi–xviii
    human capital 51–3
    infant mortality 52
    informal employment 176
    investment climate 54
    tariffs 53
    wages 51–2, 53
Asian Century 46–8, 67

Bagha Jatin Hospital, Kolkata 152, 153,
    169

Balassa, Bala 73
Bangladesh 46, 49, 51–2, 53, 54, 56, 62
banking lending to entrepreneurs, China
    caution 201–3
    and legislative membership 203–20
    private sector finance 199–200, 220–21
    reform constraints 10–11, 60
Bardhan, Pranab xvii, 228
Barro, Robert xix
Benjamin, Dwayne 233
Bernard, Andrew 98
Bhalla, Surjit 32, 39
Bhutan 29, 30
Björkman, James Warner xxix
Bloom, David E. 147
Botswana 29, 30
Bourdieu, Pierre 206
Brandt, Loren 233
Branstetter, Lee 99, 111
Brazil 62, 110
Brülhart, Marius 81
bureaucracy 158–9
Burma see Myanmar

Cai, Fang xx, 177
capital xii–xiii, 14, 30–31
capital goods import intensity 127,
    129–37
'catching up' (technological
    advancement) 17
Chattopadhyay, Raghabendra 226
Chen Jie 228
Chile
    economic growth 29, 30
    effect of Chinese exports 98
    margins of Chinese exports 99–105,
        115
    prices of Chinese exports 105–8, 115
    quality of Chinese exports 108–15

China
  agriculture 9, 11, 63, 201, 226
  consumption 59–60
  development barriers xxvii–xxxii
  development challenges 19–20, 47,
    59–64
  development drivers xviii–xxvii
  economic growth 3–4, 10–20, 29, 30,
    41–3, 46–51, 58–9
  economic reform 4–10
  economic research xiv
  education 51–2, 57, 63
  energy supplies 54
  foreign direct investment (FDI) 12–13,
    17, 53, 75
  GDP (Gross Domestic Product) 4, 5,
    12, 14, 48–51
  global role xvi–xviii, 17–20, 41–3,
    65–7
  health care 63
  human capital 51–3
  inequality 62–4
  infant mortality 52, 57, 62–3
  investment 54, 57, 59–60, 64, 66–7,
    xxi–xxiii
  literacy 51
  population 33, 49
  poverty 62
  public sector 62–4
  and rest of developing Asia (RODA)
    54–8
  social policy 47, 62–4, 66
  structural constraints on reform 10–13
  tariffs 53
  unemployment 57
  and the United States (US) 47–8, 65,
    66, 67, 98, 103
  wages 51–2, 53, 57, 63
  see also entrepreneurs in China;
    exports; informal employment in
    China; labor markets;
    liberalization; village elections,
    China
'China plus' xxiv
Chinese Communist Party (CCP) 204,
  212, 221, 225
Chiranjeevi Yojana, Gujarat 152, 153,
  162, 170
Claro, Sebastián xxii, 98, 104, 106, 113

climate change 48, 62, 65–6, 67
coal 61
competition 120–21, 122–37, 195–6
Comprehensive Labor Statistics
  Reporting System (CLSRS) 179
consumption 59–60, 66
contract-based rights 13
Contract Responsibility System 6, 12
corruption xxv, 221
countryside *see* rural areas
Craig, Patricia 147

Dahlman, Carl J. 126
democracy 58, 225–9, 243–4
demographic dividend 33
Deng, Xiaoping 6, 202
development
  barriers to xxvii–xxxii
  challenges 19–20, 47, 59–64
  drivers xviii–xxvii
Dollar, David xvii, xviii, xxi, xxiv, xxvi,
  xxviii, xxix
domestic demand 59–60, 65
Du, Yang xx
'dual-track' system 9
Duflo, Esther 226
duopoly 121

earnings *see* wages
Eastern Europe 7, 49, 50, 74
'Easy-to-Hard' reform sequence 10
economic growth
  Bangladesh 56
  China 3–4, 10–20, 29, 30, 41–3,
    46–51, 58–9
  India 23–7, 39–41, 46–51, 56, 59, 67
  Indonesia 29, 30, 46
  Pakistan 56
  Thailand 29, 30, 46, 56
  and trade 29–30, 34, 51
  United States (US) 59
  Vietnam 29, 30, 46, 56
economic reform 4–13, 23–7, 28, 38
education 38–9, 51–2, 57, 63
Emergency Ambulance Services, Tamil
  Nadu 152, 170
employment 173–4
  see also informal employment in
    China

employment shocks 190–91
energy scarcity 47, 61, 65–6
energy supplies 35, 38, 54
Engardio, Pete xix
entrepreneurs in China
  banks' caution 201–3
  finance strategies 220–21
  growth of 199–200
  legislative membership 203–20
  personal skills 219–20
environmental impact xxviii, 48
Europe 7, 49, 50, 74
exchange control liberalization 76
export intensity 127, 129–37
exports
  Africa 49
  Asia 51
  China 15, 49, 51, 59–60, 77–80, 93–4,
    98–9
  China, margins of 99–105, 115
  China, prices of 105–8, 115
  China, quality of 108–15
  Eastern Europe 49
  India 26, 43, 49, 51, 77–80, 93–4, 110
  Japan 49
  Latin America 49
  liberalization, effects of 77–80, 93–4
  and research and development (R&D)
    121–2
  United States (US) 49
extensive margin exports 99–105

Fan, Shenggen 226
Feenstra, Robert 103
finance for private enterprise, China
  banks' caution 201–3
  entrepreneurs' strategies 220–21
  legislative membership 203–20
  sources of xxxi, 199–200
financial sector, India 28
Finger, J. Michael 108
firm age 126, 129–37
firm size
  bank lending 202–3, 220–21
  finance advantages of 208–20
  research and development (R&D) 125,
    129–37
firms 31, 199–200
fiscal policy 26, 28, 33–5

Fixed-Point Survey (FPS) 229
Fontagne, Lionel 74
food markets, China 9
foreign direct investment (FDI)
  China 12–13, 17, 53, 75
  as development driver xxi, xxiv
  foreign equity participation 126–7
  India 76
  and intra-industry trade (IIT) 86–8,
    93–4
foreign equity participation 126–7
foreign exchange markets 9
Foster, Andrew 226
Four Little Dragons xvi
Free-Trade Zones 6
Freudenberg, Michael 74
Fukao, Kyoji 74

Gan, Li 226
gas 61
gasoline 61–2
GDP (Gross Domestic Product)
  Africa 49
  China 4, 5, 12, 14, 48–51
  Eastern Europe 49
  India 24, 25, 26, 40, 41, 46, 48–51
  Japan 49
  Latin America 24, 49, 50
  rest of developing Asia (RODA)
    48–51
  United States (US) 49, 50
Giant Dragons xvi
Giles, John 236
Global Development Network (GDN)
  xiv, xviii
global economy
  China's growth 17–20, 41–3, 65–7,
    xvi–xviii
  India's growth 27, 29–30, 34, 39, 41–3
  recession 47–8
globalization 57
Goldman Sachs 39
governance 57–8
gradualism in market reform 7
grassroots democracy 225–9, 243–4
Greenaway, David 82
Grubel, Herbert G. 81

Hamilton, Clive 81

Hart, P.E. 124
HCL 31
health care
    China 63
    India 38–9, 143–5, 147, 150–65
    Indonesia xxx, 39
    see also public–private partnerships,
        India
Heckit Model 216
Heckman, James 216
High-Technology Development Zones
    (HTDZs) 6, 17
Hine, Robert C. 82
Hong Kong xvi, xxiv
horizontal intra-industry trade (HIIT) 74,
    82–93, 94
Household Responsibility System 5, 8,
    11–12, 201
Hu, Xiaoling 92, 93
Huang, Jikun 226
Huang, Yasheng xvii, xxiv, xxv
Hughes, Kirsty 121
human capital xix–xx, 51–3
    see also labor markets
human resources 38–9
Hummels, David 99, 101, 102

import-penetration rate (IPR) 123–4,
    125, 129–37, 142
imports 16, 29, 120–37, 138
income distribution 225–9
income inequality 62–4, 242–4
income redistribution 227, 232–6,
    238–42, 243–4
Index 124
India
    agriculture xxx, 26, 28, 37–8
    development barriers xxvii–xxxii,
        34–9
    development drivers xviii–xxvii,
        27–34
    economic growth 23–7, 39–41, 46–51,
        56, 59, 67
    economic reform 23–7, 28
    education 51–2
    energy supplies 54
    exports 26, 43, 49, 51, 77–80, 93–4,
        110
    foreign direct investment (FDI) 76

GDP (Gross Domestic Product) 24, 25,
        26, 40, 41, 46, 48–51
    global role xvi–xviii, 27, 29–30, 34,
        39, 41–3
    health care provision 38–9, 143–5,
        147, 150–65
    human capital 51–3
    infant mortality 52, 62
    intra-industry trade (IIT) 76–7, 81–93
    investment climate xxi–xxii, 54
    labor markets xxxi–xxxii, 35–7, 76
    liberalization 75–6, 122–37, 138
    market reform 120
    population 33, 49
    poverty 24, 143–5, 147, 150–65
    tariffs 53, 56
    technological progress 120
    village elections 226
    wages 51–2, 53
    see also liberalization; public–private
        partnerships, India; research and
        development (R&D)
Indonesia
    Chinese exports 110
    economic growth 29, 30, 46
    education 52
    energy supplies 54
    health care xxx, 39
    infant mortality 52, 62
    investment climate 51, 54
    population 49
    tariffs 53
    wages 51–2, 53
industry 28, 127–8
inequality 62–4, 66
infant mortality xix, 51, 52, 57, 62–3
informal employment in China
    definition 175–7
    and formal employment sector 192–4
    market characteristics 183–8
    market implications 195–6
    measurement 174–83
    policy recommendations 196–7
    workforce characteristics 188–91
Infosys xxiv, 31
infrastructure xxvii–xxviii, 35, 36, 37
institutions xxv–xxvii, 11–13
    see also village elections, China

intensive margin exports xxii, 99–105, 115
inter-industry trade xxii, 73
interest rates 216–19
International Monetary Fund (IMF) 25
international trade *see* trade
intra-industry trade (IIT)
    definition 73
    liberalization xxii, 73–5, 76–7, 93–4
    patterns of 81–93
investment 14, 26, 47, 59–60
investment climate xxi–xxiii, xxiv, 51, 54, 57, 64, 66–7
iron rice bowl 173
Ishido, Hikari 74
IT (information technology) 43, 88
Ito, Keiko 74

Japan 33, 48, 49, 50
Jensen, J. Bradford 98
Jet 31
joint ventures 12–13

Kagan, Robert xiii
Karnataka Integrated Telemedicine and Telehealth Project 152, 162, 171
Karuna Trust, Karnataka 152, 153, 161, 162, 169
Kelkar, Vijay 39
Kelly, David xvi
Kennedy, John 226
Khanna, Tarun xvii, xxv
Klenow, Peter 99, 101, 102
Klundert, Theo van de 121
Kniest, Paul 81
Knight, John 14
Kreinin, M.E. 108
Kripalani, Manjeet xix
Kristof, Nicholas xvi
Kumar, Nagesh 125

labor markets
    China 173–4, 195–6
    flexibility xx–xxi, 195–6
    human capital xix–xx, 51–3
    India xxxi–xxxii, 35–7, 76
    liberalization 75, 76, 94
    see also informal employment in China

land 5, 11–13, 63, 243
Lardy, Nicholas 80, 99, 111
Larsson, B. Ross 126
Latin America
    Chinese exports, effect of 98, 109–10
    exports 49
    GDP (Gross Domestic Product) 24, 49, 50
    inequality 62
    informal employment 176
    literacy 51
    population 49
Lee, Jong-Wha xix
legislative membership, China
    empirical analysis of finance advantages 208–20
    role of 203–8, 220–21
liberalization
    China 75–6
    as development driver xxi–xxiii
    exports, effect on 77–80, 93–4
    India 75–6, 122–37, 138
    intra-industry trade (IIT) 73–5, 76–7, 81–94
    and research and development (R&D) 122–37
    and technological progress 119–20, 137–8
    theoretical effects 120–22
    see also openness; trade
literacy xix, 51
Lloyd, Peter J. 81
local government 207
    see also legislative membership, China

Ma Yue 92, 93
Macau xxiv
Mahavir Trust Hospital 152, 172
Malaysia 29, 30, 110
manufactured goods 83–93
market concentration 124–5, 129–37, 142
market reform 4–13, 23–7, 28, 38, 120, 195–7
Mauritius 29, 30
Mexico xiv, 62, 110
middle class 31–2
migrant labor xxix, 182, 183–8, 197
Milner, Chris 82
Mitchell, Marc 147

Mobile Health Service, The Sunderbans
152, 162, 170
momentum 27–9
monopoly 121
Mookherjee, Dilip 228
Morrisson, Christian xix
mortality xix, 51, 52, 57, 62–3
Multipolar Century 48, 67
Murtin, Fabrice xix
Myanmar 46, 49, 52

National People's Congress, China
(NPC) 225, 227, 244
National Rural Employment Guarantee
Scheme 35
natural resources xxviii, 47, 55–6, 61–2
NDTV 31
non-governmental organizations (NGOs)
definition 145
public–private partnerships 151, 154,
158, 159, 161, 163
role of 147–8, 150
non-profit organizations *see* non-
governmental organizations (NGOs)

oil 61
oligopoly 121
'open-door' policy 6, 12, 53
openness xxi–xxii, xxiv, 29–30, 53
see also liberalization; tariffs
Organic Law of Village Committee
(OLVC) 225, 227, 230
Organisation for Economic Cooperation
and Development (OECD) 109–12
organizational legitimacy 205–6

Pakistan 46, 49, 51–2, 53, 54, 56, 62
Pamukcu, Teoman 125
Parameswaran, Mavannor xxi, xxiii
partial reform theory 9
partnerships *see* public–private
partnerships, India
Pavitt, Keith 127
Peng Zhen 227
People's Congress, China (PC) xxxi,
204–8, 212, 220–21
People's Political Consultative
Conference, China (PPCC) xxxi,
204–8, 212, 220–21

petrol 61–2
Philippines 46, 49, 51–2, 53, 54, 62, 110
political status *see* legislative
membership, China
pollution xxviii, 61
population 33, 49
poverty 24, 62, 143–5, 147, 150–65
see also public–private partnerships,
India
prices 105–8, 115
primary goods 83–93
private equity markets 222
private–public partnerships *see* public–
private partnerships, India
private sector, China
banks' caution 201–3
definition 145
finance strategies 220–21
growth of 199–200
legislative membership 203–20
privatization 10–11, 38
productivity 13–17, 26
profit 125
property rights 5, 11–13, 63, 243
public–private partnerships, India
advantages 143
case studies 150–51, 152, 169–72
characteristics of xxix–xxx, 149–50,
165–6
complexities of 147–9
definition 145–6
operational management 151–9
policy goals 160–65
types of 151–3
public expenditure 226–7, 231–2, 237–8,
243–4
public sector 28, 34–5, 62–4, 145

quality of exports 108–15

Rajan, Ramkishen xvi
Rajiv Gandhi Hospital, Karnataka 152,
153, 155, 160, 161, 169
Raman, A. Venkat xxix
Ranbaxy 31
rate of profit 125, 129–37
Rauch, James 113
Rawski, G. Thomas 177

reform *see* economic reform; market reform
regional development 5–6, 8, 174–89, 196–7
   see also village elections, China
rent seeking 221
research and development (R&D)
   economic growth in China 14–17
   R&D intensity 122–3, 129–37
   role of xxiii, 120
   trade liberalization, analysis of 122–37, 138
   trade liberalization theory 120–22
rest of developing Asia (RODA) 46–58
   see also Asia
RNTCP 152, 172
roads 35, 36
Rodrik, Dani xxiii, 39, 99, 108, 110, 120
Rogi Kalyan Samiti, JP Hospital 152, 162, 171, 172
Rohwer, Jim xvi
Romalis, John 103
Rosenzweig, Mark 226
'round tripping' of FDI 17
Rozelle, Scott 226
rural areas 5, 11, 62–4, 66–7
rural–urban migration 62–4
rural–urban migration 62–4, 66–7

Sample Survey of the Population Changes (SSPC) 181
Saqib, Mohammed 125
scale intensive industries 127–37
Schmitz, Hubert xvi
Schott, Peter K. 80, 98, 99, 103, 105, 107, 108
science based industries 127–37
services sector 27
sewage facilities, India 37
Shamlaji Hospital, Gujarat 152, 162, 169
Shetty, Dr Devi Prasad 154–5
Shi, Yaojlang 226
shock therapy in market reform 7
Singapore xvi, 110
Singh, Manmohan 25
SMS Hospital, Jaipur 152, 157, 160, 169
Smulders, Sjak 121
social capital 206–7
social policy 47, 62–4, 66

social protection 188, 195
social security 10–11, 184, 195
soft-budget constraints 10–11
South Korea xvi, 29, 30, 110
Soviet Union 7, 13
special economic zones (SEZs) 6, 8
specialization 94, 105–8, 115
specialized supplier industries 127–37
Sri Lanka 29, 30
Srinivasan, T.N. xxviii
State Administration for Industry and Commerce (SAIC) 179
state role xxx–xxxii
structural changes 93–4
structural constraints xxx–xxxii, 10–13, 35–7
Subranabian, Arvind 39
Summers, Lawrence xvii
supplier dominated industries 127–37

Taiwan xvi, xxiv, 110
Tanzania xxx, 39
tariffs 53, 56
Tata Consultancy Services (TCS) xxiv, 31
technological progress xix–xx, 119–20, 137–8
   see also research and development (R&D)
technology 6, 14–17, 29, 43, 122
technology import intensity 127, 129–37
Thailand
   Chinese exports 110
   economic growth 29, 30, 46, 56
   education 52
   infant mortality 52, 62
   investment climate 51, 54
   population 49
   tariffs 53
   wages 51–2, 53
township and village enterprises (TVEs) 5
trade
   and economic growth 29–30, 34, 51
   global flows xiii
   liberalization effects xxii–xxiii, 77–80
   and research and development (R&D) 122–37

and technological progress 119–20,
    137–8
  theoretical effects 120–22
  see also intra-industry trade (IIT);
    liberalization
transparency 202, 203

unemployment 10, 57, 173–4
  see also informal employment in
    China
United States (US)
  and China 47–8, 65, 66, 67, 98, 103
  economic growth 59
  energy scarcity 61
  exports 49
  GDP (Gross Domestic Product) 49, 50
  global role xiii–xiv
  informal employment 176
  population 33, 49
  trade deficit 59–60
urban areas 5–6, 11, 35, 62–4, 66–7
Urban Slum Health Care Project, Andhra
    Pradesh 152, 157, 162, 170
Uttaranchal Mobile Hospital and
    Research Centre 152, 162, 171

value-added share (VAS) 126, 129–37
Veeramani, Choorikkadan xxii
Verdoom, P.J. 73
vertical integration 126
vertical intra-industry trade (VIIT) 74,
    82–93, 94
Vietnam
  economic growth 29, 30, 46, 56
  education 52
  infant mortality 52, 62
  investment climate 54
  population 49
  tariffs 53, 56
  wages 51–2, 53

village committees, China 227–9
village elections, China
  as development drivers xxv–xxvi
  effects of 225–9, 243–4
  empirical analysis 229–43

wages 46, 51–2, 53, 57, 63, 183–7, 189
Wang, Meiyan xx
Wang, Yidan 149
Westphal, Larry E. 126
Winters, L. Alan xxi
Wipro xxiv, 31
Witteloostuin, Arjen van 82, 86, 88, 92,
    93
Wooldridge, Jeffrey 128
working conditions 195
working hours 188, 195
World Bank 25, 164
World Trade Organization (WTO) 17, 18,
    53, 75, 173, 221
WuDunn, Sheryl xvi

Xu, Lixin 226

Yan, Shen xxv–xxvi
Yao, Yang xxv–xxvi, 226
Yeshasvini Health Insurance Scheme
    152, 153, 154, 160, 171, 172
Yueh, Linda xvii, xx, xxi, xxx, 14
Yusuf, Shahid xxi

Zedillo, Ernesto xiv
Zee 31
Zhang, Jianhong 82, 86, 88, 92, 93
Zhang, Linxiu 226
Zhang, Xiaobo 226
Zhong, Yang 228
Zhou, Chaohong 82, 86, 88, 92, 93
Zhou, Wubiao xxxi
Zhu, Rongji xiv